LEANING

–ON–

THE ARC

M. GERALD SCHWARTZBACH

LEANING

–ON–

THE ARC

A PERSONAL HISTORY OF CRIMINAL DEFENSE

ANKERWYCKE

Cover design by Monica Alejo/ABA Publishing.
Interior design by Betsy Kulak/ABA Publishing.

Printed in the United States of America.

20 19 18 17 16   5 4 3 2 1

Library of Congress Cataloging-in-Publication Data
Schwartzbach, M. Gerald, author.
  Leaning on the arc : a personal history of criminal defense / M. Gerald Schwartzbach.
    pages cm
  ISBN 978-1-63425-137-2 (alk. paper)
  1. Schwartzbach, M. Gerald. 2. Lawyers—United States—Biography. 3. Defense (Criminal procedure)—United States. 4. Criminal justice, Administration of—United States. I. Title.
  KF373.S348A3 2016
  340.092—dc23
  [B]   2015035971

Discounts are available for books ordered in bulk. Special consideration is given to state bars, CLE programs, and other bar-related organizations. Inquire at Book Publishing, ABA Publishing, American Bar Association, 321 N. Clark Street, Chicago, Illinois 60654-7598.

www.ShopABA.org

*For her enduring love, support and inspiration
I dedicate this book to my wife
Susan Homes Schwartzbach.*

The arc of the moral universe is long, but it bends toward justice.
—*Martin Luther King, Jr.*

Contents

— 1 —

Opening Statement: Confessions of an Unrepentant Criminal Defense Lawyer

---

"He will never be rich and he will never be famous, because he knows nothing about money and he has no idea what to do with you people, but by God he can save lives, and that will keep him warm on any cold night in his life."

—*Robert Blake at his press conference immediately after he was acquitted of murdering his wife*

True story:

In major cases, and especially in capital cases, prospective jurors may be required, if the presiding judge assents, to fill out questionnaires that let the lawyers for both sides gauge the jurors' attitudes toward wider issues that may be pertinent to the case.

In one of the cases you will read about in Chapter 8 of this book, such a questionnaire was given to the pool of potential jurors, and among the questions were two that sought to find out each individual's views on prosecutors and criminal defense lawyers.

One man wrote about prosecutors that "They keep us safe." For criminal defense lawyers, he put down "Sleazy." When I had a chance to question him later, I assured him that although I was and am a criminal defense lawyer, since he and I had never met, I wouldn't take his assessment personally.

"I meant it in a good way," he replied.

Benevolently intended or not, his view of criminal defense lawyers is not unusual. Just witness that small but toxic slice of lawyer jokes reserved for us—like these:

Question: Why don't sharks eat defense attorneys?
Answer: Professional courtesy.

Question: How can you know it's really cold outside?
Answer: When a defense attorney has his hands in his *own* pockets.

Question: How does a defense attorney sleep?
Answer: First he lies on one side, and then he lies on the other.

Granted, much of the public sees or hears of us only in connection with some high-profile proceeding, usually one involving a celebrity or highlighting mayhem among the very rich, but sometimes unfortunately it's a case involving the most twisted kinds of crimes—a parent murdering a child, for example—or touching our most secret fears and reigniting our sense of our own vulnerabilities—like the "alien among us" committing some sort of terrorist act.

As if the association with such milieus were not enough, we are seen by a large part of the population as trying to get accused criminals, typically referred to as "scum," off the hook, which is indeed our job, and doing so with a certain "slickness," then pocketing an enormous payoff. Along the way, we're perceived as engaging in behavior that is at least somewhat antic and at most downright crude. We are often described as "colorful," frequently as "sharply dressed," and occasionally as "cigar-smoking" or even "cigar-chomping"—descriptions that seem to invite the reader or listener to understand that being a criminal defense lawyer is synonymous with a certain crassness, a failure of taste, and just a whiff of subversiveness.

I will resist the temptation to state that such characterizations could not be further from the truth and that the right to a defense attorney is so central to our nation's values that it is enshrined in the Bill of Rights of our Constitution. I will not ask why a lawyer's smoking habits or manner of dress should be considered relevant to anything at all, and I will forego demanding to know who does not insist on being paid for his or her work. I will also concede that there are certainly criminal defense lawyers who merit criticism, as can be said of any profession.

But having achieved the biblical "three score and ten," I thought I would answer the skeptics, the cynics, the suspicious, and the merely dubious by simply telling the story of what it has been like, over a 45-year career, to dedicate my professional life to representing the very poor, the very unpopular, the very famous, and the very rich on those occasions when they are charged with a crime.

I do so because there is a theme that runs through criminal defense lawyering that troubles me to the point of wanting to raise it again and again. It is found in the experience that underlies the legal process and that is shared by all criminal defendants, whether poor, unpopular, famous, or rich—the experience of being objectified.

Robert Blake, the Hollywood actor accused of murder, whom you will read about in Chapter 9 of this book, was objectified into a symbol of the powerful—a hotshot who thought he could get away with murder. Buddy Nickerson, an admitted lawbreaker, whom you will meet in Chapter 8, had been objectified into everyone's idea of a racist thug who therefore had to be guilty of something and thus could easily be hung out to dry by police looking for an easy win and by a prosecutor willing to look the other way. A car burglar I was appointed to defend early in my career— and whose story is so common I do not relate it in this book—was easily objectified into just another "ghetto" guy grabbing quick cash for a fix, like so many ghetto guys before him. The judge in charge of monitoring how much I was being paid for my court-appointed work chided me for spending "too much time" on my client's case. "Your honor," I replied, "I don't think you would feel that way if you were my client."

Objectifying people strips them of their humanity; as in the case of my car burglar, even a judge, who had sworn an oath not to objectify those who come before him, can fall into the trap and become blind to the individuals inside the stereotypes. That makes it easy to separate those people—Blake, Nickerson, the car burglar—from the rest of us. When that happens, the rights we consider inalienable and endowed in us at birth can start slipping away, and any one of us can find ourselves in jail with the key tossed away. That is the real danger, and it is scary. If the Constitution does not work for the guilty, there is no assurance it will work for the innocent.

This is the space in which the criminal defense lawyer operates. This is my workplace. It is where I have spent every working day of a very varied, very rich, very rewarding—albeit in no way lucrative—professional career, and in this book, I want to communicate the granular quality of the space, the work, and the characters who have shared it with me.

There have been costs. When the breadwinner's primary goal is to help people, and only secondarily to make a living, that takes a toll on a family. It was summed up for me during my first capital murder trial. I had had a very difficult day in court and could not wait to get home and, finally, after so many late nights at work, have an evening at long last with my wife and son. I opened the door and called out my hellos. I could hear the yelps of my two-year-old as he raced down the hall to greet me, his arms already thrust outward. I opened my arms for his embrace, but when he reached me, he pushed me from him. "Go away!" he shouted, punishing me more harshly than he could possibly have known for all the evenings I had failed to be there and all the stress I had brought home with me.

Yet it is also true that that little boy grew up to join me in my profession, while my wife, as committed to justice as I, not only enabled me to keep doing the work but often shared the labor.

Because you really cannot stop this work. You cannot put it down for a while and get back to it when you feel like it. You have to keep at it all the time because the process of objectifying people goes on all the time. And while that process may be a very human response, something everybody does, and fertile territory for study by psychologists, sociologists, and even political scientists, there is still one place where it is absolutely not allowed, and that is in the justice system. We can define the job of a criminal defense lawyer, as I do, as defending the Constitutional rights of clients and, therefore, by extension, all of us. But the work required to do that job necessitates guarding against objectification seeping into the system, and when it does seep in, fighting it tooth and nail. While it may not be all that difficult to throw away an inanimate object, it is a lot harder to toss into prison or—worse—to execute a human being who, just like me and thee, has a life story.

But of course, objectification seeps into the system repeatedly. For the system is as flawed as the human beings who operate it—from the police and prosecutors who begin the process to the judges and juries who resolve it one way or the other. Any one of them can, and many of them in fact do, abuse and pervert the system from time to time, in this case or that, for this reason or that purpose, because it is easier or no one's looking, or it's time to head home for the weekend.

Wielding his or her only available tool, the law itself, the criminal defense attorney confronts the gamut of human resentments and prejudices, desires, and disappointments in trying to thread a path through this system toward justice. It very often takes much more time and far more effort than it should to arrive at that goal. This may be why someone once told me that criminal defense lawyers are the jazz musicians of the profession. I suppose we have to be as highly skilled, as knowledgeable, as able to hear the music in our heads, as facile at improvisation as a Miles Davis or a John Coltrane. This makes for a precarious existence, but it constitutes the most enriching experience a lawyer can have.

The 10 succeeding chapters and the 12 cases they highlight are aimed at showing you why. They run the gamut from murder to domestic abuse to protecting the right of dissent and expanding rights for defendants. The cast of characters includes New England bluebloods and Western rednecks; reactionaries and radicals; the moneyed and the indigent; the famous and the notorious; some who committed crimes and some who had crimes committed against them; and some, like Buddy Nickerson, who qualified in both categories.

All took place against a background of wide-ranging social change. I began practicing law in 1969. Civil rights, the sexual revolution, protest movements of every sort were roiling the nation and the world, shifting the very ground beneath our feet, transforming our laws and our politics. The cases I tried reflected those changes, but the goal was always the same—justice. More often than not, I met the goal.

Here's the story of how I did it. I understand that in telling the story, I'm putting myself in the dock; you be judge and jury.

— 2 —

An Accidental Lawyer Steps—or Is Dropped—into the Cauldron

In 1966, the year I was to graduate from college, if you were male, at least 18 years old, and neither a clergyman, a farmer, a sole surviving son, in a job essential to the national interest, disqualified by reason of physical or mental impairment—the category known as 4-F—a certified conscientious objector, nor in some serious sort of graduate school in some serious way, the threat of being drafted and deployed to Vietnam loomed as a very real possibility.

Unwilling to fight in a war to which I was very much opposed, I ducked it by going to law school. To this day, I'm not certain why I chose that particular draft-avoidance path over other, albeit limited, options. It was a reflex response, conditioned no doubt by my upbringing.

That upbringing took place in Northeastern Pennsylvania, in the borough of Kingston, a municipality comprising some 20,000 or so people at the time on the west bank of the Susquehanna River, just across from Wilkes-Barre, where I was born. Kingston was as average an example of middle-class small-town America—that is, of middle-class *white* small-town America—as you could find in the 1950s and early 1960s, and my upbringing was as average an upbringing as can be imagined.

I was the youngest of the family, with a sister, Barbara, almost eight years older, and a brother, Stephen, almost five years older. To my foreign-born immigrant grandparents, who as children had fled the oppressive persecution of Eastern Europe, and even to our American-born parents, Sanford Schwartzbach and Rachel, formerly Finkel, Schwartzbach, to whom opportunity beckoned but in limited ways, life in our suburb in that era must have seemed like heaven on earth. In Kingston, as in so many similar suburbs, narrow gabled houses were arranged neatly side by side along leafy streets, while a nearby "downtown" offered a few shops, a bank, grocery store, insurance and law offices, and the requisite houses of worship for Catholic, Protestant, and Jewish congregations.

We lived in a small pleasant house in a friendly neighborhood that could boast diversity of religion and of ethnic background. Tolerance governed virtually every interaction between groups; intimacy was harder to come by, and in fact, we really lived within a segregated Jewish community.

For one thing, ours was an ostensibly observant home. We "kept kosher," as the saying goes, spent hours in the synagogue on Saturdays, and I went to Hebrew school three times a week.

Perhaps even more to the point, our social life was pretty much exclusively Jewish. This was perhaps not surprising. "Greater" Wilkes-Barre, of which Kingston was a part, had a large and vibrant Jewish community, served by half a dozen separate synagogues, and at the center of this bustling community was the Jewish Community Center (JCC), a lively bazaar of classes, cultural events, lectures, social functions, and sports, which were then and are now my passion. I have always been mad about basketball, baseball, football—any endeavor in which grown men compete over a ball, no matter its size or shape. I came by this love naturally; my father had been a professional boxer and had played semi-pro baseball and football before "getting serious" and going into business. He took my brother and me—not my sister—to every available sporting event of every stripe. We had season tickets to the local minor league baseball and basketball games, and when we visited New York, we even got to go to games at Madison Square Garden, at beloved Ebbets Field, at the hated Yankee Stadium, and, if I recall correctly, at the Polo Grounds, original home of the Giants I now root for. He also encouraged our participation in sports. He helped start the local Little League, sponsored our team, and coached the players. It was not surprising that my brother and I both grew up to be good all-around athletes and better-than-good high school basketball and baseball players.

Above all, my father was a fanatical fan of the Brooklyn Dodgers, and whenever the Dodgers were in the World Series, my Dad went to all the games and took Stephen and me to the two on the weekend. In 1952, he was present without us when the Dodgers lost—yet again—to the Yankees in the final game at Ebbets Field. When he went into work at his trouser factory the next day, the Yankee-fan owners of the gas station next door staged a mock funeral, complete with coffin containing a dummy corpse dressed in a Dodgers' uniform, a priest, pallbearers, and a hearse that carried the coffin to a cemetery to bury it and the team's hopes for another year. The local newspaper covered the story with a report and a group photograph.

So although my father clearly did not believe it, he always told my brother and me that sports were just not that important. His own immediate family had focused far more than he on education and intellectual endeavors, and he believed, without quite adhering to the belief himself, that our chances of success in life would depend on the quality of the education we received. It is why he and my mother made whatever adjustments and sacrifices were necessary to send all three of us to private school, the prestigious Wyoming Seminary, a highly regarded prep school founded in 1844 that was the pride of Kingston. "School is what counts," declared my father, who for himself had little patience with school; "more than sports." So against my will—I wanted to stay at Kingston High School and play basketball on a championship team—I went off to Wyoming Seminary.

In my first year there, my father died quite suddenly. He complained of neck pain. It was 1959 and there weren't the medical diagnostic tools we have today. As a result, there was an inaccurate diagnosis. He had suffered a cerebral hemorrhage; a week after the misdiagnosis, he fell into a coma and died.

It was devastating. My father was a young man when he died, and he had been larger than life, a Technicolor personality who never did anything small. His joys, his humor, his principles, his affection, his temper were all big, forceful, and on a bold scale. So the emptiness that followed his death was palpable. Among other effects, the emptiness evidenced itself in my academic performance. I had always been an A-student, but my grades plummeted after my father died.

Still, at 14, you are amazingly resilient, and my mother worked hard to keep our life unchanged in all other respects, especially as I was the only child still at home.

Despite my suddenly-less-than-stellar performance as a scholar, I was still something of a big man on campus—captain of both the basketball and baseball teams, engaged in numerous extracurricular club activities, and president of my senior class.

I soon gained a reputation for being highly competitive in just about everything I did—academics excepted. A yearbook picture from the time shows me with a huge black eye, the result of being elbowed by a bigger opponent in a basketball game. I just did not know how to back down, not when I was competing.

It was a good time to be young and competitive. So was JFK—President John F. Kennedy—a hero to me and all my classmates with his muscular approach to the use of power to right wrongs. Justice was my other great passion, on a par with sports, and I had come by it just as naturally. It was in the air in that era of liberal thinking and certainly in the circles in which I moved—at home, in the synagogue, at the JCC, at school, among my friends. I focused my passion for justice on a kind of hero-worship of Clarence Darrow, the great defense lawyer and civil libertarian. A fierce litigator, a champion of the underdog, an advocate for rationality and the primacy of the mind, he defined for me what it meant to fight for justice. No one stood higher in my esteem. But I do not think I ever thought of following in his footsteps and making my living as a lawyer.

Instead, I saw a future in which I was somehow connected with the business of sports, living in Kingston, and surrounded by all the people I was then surrounded by for the rest of my life. I could envisage no greater contentment.

––––––

I majored in History at Washington & Jefferson College, some 300 miles west of home in Washington, Pennsylvania. A small liberal arts college with an excellent reputation, I was accepted despite my not-so-great grades, because of my athletic experience, the fact that I had been senior class president, and because my brother had been a student there. I applied myself—inspired to some extent by my roommate, a premed who studied nonstop—and my grades reflected the effort.

But this didn't mean I gave up sports. I played baseball all four years of college—center field—but I deferred to an ankle injury and a better point guard and got off the basketball team after two years of play. College also gave me a brief brush with discrimination—and with the benefits of a more active diversity than I had known growing up in Kingston. Washington & Jefferson was an all-male school back then, so if you wanted any form of social life, you had to join a fraternity. There were two on campus that accepted Jews and blacks, so the brush with discrimination was that my fraternity options were limited, while the great benefit was that for the first time in my life I had the experience of living with African Americans. That was a valuable learning experience for us all, and at a college where life really centered around the fraternity, it stretched our sense of common ground and our sharing of community.

For all of us, whatever our creed, race, or background, the searing event that marked our time at college was the assassination of JFK. "Where were you when you heard?" was as common a question then as "Where were you on 9/11?" became for a later generation. I was a sophomore, living with two fraternity brothers in a funky, small first-floor apartment off-campus. On that Friday, with its easygoing end-of-the-week feeling, I was alone in the apartment and decided to kick back and watch a little TV. I remember the first announcement of "a shooting," delivered in an unbelieving tone. Then the gradual filling in of details, confusion, fear alternating with hope, and the somehow stunning impact of the distinguished CBS news anchor Walter Cronkite in shirtsleeves. How profound it was, and—for my generation—how unwanted a turning-point it would prove to be.

A year later, my classmates and I began worrying about the draft and talking of little else. I knew I had to find some form of graduate education that would qualify me for a draft deferment at least for a few more years so I could edge toward the age of 26 when I would magically become too old to be eligible. I sure wasn't cut out for medical school or a PhD in scientific research. Almost reflexively, I decided to apply to law school.

I disliked it intensely. Immediately and virulently. It was a fine educational institution—George Washington University Law School—and it was located in the heart of the nation's capital, but I hated it anyway. At our first convocation, whoever was giving the welcoming speech offered the usual clichéd instruction: "Look at the person to your left, look at the person to your right. One of you will not survive the rigors of this course of education." This was his way of warning us, as he went on explicitly to say, that we had to study very hard if we wanted to get the recruiters from the hotshot law firms to notice us so we could get the good job offers and become rich lawyers.

It all struck me as having very little to do with what I thought of as justice, and to show my displeasure, I simply stopped studying after Thanksgiving. Naturally, my grades nosedived. I didn't care. Better to take my chances fighting my draft board, I thought, than to put up with the incessant money-grubbing and the stifling boredom.

As if in confirmation of that stance, toward the end of my first year, I was offered a high school basketball coaching position, that would start in the fall. It was just what I wanted, and I was looking forward to telling the Dean I was dropping out of law school when I learned I had flunked Constitutional Law. It was hardly surprising; if you stop studying, as I had done, something's got to give. But the failure stuck in my craw, and all my old competitive instincts kicked in. I was damned if I was going to be defeated by the capitalist thuggishness of law school. My plan was to go back for my second year, do well, and then quit. That would show them.

So I duly returned for a second year, and I duly applied myself, and I did in fact do well. But a funny thing happened on my way to quitting and showing them. I was selected to be part of a clinical law program—one of the first in the country and a real novelty at the time—in which law students represented poor people in small-claims court. To say this experience was an education for me is an epic understatement. I spent time in public housing projects; got to know people living in abject poverty; saw how they were exploited by landlords, store owners, the government, and the legal system; saw racism up close and personal. When I say I got to know these people, I mean that exactly: I established relationships with my clients, thereby learning about them as individuals, befriending them as individuals—in this case, individuals forced to live in conditions that I could see for myself were outrageous and under pressures I could feel for myself were oppressive. It changed my mind—literally—and it changed my life.

What I suddenly saw through the experience of that clinical law program was that the law was not just a bunch of words in black and white on a page, not just codes and regulations, arguments and counterarguments. The law was a tool—and when necessary a weapon—that people could use on their own behalf to fight for their rights, to counter the discrimination visited upon them, to battle back against those who would take advantage of them. All it needed was a lawyer willing to battle with them.[1]

I finished law school, and when I graduated, I signed up to be a foot soldier in the battle. I became a VISTA legal volunteer; my assumption was that I would be assigned to the Deep South to work on the frontline voter registration issues that seemed to me back then to define the search for justice. But as anybody who has ever volunteered for anything knows, it does not work that way: They sent me to Detroit.

I knew it as Motown, home of the sound that started my feet tapping throughout high school and college. But that was a portmanteau name; its real identity was "The Motor City," the tough, raw industrial boomtown shaped by galloping capitalism, by powerful unions led by the likes of Jimmy Hoffa and Walter Reuther, and by racial tension. Especially during World War II and in the years immediately following, Detroit's auto manufacturing assembly line jobs had lured both immigrants and

---

1. The best advice I received while in law school was from my then 91-year-old grandfather, who had spent his adult life in the garment business. He said, "You gonna be a lawyer, be a good lawyer, be an honest lawyer, be somebody people can trust."

migrants, including large numbers of African Americans from the rural South. They came to get their piece of the middle-class economy that had been forged in the confrontations between the manufacturers and a thriving labor movement, an economy that pretty much guaranteed a man—and it was mostly men—the wherewithal to buy a single-family house and a car, enjoy paid holidays, and count on a secure retirement even if he had only a high school diploma.

In time, close-knit white neighborhoods began to resent the influx of a rising black middle class that could afford to move in next door, and when auto industry job growth began to dry up in mid-century, thereby diminishing the size of the pie everyone was trying to eat, tensions rose. Two years before I arrived in Detroit, both the National Guard and the U.S. Army were called out to quell the so-called Twelfth Street race riot, which left 43 people dead and devastated the majority-African American neighborhood in which it had started. As the economy continued to decline, so did jobs and population; meanwhile, poverty and ghettoization were in the ascendant. By the time I got there in September 1969, Detroit was the byword for urban blight.

It was also a hotbed of the kind of revolutionary activism the counterculture had ignited starting in the 1960s, and I was plunged into it without delay. The day I arrived in Detroit, a summer-like day in September 1969, a group of mothers who were on welfare staged a sit-in at the Department of Social Services; the aim was for the women to get themselves arrested for criminal trespass as a way of bringing attention to their plight. My VISTA supervisor, knowing that I had worked as a criminal investigator while in law school, immediately assigned me to assist the three criminal defense lawyers handling the mothers' case.

The three lawyers were Sheldon Otis, Ken Cockrel Sr., and Justin Ravitz, always called Chuck, and they were all prominent professionals and well-known left-leaning activists. Ken would later serve on the Detroit City Council, and Chuck was later elected to the bench. All three were superb attorneys, and for a young lawyer just out of the gate, with similar political instincts, spending time with the three of them was an extraordinary opportunity for a young lawyer.

It was also the best education a criminal defense lawyer could ever have. These were three brilliant men—each brilliant in a different way;

they were realists; they were rational; they were principled. They also worked harder than I had ever seen anybody work. Being around them trained my own mind, sharpened my instincts, and made me want more than anything in the world to be a criminal defense lawyer.

The one who exerted the greatest influence on me—as well as on Chuck and Ken and an entire generation of Detroit criminal defense lawyers—was Sheldon Otis. A troubled soul, as events would later tragically demonstrate, Sheldon was, to my mind, the absolute epitome of what a lawyer could and should be. He combined superb legal scholarship—Sheldon knew every detail of the law in all its majestic breadth and depth—with the trial skills of a Cicero, and he channeled all of his wisdom and virtuosity to his clients' advantage. He instantly became my role model—a position he still holds in my legal life—because he did everything I was taught lawyers should do and showed heart and courage in doing it.

What's more, there was just something about the man. Not particularly prepossessing in appearance, Sheldon could nevertheless walk into a room and, without trying, make everyone instantly aware of his presence.

He would go on in later years to represent some of the best known and most notorious radicals of the 1960s and 1970s—Steven Soliah, Angela Davis, Huey Newton. To the great mass of the population, these people were incomprehensible, and they were scary, on the fringe, alien. Defending them defined who Sheldon Otis was. It was in his blood to fight for unpopular defendants against aggressive prosecutors and before hostile judges with the press and the public at large against him—and win.

In those first days and weeks in Detroit, I watched to see how he did it. I think he did it above all through meticulous and rigorously disciplined preparation. Sheldon left no stone unturned—not the tiniest pebble. He challenged every assumption, investigated every lead, researched every fact, and checked every legal possibility; he left nothing to chance in making a case. His reputation was as a master of the courtroom, and I believe it was simply because he knew his case inside and out, up and down, in every detail. The very thoroughness and precision of his preparation were precisely what enabled him to be himself in the courtroom—and to be ready for anything the prosecution could throw at him or for eventualities even he had not anticipated. It was discipline that made

Sheldon an artist in the cause of justice and a successful artist at that. It is a lesson I've never forgotten.

He also had little respect for the justice system, and he literally wore that opinion on his sleeve—or rather on his wrist—in the form of the Mickey Mouse watch he used throughout his life. In his view, the system had simply failed; it was corrupt, and it could only be dealt with if that was understood. But he also saw himself as Don Quixote, tilting at windmills as he tried to revive the system and restore it to its true glory. Sheldon Otis would not back down before any judge or prosecutor, but his defiance and resolve were always at the highest levels of professionalism because he knew precisely what the law was and how it should work. That has always seemed to me the perfect formula for a lawyer to follow. For years, when I was unsure of a move or if my emotions got hold of me during a trial, I would ask myself "What would Sheldon do?" It invariably clarified the issues for me, quieted the noise, disciplined my thinking; it was as if, from the grave, Sheldon Otis could point me in the right direction for my client and my case.

At the time, however, my attitude toward Sheldon was one of hero-worship. Unaware, as so many of his colleagues and friends were, of the personal demons that would one day bring him low, I was content—I was thrilled!—to be within his orbit and to soak up like a sponge everything I could learn from him.

At first, all the VISTA volunteers assigned to Michigan bunked in a convent recently emptied of its nuns. I soon moved from there, sharing a house with two other legal VISTAs. It was hardly a palace—I think the stipend for VISTAs at that time worked out to about $125 a week—but I had my own basement room, which I rarely saw anyway. I worked long hours and found every minute of every hour exciting.

In fact, it was more than exciting, and it was about more than just practicing law. Not far away, less than 300 miles as the crow flies, the trial of the Chicago Eight was proceeding apace. The charges against the original eight arose out of the tumultuous antiwar protests surrounding the 1968 Democratic National Convention in Chicago, protests that were countered by what U.S. Senator Abraham Ribicoff of Connecticut styled at the time the "Gestapo tactics" of Chicago police. The eight defendants and their lawyers constituted a who's who of 1960s' protest counterculture: Abbie Hoffman, Jerry Rubin, David Dellinger, Tom Hayden, Rennie Davis, John Froines, Lee Weiner, and Bobby Seale were the defendants, although Seale's case was later severed, and their lawyers included William Kunstler and Leonard Weinglass of the Center for Constitutional Rights, known as the gathering place for radical lawyers. The judge was Julius Hoffman, a close associate of Mayor Richard Daley, the very mayor whose police had run riot during the convention. Hoffman was also an abrasive personality and a man singularly lacking in what we might call "judicial temperament."

I had been in Detroit only a few weeks when Judge Hoffman held the defense lawyers in contempt, prompting the National Lawyers Guild, the association of progressive lawyers and jurists founded in 1937, to organize lawyers around the country to respond. From Detroit, a small contingent of lawyers, myself included, headed to Chicago to support the defense team, and at a rally in a Chicago church, we heard from Bill Kunstler and Abbie Hoffman themselves. It was mesmerizing. Abbie Hoffman was as hilarious as a Borscht Belt comic, and Kunstler was a compelling speaker. I was hooked—committed on the spot to what was for me a new kind of political activism.

The Guild then recruited me to stage a fundraiser in a Detroit church, this one to "star" Jerry Rubin. Rubin was a master organizer and creator of protest as theater, so the crowd was bound to be huge, and once I had handled the details of the event, my task the night it took place was to be Rubin's "handler" and usher him around.

It was disillusioning to come away from that experience with an impression of Rubin as immature and self-absorbed. While Kenny Cockrel, a dynamic speaker, held the crowd in thrall, Rubin kept nudging me to "get him off the stage. It's me they've come to see."

In the end, the event was wildly successful—at least in terms of the size of the crowd and its enthusiasm. But like so many events staged by and for the counterculture, just about nobody paid to get in or donated once there. And that result made me not just a failure as a fundraiser but actually suspect. This was, after all, the era of COINTELPRO, the FBI's Counter Intelligence Program that specifically targeted liberal and left-leaning domestic organizations through a range of covert actions including infiltration. The Guild was a favorite target of COINTELPRO, and in the minds of some Guild members, it was not beyond the realm of possibility that this short, curly-haired, hitherto unknown "new guy" from somewhere "back East" was an informer or an agent. It was only thanks to Sheldon, Ken, and Chuck personally vouching for me that I maintained my standing with the Left—and stayed alive. In fact, I went on to expand my political involvement with the Guild, becoming a diligent foot soldier in the organization's repeated challenges to the way justice was delivered—or more usually denied—in Detroit.

In this and in the job I went to each day, I felt like I was part of a significant change. Everywhere I looked—at the mothers taking on the establishment and unafraid to do so; at the courtroom victories defense lawyers kept gaining, case by case; at the challenges to entrenched thinking going on not just in the newsworthy Chicago trial but in neighborhoods, on campuses, and around the world—what had begun in the sixties seemed to be blossoming, busting out all over. And I felt myself a player in a great movement that just might effect fundamental change for the better.

Was I naïve? Maybe. But I was 25 years old, and I believed I was helping to bring about legal and social change that would aid individual clients and make my country more humane. It does not get much better than that.

———

Before the year was out, I was fired.

It's not easy to get fired from VISTA, but I managed it. The supervisor who had assigned me to help out with the defense of the women on welfare that first day in Detroit simply never got around to cancelling the assignment to work with Sheldon, as he was supposed to do. Legal VISTAs were there to work with clients, not be an apprentice in the legal practice of a criminal defense lawyer, and that was effectively what I was doing. So when the powers-that-be finally noticed, I received a letter from the Washington D.C. headquarters of VISTA telling me, fairly politely, that I had been axed.

It didn't matter because I immediately got a job with what was then called the Legal Aid and Defender Association of Detroit. Sponsored by the Detroit Bar Association, this smallish office—some eight lawyers at the time—eventually morphed into a much larger office, but back then, we were just one of the options a judge might choose to appoint as counsel for an indigent defendant. One of the lawyers who preceded me was a young, politically ambitious guy named Carl Levin, who of course later went on to become a U.S. Senator from Michigan. At the time I joined the office, Carl was already a member of the Detroit City Council, but I ran into both him and his brother, Sander, later a Congressman, in pickup basketball games at the downtown YMCA.

The job was another key learning experience for me. The most experienced lawyer in the office, Jim Roberts, became something of a mentor to me. An African American from the heart of the inner city, he brought a great breadth of experience as well as a native understanding to the work. "I don't judge a person on where he is but on how far he has come," he used to say. I've always considered that a good prescription for both the practice of law and anything else in life, and it's a mantra I often repeat to myself.

But I got fired from the Legal Aid and Defender Association as well. This time, the reason was, as I saw it, a matter of principle, and it involved another lawyer named Sheldon—in this case, Sheldon Halpern, a New York lawyer who came to Detroit to defend a New Yorker on trial there and stayed to join our office.

Shelly, as he is called, was then and is now a pugnacious guy who managed to get acquittal after acquittal in cases that looked like lost causes. I always secretly thought it was because his East Coast street-fighter manner struck fear into the hearts of the jurors. Shelly had a reputation for being disrespectful to some judges. In fact, I understand that, in one case he tried after I left Detroit, a judge actually pulled a gun on him in chambers.

Many judges didn't like Shelly, and the fact was that our office was sponsored and funded by the Detroit Bar Association, so when some of these judges began pressuring the Bar Association to persuade the head of our office to fire Shelly Halpern, the Bar Association caved. The argument, of course, was that our clients would lose out if one of our lawyers kept on being a thorn in the side of the judicial community.

I was incensed at this handshake with expediency and tried to organize the office to protest against Shelley's firing. It was an ill-conceived move: I was the youngest in the office, with the least seniority. I had hoped that my friend and more senior colleague, Bill Segesta, would take the lead in organizing the office, but he was on vacation. With no one else willing to take the initiative, I did, thereby turning myself into a thorn in everyone's side—an annoyance at best, an obstacle at worst. I was out. It is a firing I'm still proud of, though; it was the moral high ground I got knocked off of.

In any event, rescue was rapid. An exceptional lawyer in our office, Art Tarnow, who would later go on to become a distinguished federal judge, was named the executive director of the Michigan State Appellate Defender office, one of the first of its kind—basically, a public defender's office for indigent people appealing their convictions, both trial and plea-based. Art, who was another good friend, offered me a job, which I, of course, accepted, but appellate work did not excite me, and after a few months, I was ready to move on.

So when Shelly Halpern opened his own law practice in a storefront in the city's Greektown district, I decided to do the same and took half the space Shelly had rented at 506 Monroe Street. I was told it had previously been the office of a bail bondsman who was murdered there, and the bloodstains on the floor had been cleaned up before we moved in.

As it turned out, bloodstains, both literal and figurative, were not unusual in that first foray into private practice. My clients ranged from revolutionaries to reprobates, with everything in between. In one high-profile case, two young men were charged with attempting to murder Detroit police officers; the defendants were also alleged to be members of the Black Liberation Army, the underground black nationalist organization committed to armed struggle. The fearmongering the case ignited was widespread and intense, combining elements of racism, fear of revolutionary takeover, police abuse of power, and plain old urban violence. The court had trouble keeping a defense lawyer on the case because of successive death threats against its appointees. But I never gave it a second thought. It was right up my alley, and, as it proved, it helped me hone my skills and develop as just the kind of lawyer I wanted to be—equipped to take on a challenge, unafraid of the power structure, and a committed defender.

Chuck Ravitz got me another case that sharpened what I think of as my counterattack skills. Three police officers had shot and killed two homeless men and had left another for dead. But when the cops learned that the third man had survived, they arrested him on a charge of attempted armed robbery, fabricating the "facts" of the case out of whole cloth.

The court had appointed a defense lawyer for the man, but he was a "dump truck"—lawyers' jargon for an attorney who looks for a large number of clients for whom he or she can quickly enter a guilty plea, then pocket the fee. The defendant's family had noticed this about the court-appointed lawyer, was worried, and contacted Chuck, and Chuck had asked me to take it on for free. I prepared the case for trial *sub rosa*—nobody knew about it—and it wasn't until I showed up on the day of trial that the court-appointed lawyer and everybody else learned that the defendant was my client. The prosecutor immediately asked for and received a postponement. I then held a press conference in which I announced that in court, I would, on my client's behalf, prove beyond a reasonable doubt that the police had committed murder and attempted murder. Lo and behold! The case against my client was eventually dismissed. For me, this was a lesson in the power of preemptive retaliation, a good tool to use when it is available, as it certainly was in this case.[2]

Tool after tool, skill after skill, I was steadily gaining competence, and as my competence grew, so did my confidence. To the roiling crucible that was Detroit in the late 1960s, I owe the steady accumulation of practical knowledge about the lawyer's job and a sense of the way litigation works and of how the players in a legal proceeding act and react. It is a crucial phase in the development of any legal practitioner, and I will always be grateful that I was able to go through it in Detroit. It's where I learned how to be a lawyer, and it's where I conceived the desire to be a great one.

———

I no longer recall who referred the Lester Stiggers case to me, but it was an unusual case in several respects. For one thing, it was an extradition case—a procedure in which a person accused or convicted of a crime is returned, by request, to the jurisdiction in which the crime was committed. Now extradition is technically an administrative matter; theoretically, the governor of the state seeking the extradition requests it from the governor of the state in which the individual is found. And it is

---

2. One of the three police officers was later charged with murder, accused of shooting and killing a man while off-duty, and following a car accident. He was also accused of having planted a knife on the murdered man so he could plead self-defense, but when hairs from his own cat were found on the knife, that defense collapsed. Instead, the cop pleaded insanity—and was acquitted.

then virtually automatic. In other words, it is a routine matter, and it is extremely rare for a governor to deny extradition. It just isn't done. The Lester Stiggers case was different.

What made it different was that Lester, 20 years old at the time I began to represent him in 1971, was a fugitive from Arkansas, where the prison system was both corrupt and barbarous—and known to be so. A few years before, in fact, the state of Oregon had denied an Arkansas extradition request on the grounds, as the hearing judge wrote, that its prisons were "institutions of terror, horror, and despicable evil." The Oregon decision may have been influenced in part by the discovery, a year earlier, of 200 unidentified bodies in unmarked graves on the grounds of an Arkansas prison notorious for prisoner abuse; the incident later gained fame in the movie *Brubaker*.

Lester Stiggers told a story that made the movie look tame, and the Oregon judge's assessment right-on. This was a young man quite different from most of my clients up to this point. He was no Detroit street kid; there was no urban savvy or swashbuckling bravado in this very quiet, humble young man from rural Arkansas. He was shy, sympathetic, and likeable, and what he told me of his life made me shiver with horror.

At age 15, Lester had shot and killed his father. The shooting followed years of physical abuse and was committed in fear and anger just as his father was about to inflict another beating. Although a juvenile, Lester was tried as an adult. His entire trial—before a jury of 11 whites and one African American—lasted only one day; his court-appointed lawyer lacked either the competence or the will to defend him—and Lester was convicted and sentenced to life imprisonment.

At the prison in which he was held, as is not unusual, some prisoners were named trustees, although these particular trustees were not simply given the privilege of helping to keep the prison clean, as is typically the case, in return for more lenient treatment. In addition to that standard privilege, some of these trustees were given guns and were encouraged to use them to put down trouble and prevent escapes; others were in the extortion business. Lester said he was put into solitary confinement for refusing to pay a trustee and was beaten daily while in "the hole."

In 1970, after five years in prison, Lester was granted a five-day leave for good behavior. His aunt immediately put him on a plane to Detroit, where he had relatives. Once there, he checked in with the Detroit police, stating he wanted to fight extradition. The police found no warrant for his extradition and told him they had no interest in him.

Lester got a job in construction and enrolled in an auto mechanics course at a local community college. For a year, he lived the life of an upstanding citizen until an extradition request was received by the Governor's Office, at which point the police arrested him.

On its face, the injustice of the extradition request seemed clear to all who became acquainted with it: Here was an abused child, a probably justifiable homicide, a travesty of a trial, and a youth thrown into a prison system as terrifying as that of Stalinist Russia. And now the law would send him back to all that?

But the injustice—the almost patent absurdity of it—did not mean that the extradition wouldn't take place. On the contrary: It remained a likely probability. The U.S. Constitution requires states to deliver fugitives to other states on request; the Uniform Criminal Extradition Act sets requirements and standards for extradition, and precedent and common practice have long affirmed the routine nature of such requests. If that requirement seemed in this particular case unjust on several levels, that is often the nature of things; even the terminally naïve can see that the requirements of law do not always coincide with justice. The principle of the law is clear and unambiguous: Fugitives should be returned to the place where the crime of which they are accused or already convicted has taken place. But principles, no matter how just or noble, do not always cover all the nuances and subtleties of human experience. A criminal lawyer needs an understanding of those gray areas, for they are often crucial in defending clients.

It was also the case that prison reforms had been initiated by Arkansas' previous governor, Republican Winthrop Rockefeller, starting in 1967 and were ongoing under the current Democratic governor, Dale Bumpurs. This fact might be seen to mitigate the implied threat Lester would face if he were returned to the Arkansas prison system.

Officially, the extradition request came from reformist Bumpurs to Michigan Governor William Milliken, a moderate Republican (and a man who later publicly and forcefully broke with his party's rightward shift). It was Milliken who would decide Lester's fate, and he appointed his legal advisor on extradition issues to pursue the matter, hold a hearing on it, and make a recommendation.

Since Lester's story was so compelling, one obvious tack for me to take in his defense was to try to get his story heard by as wide an audience as possible. I followed two paths to this end. One was to ask the Detroit natives among my acquaintance to line up some political support and exert some political pressure. My friend, Art Tarnow, who had given me the job at the State Appellate Defender's office, was close to Carl Levin, and then-City Council Member Levin of course knew John Conyers, already a member of the U.S. House of Representatives. They wrote letters of support, and their stand against Lester's extradition spurred more support among the political elite.

The other path toward getting Lester's story told was to broadcast it as widely as possible. To do that, I got myself on a radio show called *Radio Help*, a morning show on WCHD-FM, the station of, by, and for the large African American community of Detroit. *Radio Help* was the brainchild and megaphone of a rather amazing personality known as Mother Waddles—Charleszetta Waddles—an ordained Christian fundamentalist minister who singlehandedly launched and maintained a collection of community self-help services, most of which she operated out of her Perpetual Mission for Saving Souls of All Nations, in what *Life* magazine called "a one-woman war on poverty." The radio show was Mother Waddles' daily outreach and call-in show about community services for the needy; its audience was huge, and in sharing the microphone with her one morning, I managed to drum up massive support for Lester within the state's African American population and, thanks to their advocacy, in the white community as well.

Armed with this popular support and the support of the political elite, Lester and I proceeded to the hearing before the governor's legal advisor. I was nervous. The legal obstacle still needed to be surmounted, and while we had a groundswell of support, I could not be sure that it was enough to do it for us. Lester told his story and asserted his belief, based on past experience, that if he were returned to Arkansas, he would be "brutalized." I argued that the conditions in the Arkansas prison system violated the Constitution's ban against cruel and unusual punishment and that

Lester's exemplary life in Detroit justified his remaining in Michigan. All we could do now was wait for the governor's decision.

When it came, it could not have been clearer. Milliken refused to extradite, stating simply that returning Lester Stiggers to Arkansas "would not serve the ends of justice, the needs of society, nor the rehabilitation of Mr. Stiggers." Lester was free.

It is hard to describe how rewarding it is for a lawyer to succeed on behalf of his client. It's true of any case, but it is particularly true of a victory through which someone's life is not simply saved from injustice but is literally turned around. The decision ensured that 21-year-old Lester Stiggers, who had lived in terror for 15 years as the child of an abusive parent and for five years as an inmate in an abusive prison, could suddenly confront a future of possibilities—without fear.[3]

For a lawyer, nothing could be more gratifying.

---

3. Forty-three years after Lester was freed, his application for Social Security benefits again put him on Arkansas's radar, and the governor of Arkansas renewed the extradition request. The times were different in 2013—less tolerant of anybody "getting away with" anything. But at 63, the victim of two strokes, by his own description a "half-dead invalid," Lester Stiggers was no one's idea of a threat to public safety. The sitting governor, Rick Snyder said that Stiggers had "lived in our state in a peaceful fashion and (is) fairly elderly and has significant health problems." The extradition request, said the governor, was not a high priority.

Well, not for him.

— 3 —

Community Defender

In the summer between college and law school, well before I ever got near Detroit, I had done what many college graduates of that time did as soon as we graduated—maybe they still do it: I took off on a road trip. The 1966 version of that was to find a friend and start driving, and the idea was almost literally to get lost—to head somewhere you'd never been before—so as to have one final, escapist blowout before moving on to what we thought of as the grown-up world of work or graduate school.

I was an East Coast guy, with many relatives in New York City and Washington, D.C., and I would be living in D.C. come the autumn and law school. Southwestern Pennsylvania, where I had gone to college, bordered the Midwest, giving me some inkling of heartland culture, but the rest of the country was a blank slate to me, and I was eager to see what it was like. So, preceding by a year the legendary Summer of Love of 1967, my friend Rick and I packed up my 1962 Plymouth Valiant convertible and set out after commencement to drive across the country to California.

Like pretty much everyone who has ever made the trip, we were dumbfounded by the sheer size of the country, stunned by the amount of open space, dazzled by the scenery, bemused and sometimes charmed and occasionally appalled by the people we met. The plan was to stay north for the drive west and come back through the Southwest and the South. But the two tires I blew out in the middle of the Nevada desert sent that itinerary packing. When I asked the only attendant at the only gas station within hundreds of miles how much two tires would cost, he asked how much money we had. It meant that by the time we had tires on the car, we were virtually broke.

I called my cousin Donny in Las Vegas. Though he was 13 years older, we always had a special relationship. Donny came from a branch of my mother's family that had moved west in the 1950s, yet he and I had always remained close. Sure enough, Donny and Fay, his wife, welcomed us to their home where we set about replenishing our funds. I got a job as a dishwasher in a Mexican restaurant called El Cholo, and Rick worked at a gas station until we had stashed enough money to move on. When we had made it to Los Angeles, the funds again needed a topping up, so I worked as a gardener at the Hollywood Bowl—my love of orchestral music comes from hiding in the bushes during rehearsals by the Los Angeles Symphony—and my sidekick was a busboy nearby. We restocked our wallets for the next phase and headed north to San Francisco.

Of course, we made our way up Highway 1 through mountains and around sensational curves under a brilliant California sun. I was behind the wheel when we entered the city of San Francisco, the top was down, the radio was blaring, and Rick and I were probably singing along when I suddenly caught that spectacular first glimpse of the Golden Gate Bridge and the city shining like a gem at its southern end. In that moment, I think, I fell in love with the whole Bay Area, although at the time I could not have imagined I would end up living most of my life there.

So it was not that I had San Francisco or any other destination in mind when, years later, I suddenly realized it was time to leave Detroit. The realization came as a result of several unrelated motivations, but the most significant was that a close friend—a mentor in both the legal and political spheres of my life—lied to me about a matter I considered important concerning a political campaign in which I was involved. When I confronted him, he said that the lie had been "politically necessary." I did not buy it. I was then and am now a small-town boy with old-school values. They include the one that says that you don't lie, especially to a friend. For me, once trust was broken, it did not knit back together easily. I never lost my respect for my friend's intelligence and legal skills, but I never really saw him or the politics I had adopted in quite the same way, and at the time, the disillusionment felt oppressive. The irony is that today, I can no longer remember the details of the lie, but I still recall the hurt.

Mostly, I suppose, I was also just ready to move on—not just out of Detroit but away from what I had been doing. It had been a superb way to begin a legal career, a learning experience second to none, but it had been relentless. I had worked incredibly hard, under difficult circumstances, with a weight of responsibility that never let up and that created a level of stress that also never subsided. Three years of it had left me physically and mentally exhausted, and my body and brain seemed to be telling me that what I really wanted to do was go somewhere warm and be a hippie. I was even willing to accept that my life as a lawyer was over—as if I had used up all the lawyer within me through the work I had done in Detroit. So my plan, if you could call it that, was to hit the road again and see where it might take me and what might happen.

I would go first to Michigan City, Indiana, to visit my brother and his family, then drive on to San Francisco to visit my friend Bill Segesta, who had been my colleague in the Detroit Defender's Office and who had married and moved west with my friend and former neighbor, Alice. Since I was responsible for having fixed them up in the first place, I knew Alice and Bill would be glad to welcome me. After a stint in San Francisco, I figured I would let the universe and circumstances plot my course.

So in early December 1972, I put Detroit behind me and headed for Indiana and my brother's home. From there, I phoned Bill and Alice, as prearranged, to let them know when I expected to arrive on their doorstep. Alice answered; Bill was not there. The reason, as Alice briskly informed me, was that she and Bill had broken up. But she had an alternative idea for my itinerary. A schoolteacher on winter break, Alice wanted to fly to Chicago and drive with me to Mexico and then home to San Francisco. Being extremely footloose, it sounded as good an idea as any, so that's exactly what we did, arriving in San Francisco on the last day of the year—December 31, 1972. I never left.

I rented an apartment in the Watergate Apartments in the East Bay, which is what Californians call all the lands and towns on the eastern edge of San Francisco Bay. Needless to say, this Watergate was a pale imitation of the elegant Washington residence about to become so very notorious, but I did have to pay rent, and to do so, I more or less fell back into the law. It was what I knew how to do, and the only contacts I had in San Francisco were lawyers. One was Sheldon Otis's law partner from Detroit, David Rosenthal; he had gotten his law degree at Boalt Hall— Berkeley's law school—and had moved back to the West Coast, opening an office in the East Bay's Point Richmond, a small and attractive town right next to the much larger, poorer, more crime-ridden commercial city of Richmond.

I began working as David's law clerk. The job kept me in groceries while I studied for the California Bar exam, another indication of my intention to settle there. Not committed enough to take a bar review course, which is standard procedure, I failed the exam the first time around. For my second try, scheduled for November 1973, I followed procedure, took the course, passed the exam, and was duly sworn in as a member of the California Bar in June 1974.

I immediately applied for jobs at public defenders' offices around the Bay Area. By now, Sheldon had also moved out West, having been hired to head up the Legal Aid Society in San Mateo County, the large county south of San Francisco that runs virtually all the way down the coastal peninsula. It was Sheldon who suggested I apply for a job in the Community Defender program of the Bayview-Hunter's Point Foundation, a lively, multi-service community organization in a neighborhood on San Francisco's southeastern edge. He also put in a word on my behalf with the organization's leadership. Not surprisingly, I guess, I got the job.

It meant moving into San Francisco proper. I found an apartment on the street known as "The Great Highway"—just across from the Pacific Ocean and only a few blocks from Golden Gate Park. I was living in the thick of San Francisco's legendary fog, but each morning I would drive out of it, commuting southward across the peninsula to work. I felt firmly entrenched—a true resident of the Bay Area.

The Bayview-Hunter's Point Foundation had been started in 1971 by Ernie Mitchell—formally, Ernest Mitchell Jr.—a local community activist, a street guy born and bred and utterly at home in the overwhelmingly African American neighborhood, but a man also utterly fed up with the crime and drug abuse that were ripping his community to shreds. The

Community Defender program was the Foundation's alternative to the San Francisco Public Defender's Office, and it was for residents of the community only. Its aim was to make sure that Bayview-Hunter's Point residents were not disproportionately swept up into the criminal justice system as a first-resort answer to any problem—at least, not without getting high-quality legal representation and other forms of legal and social-service assistance.

The director of the Community Defender program was Richard Bancroft, an experienced African American lawyer who was well known and highly respected in legal circles. Where Ernie was a local man of the people—the classic charismatic leader—Richard was the exemplar of *gravitas*, impeccably distinguished in his speech and behavior, a man who exuded a sense of purpose. The two men made a good pair.

Our staff of five lawyers comprised four whites and only one African American. Our three investigators, two men and one woman, were all African American, while one of our two secretaries was white, the other black, as was the receptionist. Just about all the nonlegal staff were residents of Bayview-Hunter's Point, and the organization was headquartered in an old house in the heart of the community; my office was the kitchen of the house next door. That next-door building also housed two probation officers, placed there as part of the thrust to provide as many services as possible in the heart of the community.

Richard presided over all of us—except the probation officers, of course—like a father over a sometimes unruly family. His lawyer kids frustrated him from time to time, but he loved us, and we all respected and loved him. We knew we could always go to him for advice on just about anything. Perhaps it was his beneficently hovering presence that glued us together. Whatever it was, there was a sense of community within that office that was quite extraordinary.

Certainly, the sense that the work we were doing was important was a key factor in forming that sense of community. Of course, that had also been the case in Detroit, but in Detroit I had felt I was part of a revolutionary movement, and everything I did was with my teeth gritted and my fists ready. Also, although I spent a lot of my time in Detroit in the inner city—and thought I knew it—I had never really felt I had a place there. In Bayview-Hunter's Point by contrast, the Community Defender office was actually *part* of the community. We played basketball with our clients; we picnicked with them and their families. We truly belonged to the community; it was for me a different—and very special—experience.

Moreover, while San Francisco was hardly free of the corruption, lying cops, or institutional racism I had found in Detroit, the atmosphere in general seemed less seething, more laid back. Above all, the caseload was reasonable—a luxury not available to a great many public defenders, who must apportion their time and effort among cases with the precision of a Swiss watch. I knew what it was like to be overworked; my work in Detroit had been always urgent. But in the Community Defender program, Richard saw to it that there was room and time for us to deliver a very high level of quality in the legal representation we gave our clients. That made an enormous difference—to the clients, of course, but also to the lawyers. With time and support and collegiality, you really don't need millions of dollars to provide successful counsel; at Bayview-Hunter's Point, we had what we needed, for the most part, to give clients the best. We were certainly the preferred alternative to the Public Defender for those neighborhood residents who qualified for our services. Precisely because we were based there, residents trusted us; because our caseloads were feasible, we really had the opportunity to fulfill their trust. It was a virtuous cycle that fostered our sense of community and made us all feel very much a family. And it made Bayview-Hunters Point a great place to work.

I remember Richard's Friday afternoon meetings in which we would brainstorm each other's cases. The sense of camaraderie was palpable; we were trying to help each other, to help the organization, above all to help the clients. Do any one of those things, and you were doing them all.

The discussions were serious—our purpose was serious—but that didn't keep us from indulging in sharp banter and good-natured joshing. Richard enjoyed the comic relief even as he determinedly kept us focused on the matter at hand. The meetings stretched on through the afternoon, but when they ended, it felt like closing time; the court week was over, and there was that warm feeling of being off-the-hook for a while as we went our separate ways.

Work worth doing with people you admire and like for a boss who has your back: For me, it was a highly satisfying prescription. I was learning that it was possible to practice law and live a fulfilling life outside of the law at the same time—a good lesson and one for which I am grateful to Bayview-Hudson's Point.

The problem was that the program was federally funded, and getting the funding we needed was always a struggle—which is probably why Richard stuck around on Friday nights when the rest of us were heading for home. His constant worry was how to secure the money to keep the Community Defender program in business. It was never a sure thing.

The kinds of cases we mostly dealt with were typical of the violations alleged in a neighborhood mired in poverty and isolated by racial discrimination. Where unemployment is high, education low, and public services difficult to access, life on a day-to-day basis is invariably difficult, and the tensions from living it are invariably high. Petty thefts can be common, but so can the bursts of violence that arise from anger, resentment, the feeling that the world is indifferent and that no one is listening to you. Drugs were the main escape from these feelings, and the criminal drug trade fueled the neighborhood's economy.

The case of a young African American man I'll call Jimmy was typical. A known addict, Jimmy was caught up in a wide-ranging "sweep" staged one day on the corner of Sunnydale and Hahn, a legendary hangout place in the neighborhood, by a narcotics task force unit of the San Francisco Police Department. Jimmy was charged with two hand-to-hand sales of heroin to the same undercover cop and with possession of heroin, which he was alleged to have dropped on the street at the time of his arrest.

Jimmy was a slight guy—five feet nine inches tall at most and narrow as a rail—and as soft-spoken as he was diminutive. His mother, by contrast, was overbearing, formidably outspoken, and totally opposed to me serving as her son's lawyer. That was because I was advising Jimmy to let me try to negotiate a plea bargain. The reason I was advising that was because his case was going to be a very, very difficult case to win. Simply put, that he had been caught red-handed was credible; that he was innocent of all the charges, as his mother wanted to believe, was a lot less credible. If convicted, Jimmy would be subject to a mandatory minimum sentence long enough to rob him of his youth. He would have emerged from prison a middle-aged man; a middle-aged ex-con would face enormous difficulties finding a job, and studies confirm that middle-aged ex-cons who cannot find jobs are particularly disposed to committing crimes. If we plea-bargained, I argued, he would do far less prison time, and when he got out, he would still have a life of possibilities open to him.

But his mother was having none of it. She wanted her son to go to trial and prove his innocence, and she told Richard she wanted me replaced with a lawyer who would do that very thing. Richard said no. "Gerry is the lawyer I have assigned to represent your son," he said. "Your other option is the public defender."

Reluctantly, Mama agreed to keep me on, but she also continued to insist there should be no plea bargain. I argued as fervently as I could. I wanted her to understand that I cared about her son—as indeed I did, that I understood he was telling her he was innocent and that I wanted to do all I could for him, but that I thought the evidence was simply stacked against us. That evidence, I told her, would come from an African American narc, an undercover officer who would testify that Jimmy twice sold him heroin and that he saw Jimmy drop a bindle of heroin—drug slang for about 100 milligrams or five "lines"—when the police converged on Sunnydale and Hahn. A mother's belief in her son's innocence versus a veteran narcotics cop's testimony: it wasn't a good equation to put before a jury. But I was unpersuasive; in the end, I had no choice but to accede to the wishes of my client, a client heavily influenced by his mother, and go to trial.

Every defense lawyer—certainly every committed defense lawyer—knows what it is like to lie awake at night, going over the evidence in your mind, planning strategy, worrying about your client, wondering whether you have thought of everything that needs to be done, agonizing that you won't do well at trial, won't say it right, won't make the case persuasively. The weight of another human being's life—in this case, of his youth—hangs heavy in your hands. You feel the responsibility as yours alone; it is a solemn responsibility, and it can wear you down. That is even more the case when the client insists on a course of action you do not recommend, so as I prepared Jimmy's defense, there were lots of sleepless nights.

Jimmy had been one of about a dozen people arrested in what had been a very busy day for law enforcement, as one narcotics cop after another cuffed one defendant after another and hauled them *en masse* into custody. The preliminary hearings on these cases—in which officers testified in order to demonstrate that there was enough evidence to go to trial—were just getting underway as I was preparing our case, and I had the idea to try to delay Jimmy's trial while I collected the hearing transcripts of the narcs' testimony in the cases of the other guys arrested during the same police sweep. I hoped that by analyzing the testimony in these cases, I might find some inconsistency, some anomaly, some inherent contradiction that might shed light on how to defend Jimmy effectively. So I moved for continuance after continuance, one delay of trial after another, so that I could go through as many hearing transcripts as possible.

Bingo! As I read through the narcs' testimony again and again and again, comparing and contrasting what each officer stated in each case, poring over every word, it became increasingly clear that the cops had conformed their testimony to each defendant. That is, there was a basic testimony template; the cops simply tailored it to incriminate the particular defendant in court that day.

I concluded that for any one of these cops to have witnessed all the things he claimed to have witnessed in all the cases in which he testified, he either would have had to have been in a dozen different places at one time, or he was making it up. Only the latter conclusion was credible.

It happened with cop after cop in hearing after hearing, and I began to realize that my use of delaying tactics gave Jimmy a chance at an acquittal. For it suggested to me a clear trial strategy—namely, discrediting the testimony of the most critical witness against my client. My aim was to show that the officer had committed perjury in the hearings on other defendants' cases; any testimony he might give against Jimmy could therefore not be trusted.

And that is exactly what I did.

First, the narc testified about Jimmy, stating that as soon as his unit arrived on the scene, he immediately approached Jimmy and saw him drop a bindle of heroin. Then I asked the narc to confirm that he had testified at the preliminary hearings of other men arrested in the sweep— call them Anderson, Baker, and Carter—and he did so.

"Now, Officer," I began, transcript in hand, "at the preliminary hearing of Joe Anderson, you testified that as soon as your unit arrived on the scene, you immediately approached Mr. Anderson and you saw him drop a bindle of heroin. Is that correct?" I held up the transcript for all to see, and the narc had no choice but to admit he had so testified. "And at the preliminary hearing of Donald Baker," I went on, taking hold of another transcript, "you testified that as soon as your unit arrived on the scene, you immediately approached Mr. Baker and saw him drop a bindle of heroin, didn't you?" Thus confronted for a second time, the witness again had to admit to having given that testimony. "And at William Carter's preliminary hearing," I said, "you testified that as soon as your unit arrived on the scene, you immediately approached Mr. Carter and as you did so saw him drop a bindle of heroin." Pause. "Is that also correct, Officer?"

"Yes, it is," the narc testified.

"Anderson, Baker, Carter, and now you have added my client to the list. Sir, you have testified under oath that as soon as your unit arrived on the scene, you immediately approached four different people, who were in four different places, and saw each one of them drop a bindle of heroin. Isn't that true?"

There was little for the narc to do at that point except squirm. His lying under oath on multiple occasions so outraged the jurors that they deliberated for less than an hour before acquitting Jimmy on all counts.

I had not been surprised that the officer lied; at this point in my career, I believed that many witnesses lied—cops most of all. But I was proud of the jury for overriding whatever qualms they may have had about Jimmy's conduct to focus on the fact that the police were perverting justice, and that the District Attorney's Office that prosecuted all these men knew it.

And of course, I was thrilled by the verdict, for my sake certainly, but for Jimmy's above all. Just as gratifying as his acquittal was that he obtained treatment for his addiction and never got into trouble again. So in addition to reinforcing my belief in thoroughness of preparation—and imparting the lesson that delay can sometimes be a helpful litigation tool—Jimmy's case also confirmed my conviction that people are capable of redemption. People, I believe, are like houses. Houses that lack a solid foundation are likely to have problems, but even houses with problems can be rehabilitated. It is this belief in people that motivated me to become—and remain—a criminal defense lawyer.

And yes, his mother ended up thanking me.

I was in my early 30s at the time of Jimmy's case, and life was good. I had my quirky apartment in the fog—but with beautiful sunsets—and I had a little bit of money in my pocket. I was nearly as fit as I had been in college and was involved in both basketball and softball leagues as well as playing pick-up basketball most weekends in the park or at the gym. I even took up racquetball and played it regularly with a guy named Micah Brown—a good guy with, I thought, a great first name.

My work was highly satisfying, and I was gaining experience along with skill every day. I was also meeting people who would play important roles in my professional life, for I certainly knew by now that the Bay Area was where I wanted to be and criminal defense law was what I wanted to do; my hippie fantasy had entirely vanished.

One of these new connections was made during another case in which the strategy was to impeach a police officer's testimony. To do so, I needed the officer to admit that he had initialed a key document in the case, but the scrawled letters were hard to read, and in court, the cop said he couldn't make it out; neither could the judge, who would not allow the document to be entered as evidence unless the officer authenticated the scrawl as his.

I had a photograph of the document, and I thought that if it could be enhanced such that the officer's initials were clearly legible, I could win the point. But, in those days, getting the photo enhanced at all required the expert technical assistance of a forensic scientist, and compounding the issue was the fact that I needed the enhancement before the trial resumed in the morning. So far from knowing the right forensic scientist who could do this job and do it fast, I knew no forensic scientists at all, and it was late afternoon by the time I got back to the office and began searching the phone directory. Cold calling is never fun, and in this case, it wasn't surprising that I came up empty time after time. At very nearly the end of the work day, I finally reached a man with the unlikely name of Lindbergh Miller—"Call me Ed," he said. I explained my dilemma and added the bad news that I worked for a community organization and didn't know whether money would be available to pay him. "We can worry about that later," said Ed. He and a photographer worked all night in the lab, and Ed met me on the front steps of the San Francisco Hall of Justice in the morning with a huge photographic blow-up of the document that clearly showed the cop's initials. The judge admitted the document, the cop was shown to have lied, and my client was acquitted. Ed and I established both a professional and personal relationship that has lasted for years—to the great benefit of many clients.

———

In 1976, I got an offer I couldn't refuse. My mentor and hero, Sheldon Otis himself, decided to open his own law office and asked me to come in with him. Sheldon had a very particular idea of how he wanted to structure this practice, and he suddenly had the wherewithal to make it happen. In an elegantly renovated Victorian at 1632 Union Street in one of San Francisco's classically scenic neighborhoods, he created two trial teams, each comprising two lawyers, one serving as a trial lawyer and the other as a research and writing specialist. Sheldon headed one team with Neil Morse as his research/writer specialist, and I headed the other with John Mitchell, who had been the motion and writ specialist at the Bayview-Hunter's Point Community Defender office. Each trial team was supported by a secretary-cum-administrative assistant—in our case, Karen Chedister, who had been a secretary at the Community Defender. In addition to Sheldon's secretary, another staff member carried out the essential role of office factotum and jack-of-all-trades.

In the basement, Sheldon had a mock courtroom constructed and outfitted with a video and audio taping system. He wanted this set-up to practice giving opening statements and closing arguments and to have clients and witnesses experience testifying on direct examination and undergoing cross-examination. This was unheard-of in 1976; in this, as in so many things, Sheldon was way ahead of his time. Just as coaches use video of athletes' performance to note their flaws and teach them the right way to execute a maneuver, for lawyers and especially for witnesses, it is tremendously helpful to see yourself present an argument or answer questions. Watching yourself stumble over your tongue or freeze up in mid-thought while you search for a word is highly instructive, and clients in particular can see that for themselves. It was another facet of Sheldon's meticulous thoroughness.

Sheldon's concept of the structure of the firm and the depth of the legal practice he sought to provide were certainly exciting. Yet when I think back on those years at his firm, my main recollection is that John and I did not have very much to do. I worked with Sheldon on a number of his cases, and the opportunity to watch him in action and to see "inside" his thinking was invaluable. But our team really had no cases of our own, and the work, while interesting, wasn't sufficient to keep us occupied. We were at sea in this fantasy law firm—financed, it turned out, by the very successful marijuana importer who was one of Sheldon's biggest clients.

John, a brilliant lawyer as well as a dear friend, soon left to become a law professor, first at Boalt Hall and then for many years at Seattle University—to the benefit of generations of students. I stayed on, and little by little, I began to get a sense of some of the stresses and distresses that haunted Sheldon. Indeed, as his life grew more complicated, I found myself taking on more of his work, including two murder cases, as I watched him become increasingly mired in a kind of downward spiral that was both puzzling and alarming.

For one thing, I had always been baffled by his leaving Detroit, his beloved hometown and the place where he had trained and influenced a generation of criminal defense lawyers. Even more astonishing was that when he moved to California, he had left some Detroit clients in the lurch. It was so antithetical to everything about the man that it shocked everyone who knew him; we all accounted it an aberration. I was aware that the Michigan Bar had investigated the matter, but nothing came of the inquiry, and the word was that influential lawyers who had known and respected Sheldon got the issue dropped.

But then rumors began to swirl about irregularities in Sheldon's handling of some funds back when he was running the San Mateo Legal Aid Society. He had not stolen any money, simply borrowed some from the agency's bank account, replenishing the account later. Such an act is of course technically a crime, as Sheldon, the consummate lawyer, would certainly have known; he must also have known that it would eventually be discovered. It was, and the discovery was enough to cost him his job and put him under investigation by both law enforcement and the California State Bar. Whatever was at the core of Sheldon's personal turmoil, it was tragic to see it put a premature end to his legal career. To this day he remains for me the exemplar of what a criminal defense lawyer should be. He had the knowledge, the knack, the commitment, the eloquence, and something else: a kind of edge—a sharp, impressive something he could bring to bear from just outside the margins within which most people operate. Wherever that edge comes from, it made Sheldon Otis a weapon for justice and unquestionably the best lawyer I have ever known. His fall from grace was painful to me in so many ways.

Yet in the midst of all this, my own life was in the throes of elemental changes that included both profound loss and life-changing gain.

There are some phone calls you always remember. In May 1977, I was in San Jose trying a murder case with Sheldon when I got the call that my mother had been taken to a hospital in Philadelphia. "Come at once," I was told. Some years before, she had been diagnosed with cancer, but the treatment had produced a remission that had now gone on for five years, and I suppose we all thought she had beaten it.

She certainly had the strength to do so, if inner strength were enough. My mother, born Rachel Finkel—always called Rae—had left school in the eighth grade in order to work in the bakery that sustained her family. She had been widowed young, and for what was by now the majority of my life, she had been my sole parent, an unfailingly loving, wonderfully supportive woman. She was proud of all her children, but I always liked to think she was particularly proud that I was a lawyer, and despite the distance in miles that separated us, we were always close.

I flew to Philadelphia that night, arriving just in time. She was in fact almost certainly dying of the cancer that had returned with a vengeance, but before the disease could finish the job, she had fallen victim to a sudden, explosive cerebral hemorrhage, the same thing that had killed my father. My mother did die and was buried on Mother's Day, the very same day on which we had buried my father 18 years earlier. Her death carved a deep hole in my heart.

Yet just a few months later I met the woman who would be my partner for life. Susan Elizabeth Homes was born in England and grew up in the tiny village of Middleton-on-Sea, one of the south coast staging-areas from which the Allies launched the invasion of Europe on D-Day, June 6, 1944. She came to the United States as a young woman, traveling with a friend, hoping to see the sights and find adventure. She succeeded at both by taking on the paying assignment, along with a couple of friends, of driving a car across country from the East Coast to California—not an uncommon thing in those days if a company or individual needed a car brought to another destination.

In the Golden State, she supported herself at first by making women's clothes and managing a legal secretarial agency. Then she enrolled in the California College of Arts & Crafts in Oakland where she studied fabric arts and photography, excelling at both. She also took a part-time job at a downtown law firm and happened to be working the reception desk on the day I arrived there to meet a friend for lunch. The moment I saw Susan, I quite literally knew I was going to marry her. We were "officially" introduced a few weeks later at a political fundraiser back in Bayview-Hunter's Point; although we talked the night away, I could not tell you then and cannot tell you now what we talked about for all those hours. Ten months later, we were married. Susan has been both the love of my life and the hinge that has made everything else in my life possible.

In 1978, in fact, shortly after our marriage, we agreed that it was time for me to go out on my own.

We were living at the time on Lincoln Way near Golden Gate Park, in a small house that had been gutted and completely renovated a few years before by some young guys starting up their own construction business. The interior was all raw redwood; the sculptor next door had built a wrought-iron spiral staircase to the new upper loft; and a retired brick-layer pal of the builders had crafted a large corner fireplace in the downstairs. With an unsolicited and totally unexpected windfall I received from making a referral to a Detroit colleague, I had bought the place before it ever went on the market, even though it probably violated every housing code on the City's books. Although it would eventually prove too small for a family, it was so quirky and so quintessentially San Franciscan that it had served as the perfect bachelor pad and was now a welcoming nest for Susan and me.

Outside the nest, however, Sheldon's dream law firm was falling apart. Sheldon himself was in the process of being disciplined by the Bar and was closing his practice, leaving me responsible for the two murder cases—but of course with no office from which to conduct the work of defending the clients. John Mitchell was long gone into academia, and Neil Morse and I were the only lawyers left. Although we were both ready to undertake solo practices, we decided to get an office together, and the one we found was only a block away from Sheldon's office—a space occupying half the third floor of yet another Victorian.

Neil and I shared that space and one another's company, occasionally working together on a case, for a decade. I worked on some formidable cases from that office. It is where I argued and won, in the 1978 state Supreme Court ruling in *Hawkins vs. Superior Court,* the right of all California felony defendants to a preliminary hearing, whether they had been indicted by a grand jury or charged by a district attorney.

It is where I obtained the acquittal of Reuben Vizcarra, who had been charged with masterminding the assassination of the police chief of Union City, a suburb in sprawling Alameda County. It is also the office from which I represented Stephen Bingham, as you will read in a later chapter. And it is where I had my own eyes opened to the way the justice system often worked—or failed to work—for the 51 percent of the population that is female.

— 4 —

Taking Women Seriously

It's hard to credit now, but there was a time—and it is not so very distant—when cops responding to a call about a "domestic dispute," either from a wife claiming she was being beaten up by her husband or from a neighbor hearing the screams, would routinely settle the guy down and walk back out the door. No charges would be filed; no record would be kept. This was the couple's business, nobody else's.

It was a time when wife-beating was the punch line of a joke. A famous brand of coffee ran a magazine ad showing a husband spanking his wife—appropriate punishment, the ad suggested, for her having failed to "store-test" the freshness of the coffee. The term "battered woman" had barely entered anyone's vocabulary, not because the reality didn't exist but because it was not spoken of. The various forms of spousal abuse we articulate today—beating, coercion, kidnapping, and worse—simply weren't on the radar screen. In a very real sense, violence toward women was simply not taken seriously by the criminal justice system; it was the ultimate in objectification of women and the ultimate in institutionalized solipsism—i.e., if you don't look, you can't see it, and if you don't see it, it doesn't exist.

I had by now been practicing criminal defense law for a decade, yet I was as ignorant and insensitive about these matters as was the bulk of the population. I suppose I naively thought, if I thought about it at all, that domestic violence was something that happened "somewhere else"—probably in the deep heart of the places where poverty ran deep and where an entirely different culture, steeped in an alien machismo, prevailed.

Yet the truth is that I was as much a part of the culture steeped in machismo as any man anywhere in America—and as most women as well. The most benign way to regard that culture is to say that it considered that whatever happened within the sacred precinct of marriage or a cohabiting relationship was absolutely private and not subject to public scrutiny. But in fact, the macho culture was really all about power and money, with the man still regarded in some sense as the owner and the woman as his property, to do with as he pleased. I did not consciously hold to that view—I certainly would never have expressed it in those words—but it was woven through the social fabric and had threaded its way into our legal system so deeply that most of us weren't even aware of it.

I became aware of it, with a vengeance, in the spring of 1981 when I got a call from the then-director of a women's collective known as La Casa de las Madres, San Francisco's first and, at the time, only shelter for battered women. The director, Jan Lagerlof, was calling about the case of a woman named Delores Churchill, who had shot and wounded her unarmed husband in the lobby of a downtown office building and had been charged with attempted murder and assault with a deadly weapon. Herself a member of the Bar, Jan was dissatisfied with the lawyer Delores had and was looking for someone who might be willing to take the case. The footnote to her search was that there was only minimal assurance that the lawyer would be paid. Delores was on leave from her job at a bank and could not afford an experienced criminal defense lawyer, so her only support at the moment came from the few women in the forefront of the local domestic violence movement. Jan Lagerlof had galvanized this group into action, but just how much money could be raised was unclear.

I was tentatively willing to consider the proposition, but I, of course, needed to know more and to meet my prospective client who was free on bail. We set up a meeting, and Jan and Delores trudged up the two flights of stairs to my Union Street office.

There is a lot about the practice of law that has nothing to do with legality or statutes or courtroom strategy. Rather, it has to do with human connections—specifically, with the very important connection that is forged between lawyer and client on the plane of feeling and behavior. For me, such a connection is very helpful if I am going to be able to succeed as the client's advocate, advisor, counselor. It isn't a matter of affection or of liking the person or being liked by him or her; it is about trust, about confidence that our interaction is taking us toward the same goal, about a shared self-interest.

That is why the first meeting with a prospective client is often so important. It can tell me whether a connection is possible, whether the prospective client and I can establish the mutual trust we will need to go forward.

Delores Churchill, when she and Jan came to my office that day in 1981, was in her late 20s and in the time we spent talking showed herself to be emotional, articulate, and courageous. For me, the meeting was the beginning of what would be a comprehensive, detailed, and disturbing education about spousal abuse and domestic violence. For Delores, I cannot even imagine what it must have taken to relate in excruciating detail the violence she had endured over years of abuse by the man who had been her high school sweetheart and was now a police officer. Consider that she was describing assaults, many of them sexual in nature, not only to a man but to a white man, and not only to a white man but to a white man representing the law. To a black woman growing up in the 1960s and 1970s, the law as an institutional reality was, for good reason, rarely seen as protective. In addition, Delores had listened for years to her husband's bombastic boasts at the end of a day in court about how he had "lied so well" when he testified before judges and juries, as police officers are routinely required to do. For her to have any faith at all that the legal system could work for her was a testament to Jan and the other women supporting Delores emotionally as well as financially, and the courage Delores showed in embracing that faith was inspiring to me. I took the case; I'd worry about money later, if ever.

The facts of the shooting were not in dispute. Although the couple was separated at the time, Frank Churchill had driven his wife to her job in downtown San Francisco. Just before Frank got into the car, Delores had taken one of his guns—not his service revolver—out of the glove compartment. During the ride, the two argued about Frank's demand that Delores sign a quit-claim to any rights in their house. They were still arguing when Frank pulled up in front of the large office building where Delores worked; she got out of the car quickly, slammed the door, and ran toward the building. Frank drove up against the curb and left the car in a non-parking zone on Market Street, one of San Francisco's busiest thoroughfares, as he chased after Delores. He caught up with her in the lobby of the office building, and at his approach, she turned to face him and fired the gun twice. Both shots struck Frank.

The cops and an ambulance soon arrived at the scene. Frank was taken to the hospital where his wounds were attended do, and Delores was apprehended and taken into police custody. The prosecutor determined there was "no justification" for the shooting, claimed Delores had shown "a reckless disregard for human life," and filed two charges against her.

———

Again, there was no dispute about any of these facts. Delores had indeed taken the gun out of the glove department, and she did indeed fire it twice at her unarmed husband. What was in dispute, however, was everything that led up to the moment when she pulled the trigger. That "everything" consisted of seven years of brutality, of physical and sexual assaults, and of what the law calls domestic abuse or wife-beating.

At the time I heard what Delores had to say about her life with Frank Churchill, I had been a defense lawyer for more than ten years. I had come up against some pretty rough characters and had been exposed to a number of lives lived in harsh circumstances. I knew how difficult life could be—especially among the poor, the frail, those hurt in body and mind. I had listened to testimony that curdled my blood. But none of it quite prepared me for what I heard from Delores.

She described threats and assaults. She said Frank told her he had "nothing to lose" by killing her, then their daughter, then himself. He told her he knew lots of junkies, and that he could get one of them to kill her for the price of a cheap fix. He assured her he could kill her and plead the stress of his job—"like Dan White," he said[1]—and serve maybe three months "in a carpeted cell" before being released.

There was violence. When Delores told Frank she was pregnant, he fired his .38-caliber pistol through a pillow she was holding and into the wall. Then he punched her in the stomach.

There was the time he held a gun on her and threatened to shoot her if she didn't have sex with a friend of his who was waiting downstairs. When she refused, he began to strangle her with an undershirt until she "saw black dots" and could no longer breathe.

There was the time an enraged Frank broke off a broomstick handle and raped Delores with it.

There was that very morning of the day Delores fired the gun. She left her house early for work, then called Frank to make sure he had picked up their daughter and taken her to school. Frank said he didn't know where their daughter was. They met at Delores's house where they found the little girl under her bed. Frank beat and raped Delores, then took her to his house to find the quit-claim deed he demanded she must sign. She refused, and he again assaulted and raped her. That's when she took the gun out of the glove compartment, wondering what he might do next.

When she heard him coming after her in the lobby of the place where she worked, is it any wonder she assumed he was coming to attack her yet again?

That, in fact, became the fulcrum of our defense strategy. The law is clear that if attacked, a person may use reasonable force to thwart the attack; that is the time-honored principle of self-defense. What was relatively new about the argument I would make in court, however, was that given the history of Delores's experiences with Frank, it was rational—it was indeed reasonable—for her to perceive a threat to her life in his coming

----

1. Dan White was the San Francisco County supervisor who killed Mayor George Moscone and fellow supervisor Harvey Milk, pleaded the "Twinkie defense," and served only five years in prison.

up behind her; therefore, the gun she used to counter the threat was reasonable force. For this defense to prevail, I would have to prove that Frank had abused Delores in a variety of ways over the course of years, and that she was justified in believing that she was about to be violently assaulted when she pulled the trigger to stop him.

It was a defense based on what became known as the "battered-wife syndrome," a subject about which I had known nothing but learned a great deal. From Jan, whose knowledge of the subject was gained through serving so many battered women in La Casa's shelter, from a Colorado-based psychologist named Lenore Walker who was the preeminent expert on the subject, and of course from Delores Churchill herself, I learned how repeated cycles of violence and "contrition" can make the victim believe the violence is her fault and can dull her into a state of learned helplessness. Feeling both responsible and powerless, the abused person is unable to leave the situation and unable to change it—until in many cases, as with Delores, she lashes out self-protectively.

Yes, to most people, a husband racing to catch up with his wife in an office building lobby, even an angry husband, does not look like a life-threatening situation. Frank had no weapon on him, after all, and they were in a public place. What the defense had to show a jury was that if you had experienced the history Delores had lived through, and you turned and saw your violent husband racing toward you, with a look on his face that you knew all too well was a prelude to a beating at best, it would not have been unreasonable of you to have perceived his approach as a threat. On the contrary: It would have been unreasonable not to.

The trial was scheduled for June 1981.

———

Just a few months before we went to trial, the most life-affirming of all events happened to our household. Our son Micah was born in March, and I was present in the delivery room for his birth. This was years before cell phones appeared on the scene, so my pockets were filled with enough dimes and quarters to enable me to phone my family back East in the States and Susan's family way back East in England. Three months later,

Micah would attend his first trial; he would be present in Susan's arms for my closing argument.

But first, we had to get through the trial.

It began with a loss for all the lawyers. Over my objections and those of the prosecutor, the judge allowed a television camera in the courtroom; to my knowledge, it was the first time any trial in San Francisco was to be televised. I had objected because I knew the substance of Delores's testimony, and I knew it was going to be difficult enough for her to relate the grim details to a jury, a judge, and the normal collection of courtroom spectators; how much more difficult it would be before a vast television audience of strangers was something I could not even calculate. As it happened, for reasons I never learned, the camera was not present the day she testified; it was a most beneficent stroke of good luck.

Before we ever got to that point, however, Jan Lagerlof, Lenore Walker, and I had given serious attention to the jury selection process, during which I had another somewhat stunning revelation. I had assumed that women in particular would be sensitive to Delores's plight, so I was astonished to find that male prospective jurors were far more so. For many women, it was a matter of insisting that Delores "should have left sooner" and of being certain that, in her shoes, they would have done so. Lenore Walker had alerted me to this phenomenon, and no one knew more about the subject: Dr. Walker had founded the Domestic Violence Institute, had documented the cycle of abuse, and was the author of *The Battered Woman*, effectively the bible on the subject, for which she was honored with the 1979 Distinguished Media Award. Her insights, along with those of Jan, and her testimony in the courtroom were invaluable in the case.

It was invaluable because we would need not just to present the evidence of Delores's abuse but also to educate the jurors. They would have to learn that there was a syndrome at work here, and that it was the syndrome that caused Delores Churchill to pull the trigger. To ensure that we could engage Walker and do the other preparation needed for the trial, Jan and the still small but growing women's movement in the Bay Area went to work raising money and awareness—both extremely useful. Two activists in particular, both of whom went on to greater prominence, were among the frontline supporters helping our efforts back then—Eva

Patterson, the lawyer and founder of the Equal Justice Society, and Esta Soler, who founded Future Without Violence. Press attention followed in their wake, and that too helped our cause, at least by planting some fresh thinking about domestic violence in the public's mind.

―――――

The prosecution presented its case first, and the case was simple: There was no justification for the shooting, Delores showed premeditation in taking the gun from the glove compartment, and Frank Churchill insisted he had never laid a hand on his wife in anger. End of story.

I began my cross-examination of Frank with some benign questions about his work history and the marriage. Then I said, "You have struck Delores, have you not, sir?" I asked.

He conceded that they had had what he called "mutual combat."

"So that it is clear when I am asking whether you have struck Delores, I am saying have you ever hit her with your fist?" He denied it. I asked if he had ever kicked her. He denied it. Choked her? He denied it.

Yes, he conceded that his size and strength relative to his wife's were much greater and he acknowledged that he was indeed a member of the police SWAT team. But when I asked if he had ever slammed Delores's head into a wall, he denied it.

Ever hit her with a broken shower curtain rod? Denied.

Threatened to kill her? Denied.

Shot a gun at her or near her? Denied.

Pointed a gun at her threateningly? Denied.

Ever hit her in the eye? Denied—with a footnote. As Frank explained, "she got hit in the eye as a result of coming between myself and her brother who was attacking me."

He claimed further that Delores had signed an initial quit-claim voluntarily. But because her name had been misspelled, she needed either to correct the spelling on the original or to sign a new one. That, he said, was why he had brought her back to his house, and it was what the two of them were discussing on the day of the shooting.

Yes, he admitted that having a .38 caliber gun in his car was a violation of Police Department regulations, and he admitted also to having ammunition for the gun in the center console of his car and on his person at the time of the shooting.

So the impression he wanted to leave us with through his testimony—and by denying every suggestion of violence during cross-examination—was that this was an officer of the law who was maybe a little too zealous in his preparedness but who had never, ever been a violent husband.

Our defense presentation utterly discredited that impression. Witness by witness, we proved that he had abused his wife in many ways: He had humiliated her in public; he had beaten her in front of eyewitnesses; he had left visible and invisible scars. With all of the witnesses I put on the stand, the aim was to undermine Frank's credibility and his character while building sensitivity for what Delores had suffered. I wanted the jury to feel the fear Delores felt when she turned and saw him coming after her. I wanted them to understand how utterly reasonable it was for her to be afraid he was going to harm her yet again, how reasonable it was that she should do whatever she could to thwart him.

Her own testimony, when it came, was unsparing. Rarely—if ever—had so degrading an experience been so precisely particularized in a San Francisco court room. In implacable detail, Delores recounted instance after instance of assaults, beatings, debasement, sexual violation, and death threats. For her sake, I was thankful the television camera was not there, for the presence of that large camera, centrally placed, would have been unnerving in the extreme, and needless to say, giving the testimony had been distressing enough.

Delores Churchill had come a long way down a difficult emotional path of awareness and self-awareness, supported and sustained in ways I as a man could only imagine by the women of La Casa and the advocates on her side. In the course of that journey, she had developed the inherent strength she never knew she possessed. Under cross-examination, she kept her composure and was steadfast in her answers. It was compelling testimony.[2]

I suppose what made it particularly compelling was that it was being aired for the first time. Delores had never told her parents what their

---

2. So compelling that the prosecutor in his closing argument to the jury would eventually acknowledge that Frank Churchill had brutalized his wife.

respected and in so many ways successful son-in-law had done to her; she had kept all that hidden—out of shame, perhaps, but certainly to protect them from the awful truth about her life, and perhaps also to protect Frank. For on the day she gave her testimony, her father, Willie Washington, quietly left the courtroom and drove to Frank's house. Lucky for them both, Frank was not there.

On three occasions when Delores had tried to report Frank to the authorities, they never followed through. She must have felt, justifiably, that she simply wasn't being heard—wasn't even being listened to.

So when finally she was asked directly, and then in cross-examination, to repeat and explain what had happened to her, it may well have been in some sense a relief. Delores had few expectations of acquittal; she always believed, as Frank had always told her, that his badge would protect him. This was her moment of truth, and she told it clearly and simply and with the immediacy only someone who lived it could have managed.

I then called Lenore Walker to the stand—in a sense, to shed the light of science onto the monstrously dark testimony the jury had just heard. Lenore explained the psychology of the abuse dynamic and how the repetition of the cycle—tension, release of the abuser's tension through violence, blaming the victim—eventually "teaches" the abused individual the helplessness and passivity Delores had testified to. In her expert opinion, Lenore said, having examined the history of abuse Delores had suffered, it was entirely reasonable of her to perceive that Frank was about to harm her. As for the often asked question, "Why didn't she just leave?," the answer was powerfully evident: She had left, and it didn't save her from his abuse. The jury paid close attention. Their deliberations, once the judge had charged them, lasted only two hours. They acquitted Delores of all charges. It was banner-headline news.

It should have been; for in my view, the Delores Churchill trial constituted an important lesson, one the public at large was beginning to learn. The first use of the battered-wife syndrome defense in San Francisco—and one of the first instances of its use anywhere—this case raised the consciousness not just of the members of the jury but, through press coverage, of the wider public about the very ugly realities of domestic violence. After you had read a news article or seen the TV coverage about the trial of Delores Churchill, you probably stopped telling "wife-beating" jokes, you probably stopped getting irritated at abused wives who didn't just leave their abusers, and you may even have realized that domestic abuse didn't just happen to certain people you couldn't possibly know.

That is certainly the transformation I had undergone in getting to know Delores and in working on her case. It was an important learning experience for me, and as gratifying as the acquittal was, it was even more gratifying to have articulated what became known as the battered-woman defense, something long overdue in our courtrooms, in the press, and in public discourse—an eye-opener for a great many people and perhaps a harbinger that the law was taking women seriously.

Not quite. As the case of Suzanne Wickersham showed, law enforcement authorities are too ready to be governed by old assumptions, tired clichés, and gender as well as racial profiling. Latching onto a stereotype is easier than starting from scratch to find the truth, and when the public is clamoring for someone to be punished, the easy way seems very appealing. That's what happened in the Wickersham case.

As with Delores, Suzanne's story was about a bad marriage, a gun, and a husband shot—in the Wickersham case, killed. But just about everything else about the cases was different.

Suzanne and Curt Wickersham were married in 1966 and separated in 1979. They had five children. Suzanne had been a full-time mother, while Curt, with his military background, worked in law enforcement, most recently in Customs. The family moved a lot and had settled in Novato, in the top end of Marin County, north of San Francisco, in 1977. Curt traveled a good deal for work, drank, was a somewhat irresponsible although loving father, and tended to be despondent. The couple tried marriage counseling, but Curt was not responsive. On a few occasions, he threatened Suzanne, primarily by insisting that he would block her from having custody of the children if she left him.

In the end, it was Curt who left, taking up with a younger woman. He had removed most of his belongings at the time of this separation, but on the day in question, he had come back to the house for whatever was left.

He and Suzanne were in their bedroom; Suzanne was helping him pack up. According to her account, there was a stack of Curt's folded shirts on an upper shelf in the closet, and she reached up for them. There was a gun under the shirts, which Suzanne said she had forgotten was there for protection if needed. But when she scooped up the shirts, she picked up the gun along with them. Curt saw the gun, freaked out, and grabbed at it. In the ensuing struggle, the gun went off twice; at the second shot, Curt fell, mortally wounded in the chest.

In a panic, Suzanne dialed 911. The police arrived to find, as they described her, a "hysterical" woman. The first officer on the scene said she was "yelling hysterically." The second officer on the scene said Suzanne had run up to him "in a hysterical-type condition." This impression—of a hysterical woman—became the colored filter over the lens through which the police and the prosecutors viewed the evidence and the witnesses, and the stereotype of "a woman scorned" became the accepted narrative that blunted any deeper form of investigation.

What the police did *not* find, in their survey of the scene, was the first bullet. Only the second, lodged in Curt's body, was accounted for, although two bullets had clearly been fired. The prosecutor would claim that the first, unaccounted-for bullet had been "a practice shot" by a wife rendered overwrought because she had been put aside for a younger, fresher romance. The police also found witnesses—a woman "friend" of Suzanne and the man with whom she had been having an affair—who claimed she had asked their help to kill Curt. Other witnesses would testify that she had a tendency to act "erratically," something hysterical women supposedly do a lot.

I have learned only recently that the word "hysterical"—indeed, the use of the term "hysteria" as a psychological disorder—comes via Latin from the Greek word for womb or uterus. The term "hysteria" was coined in the seventeenth century precisely because it was assumed that the behavior it described was specific to women and was in some way associated with female physiology. Three centuries later, the term "hysterical woman" still resonated; that is what the cops found when they arrived at Suzanne's house, and that is what the subsequent investigation confirmed. Hysterical as only a woman could be, Suzanne and her story were easily dismissed.

She was charged with murder, tried, convicted of the charge, and sentenced to life in prison.

————

That is when Suzanne Wickersham came to me. She believed she had grounds for appealing her conviction, and since I do not specialize in appeals, I referred her to a lawyer who did. This lawyer indeed found a basis for appeal—namely, that the judge in Suzanne's murder trial had failed, in his charge to the jury, to instruct them on both second-degree murder and voluntary manslaughter charges as well as on the charge of first-degree murder. The judge had refrained from doing so at the request of Suzanne's own defense attorney, but the defense attorney's request was never placed on the record, and therefore, as far as the appellate court knew, the request had never been made. In other words, there was no record of the defense having waived the right to object to the judge's failure to instruct the jury on the lesser offenses of second-degree murder and voluntary manslaughter. The issue on appeal was whether or not the judge should have given the instructions anyway, on his own; the legal term is *sua sponte,* of his own will.

Suzanne's appeal lost in the California Court of Appeals, but because the jury instruction issue was deemed to be unresolved and of statewide importance, it was accepted for review by the state Supreme Court. On September 2, 1982, the Supreme Court ruled that the judge in the trial should have instructed the jury on the other charges, and it reversed Suzanne's conviction. She came back to me and asked that I represent her at her retrial on the charge of murder.

————

Suzanne Wickersham was in many ways a challenging client. I liked her, and I believed her to be innocent, but she was a highly emotional individual. Although I'm not sure how I would have acted in a similar situation, her emotions often ran ahead of her thinking. She also believed she had been ill-served by her previous defense lawyers; the lawyer in her first trial thought her innocence so obvious he didn't do much to defend her, and he supposedly was distracted by a drinking problem to boot. But her case as I saw it, and as events confirmed, was to a great extent a matter of forensic evidence—the sloppy forensic evidence the prosecution had presented in her first trial and the appropriately analyzed forensic evidence we offered in the retrial.

I turned once again to Ed Miller, the forensic scientist I had first met back when I worked at Bayview-Hunters' Point and with whom I had collaborated a number of times since. The first thing we did was go back to the house where the incident had occurred. Keep in mind that this was five years after the fact. The bedroom had actually been refurbished shortly after the crime, the idea being that when Suzanne was released on bail at the time of the first trial, she would not have to come home to a bloody carpet and a room reeking of tragedy. It was quite a different room now from what it had been the day Curt was shot, and it was here that we asked Suzanne to reenact her account of what happened.

She did so. Then Ed thought for a moment, nodded, and said to me, "Grab an edge." He and I then literally pulled up the edge of the carpeting at the entrance to the bedroom and stretched it back across the room so Ed could focus on the portion of the floor where Suzanne said she and Curt had struggled over the gun. He zeroed in on an impression in the floorboard that he said was consistent with a bullet ricochet impression. Then he pulled out an instrument for measuring angle and direction, fiddled with it, walked across the room to the far wall, and pushed aside a curtain. He explored the wall and about a foot off the floor, found a hole in it. With a flashlight and a pair of tweezers, Ed now proceeded to pull the bullet the cops had missed out of the wall. That piece of evidence and its location in the wall were completely consistent with what Suzanne had told the police officers on the scene and completely *in*consistent with the prosecutor's argument that Suzanne had taken a practice shot.

Another piece of evidence took a bit more time to analyze. The California Department of Justice criminalist testifying for the prosecution in the original trial had told the jury that the bullet holes and the smoke and gunpowder burns in the pile of shirts Suzanne scooped out of the closet could only result from her having wrapped the shirts around the gun. The implication of this version of course was that Suzanne had her finger on the trigger, ready to shoot, and wrapped the shirts around the gun to hide the fact. I asked for the stack of shirts to be released for analysis and went over to Ed's lab in the East Bay to see the results. He showed me how the bullet holes and gunpowder burns lined up precisely—just as they would have in a stack of shirts fresh from the cleaners. It made for a more than reasonable doubt that Suzanne's version was the truth: She pulled down the shirts to pack them, and the gun came with them, startling Curt into struggling with her for it.

The retrial was dramatic. The prosecutor recalled that same criminalist, and he repeated the testimony he had delivered in the first trial: The pattern of the bullet holes and the burns from smoke and gunpowder were evidence that Suzanne had wrapped the shirts around her hand to conceal the fact that her finger was on the trigger.

When it was my turn to cross-examine the witness, I asked the judge for a brief recess first and folded the shirts in the way that Suzanne had told the police they had been folded. I showed the stack of shirts to the expert criminalist and asked him to examine again the bullet holes and burns. "They line up, don't they?" I asked. He began to blush with embarrassment as he admitted that they did. His credibility was shattered.

In the defense presentation, Ed Miller's testimony finished off the forensic case. His clear, thorough, careful explanations of the ricochet impression in the floor board, the hole in the wall, and the finding of the first slug ripped the prosecution's case to shreds; it was a dramatic demonstration of an incomplete and incompetent police investigation. In fact, all the forensic evidence analyzed by Ed was consistent with the account Suzanne had given of what happened in the bedroom that day.

Similarly, the repeat performance by incriminating witnesses giving the same testimony they had given in the first trial wilted under cross-examination, while the character witnesses we called for the defense disputed the portrait of Suzanne that had gone unchallenged in the first trial. Additional witnesses corroborated Suzanne's description of Curt's depressed state of mind and his emotional instability.

My main concern as we presented our case was Suzanne's testimony. Her tendency to react quickly to how a question is asked rather than to what it asked worried me, despite time spent trying to prepare her to respond only to the question asked. She did well in direct examination, but I worried about the cross-examination. In fact, she did very well in the cross as well.

The jury deliberated for a day and found Suzanne not guilty.

Neither Delores nor Suzanne had an easy time of it after their respective trials. Delores' daughter was understandably conflicted about her parents, and that has proved challenging, although as of this writing, I can report that Delores has gone on to build a happy, self-sufficient life.

For me, her case resulted in being asked to join the Board of Directors of La Casa, which had given Delores so much support and had provided me with the education I needed to manage her legal defense. I was the first man asked to join what had been an all-female board, which was flattering. I served for eight years, two of them as president.

Suzanne is still putting the pieces back together. Her relations with her five children have quite naturally been complicated by the reality of her having killed their father, while a remarriage ended tragically.

After her acquittal, Suzanne commissioned an artist to make a framed stained-glass window of a butterfly hovering over a flower; she said it represented my having enabled her to come out of her cocoon and be free. The piece hangs in my office to this day.

These were both serious women with serious, complicated, and troubled lives. Each was an individual of complex character, and each exhibited any number of imperfections along with her strengths. The criminal justice system had started out by failing to recognize those realities; it relied instead on typecasting, and it locked the women into pigeonholes defined by its own narrative. Both women might have paid dearly for that failure.

It is an all too frequently recurring paradox of the justice system that law enforcement officials—and lawyers too—who take the "easy" path to a desired "truth" in order to win a conviction and be done with it do so at the peril of those they are duty-bound to protect and to the detriment of their professional integrity. Slowly but surely, yielding to stereotypes, clichés, profiling, and what you think you know undermines our system of justice and strips us all of the protection our law enforcement professionals are pledged to provide.

"Whoever Saves a Single Life, It Is as Though He Had Saved a Whole World"—Whatever the Price He Has to Pay

Maurice Keenan was no one's idea of a model citizen. He lived through a brutal childhood and grew up to be a brutish man—a speed freak addicted to meth and prepared to steal to get it, a thief, and in due course a convicted murderer.

Yet his name will be forever associated with a ruling of the California Supreme Court that stands as a bulwark of justice for all: a guarantee that indigent California defendants in death penalty cases are entitled to not just one but two attorneys. The ruling, providing for what has become known as "Keenan counsel," made a positive contribution to the national debate about the need to provide appropriate resources for defendants who are literally fighting for their lives. It makes it a little more likely that American jurisprudence can live up to its promise that there should be a reasonable equivalency of skills, intelligence, resources, and commitment between the two sides in a trial. Supreme Court Justice Ruth Bader Ginsburg has concluded that, "people who are well represented at trial do not get the death penalty." In other words, as Justice Ginsberg suggests, the more resources you can afford to bring to your defense, the better your chances of staying alive.

I won that ruling for Maurice Keenan, but its significance went well beyond Maurice's case. It would help generations of indigent defendants to come. Yet this was a case I had taken against my self-interest and certainly against my inclination. Maurice knew about me—and I knew about him—because I had represented his wife, Linda, in a drug case a couple of years before. Now Maurice was on trial for his life on a charge of murder, and his court-appointed lawyer wanted out of the case altogether. When Maurice learned the identity of the replacement lawyer the court intended to appoint, he let it be known that if that lawyer came to see him, he would smash the man's head against the wall. The lawyer was not interested in finding out if Maurice meant what he said, and Maurice and Linda both pleaded with me to take his case.

There was a legal stumbling-block, however—a conflict of interest existed because Linda, who had been charged as an accessory after the fact in Maurice's murder case, had retained me as her lawyer. The conflict would have to be waived.

There was another issue as well. About a year before, Maurice had called our home in the middle of the night, clearly agitated and in a temper. Linda had been arrested on a drunk-driving charge, and he wanted me to get her out of jail. When I told Maurice there was nothing I could do at that time of night, he threatened to harm my wife. I didn't take his threat seriously, but it worried Susan. I wouldn't accept any capital case without her approval—especially the case of someone who had threatened to harm her—so it wasn't until Susan was persuaded that I might be Maurice's only hope to avoid the death penalty that she agreed I should be his lawyer.

There was a particular irony in this odyssey of Maurice searching for a lawyer. Although I made concerted efforts to get other lawyers to accept a court appointment as Maurice's attorney, his reputation as a trouble-maker meant that no one was willing to take him on alone. There were two lawyers who said they would be willing to do it together, but it was understood at the time that there was no way the court would appoint two lawyers for one defendant. Therein lay the irony, for it was through the Keenan case that California law would eventually require that a single indigent defendant in a capital death-penalty case was entitled to two lawyers. In the meantime, however, a motion was filed in which Maurice requested that I be appointed to represent him. Both he and Linda waived the conflict of interest, and the court appointed me.

———

Readers of a certain age may remember the Oscar awards ceremony of 1974. That year saw the peak of the streaking fad. Hordes of college kids ran naked across campus after campus in their bid for the group streaking record, while lone streakers stalked major sports events. On Oscar night of that year, the elegant British actor David Niven was just introducing Elizabeth Taylor when a streaker dashed across the stage in full view of the cameras. Niven, unfazed, delivered the following comment, possibly not quite as unrehearsed as it seemed at the time: "Well, ladies and gentle-men," he said, "that was almost bound to happen. But isn't it fascinating to think that probably the only laugh that man will ever get in his life is by stripping off and showing his shortcomings?"

The man was named Robert Opel, and while the streak may have been the only laugh he ever got, it was not—alas—his only appearance in the headlines. Opel was a one-time journalist who would later run a small gallery, specializing in gay erotic art, not far from the San Francisco waterfront. He supplemented his meager income from the gallery with the odd drug transaction, and it was in search of drugs, plus the cash that drugs generate, that Maurice Keenan and an accomplice, Robert Kelly, made their way to the gallery on the night of July 7, 1979.

There is little dispute about what happened at the gallery that night. Maurice demanded "drugs or money." Opel denied he had either. Two Opel acquaintances were there as well, and Maurice directed Kelly to lead them into the other room and "take them out." Kelly instead held a sawed-off shotgun on the two and rifled through their possessions. The three heard an altercation in the next room, threats, a shot, and "the sound of a falling body." Maurice, armed with a handgun, had shot Opel, who died from his wound within minutes. Maurice, Linda, and Kelly were apprehended a few days later at San Francisco International Airport, still in possession of all the relevant physical evidence, including the weapons.

This was not Maurice's first brush with the law. Among other arrests, he had been taken into custody in connection with a 1977 armed robbery and a 1979 burglary-plus-witness intimidation. In addition, the night before the Opel murder, while high on meth and paranoid as hell, he had shot a drug dealer friend for absolutely no reason. Later, while awaiting trial, he assaulted a fellow jail inmate and would manage three nonviolent escapes from prison, on one of which he made it all the way to Miami, Florida, where he was apprehended, without resistance, while lunching at a pancake house.[1] As I said: hardly anyone's idea of a model citizen.[2]

But he was, of course, an individual entitled to the presumption of innocence and a vigorous defense. Moreover, Maurice Keenan hadn't been born this way. It wasn't by accident that he came to be ruled by resentment and hatred, nor was it by chance that he habitually expressed his resentment and hatred in vicious bursts of anger. It was built up in him, step by step over the years. You've got to be taught, as the great Rodgers and Hammerstein song says, until you get to a point where you lash out with violence when you're frustrated or hurt. You've got to be taught, as Maurice was, probably from the age of 12, to reach for drugs when the day isn't going your way. You've got to be taught to take whatever you think you have to have because nobody has ever given you anything anyway. That is what I believe of people like Maurice Keenan, and it is probably one reason why I became a criminal defense lawyer.

---

1. Lakeland (FL) *Ledger*—August 2, 1979 http://news.google.com/newspapers?nid=1346&dat=1 9790802&id=FYIsAAAAIBAJ&sjid=u_oDAAAAIBAJ&pg=1641,559371.
2. After Maurice attempted another escape jail authorities searched his cell. They found a note Maurice had left for the Sheriff, who was then running for reelection. The note read: "Dear Sheriff Brown. By the time you read this note I will be in Mexico. Good luck in the upcoming election."

It is certainly what overcame my resistance to taking the Keenan case. My hesitation to represent him didn't spring solely from the fact that Maurice was such a difficult client. On a practical level, I couldn't afford it. It was 1979, and in San Francisco, a court-appointed lawyer in a capital case was entitled to $20 an hour for out-of-court work—preparation, research, brief-writing, and the like—and $24 an hour for time in court. I'm an all-out kind of lawyer. I put everything I have into every case. It's my nature; if I were a plumber, I would spend every second and gather every available resource to fix the broken pipe so that it never breaks again. "Every available resource" for me in the Keenan case meant my office with its library of law books, a full-time secretary, Tricia Cambron, and a law associate, Bruce Cohen, in addition to my own efforts. The office cost a monthly rent, Tricia and Bruce reasonably expected to be paid for their work, and I required a certain amount of wherewithal to support my family. It would be challenging, to say the least, to stretch the court-determined compensation to cover all that, especially because it was often difficult to get the court to pay up.

But there was another reason I didn't want the case—beyond the practical. When I say that it is my nature to go all-out on every case, I don't mean just in time and effort. I also mean in emotion, in the intensity of the effort and feeling I expend, in the sheer heat of passion I experience. The heat is often useful in helping me burn through issues and ignite the case for my clients, but it can often become self-immolating.

I am a fervent opponent of the death penalty. In the deepest part of me, I believe that when the state kills someone, it is committing murder just as Maurice Keenan committed murder, and it is just as inherently wrong— in fact, even more so because the state is the organized civil community that represents all of us. I saw the death penalty not as punishment that fits the crime but as reprisal without the chance of redemption—something I find both immoral and innately unjust. Although I had tried several murder cases, I had never tried a death penalty case; it struck me as belonging to another realm of the practice of law.

In California as in most states, a death penalty case is typically divided into two phases—the guilt phase and the penalty phase. During the former, prosecutors of a first-degree murder charge must prove guilt and at least one special circumstance beyond a reasonable doubt, and the decision of the jury must be unanimous. If both are proven, the trial moves on to the presentation of evidence in the penalty phase: evidence of aggravating circumstances by the prosecution, and of mitigating circumstances by the defense. Sifting and assessing the evidence, jurors must then decide between a sentence of life imprisonment without possibility of parole or the death penalty. A sentence of death must be unanimous. For the defense lawyer, that means that to save your client's life, you need persuade only one juror against the death penalty.

This means that if you defend a client eligible for the death penalty, you are not simply preparing a defense—not that there's anything simple about preparing a murder defense. You must also prepare for the possible penalty phase of the trial. To do that, you have to get to know more about the defendant's life than the defendant knows. You have to delve more deeply and explore more thoroughly than you ever have into anyone's life, including, quite probably, your own. There's nothing abstract about it; what you find is concrete and precise: a life history from birth to now.

What I found unsettling, even disturbing, about this wasn't just that such work is difficult, time-consuming, exacting, and emotionally exhausting. It's the responsibility it imposes on you. I did not relish the responsibility of Maurice Keenan's life in my hands.

———

But of course, I took the case. Maybe I did so because that is what lawyers do; it is the lawyer's job. Somebody had to defend Maurice. Like you and me and everyone else, he had a right to his day in court and to the best representation possible. I seemed to be the last lawyer standing. And I wanted very much to save Maurice from the death penalty.

It was going to be hard work. The previous lawyer had done relatively little on the case; it is difficult to be motivated when you are under a steady barrage of defamation from your client. But it meant that I had a lot of catching up to do.

Unfortunately, the justice system wasn't about to give me the time. I was appointed to the case on October 7, 1980; two days later, the judge set a trial date of November 24. Impossible. No way could I be ready before January 1981, at the earliest. And I was adamant: I was absolutely not going to go into any trial, no less one in which a human life was at stake, unless I was totally ready and consummately well prepared.

So I pushed back and filed a motion in the San Francisco Superior Court asking for an additional lawyer to share the work burden. I argued that a death penalty case is different in character and quality from a murder case and warrants a second attorney, and I maintained that the law giving an indigent defendant the right to request funds to pay for "investigators, experts, and others for the preparation or presentation of the defense" constituted authority for that second attorney.

The motion was denied. An appeal was denied on November 23, the day before the scheduled trial date. We immediately sought to have the motion reviewed by the state Supreme Court, but just filing the appeal did not slow the juggernaut; we were still scheduled to go to trial the next morning. Our only hope was an emergency petition to the state Supreme Court for delay of the trial.

We worked through the night to prepare such a petition. Bruce and I began rewriting our brief into an argument as to why the Supreme Court should postpone the Keenan trial while it considered our appeal of the Superior Court's ruling. Tricia typed draft after draft. We were all bleary-eyed. This was pre-computer days, even pre-copier days; every correction and revision had to be whited out and redone on both the original and the carbon copy. Tricia went nuts every time I edited the petition.

When morning came, Bruce took the petition downtown to file it the minute the Supreme Court opened for business. Meanwhile, I presented myself in the courtroom where cases were assigned for trial. You have seen how this works: The judge asks the prosecution if it is ready to try the case. "Ready, Your Honor," says the prosecutor. The judge turns to defense counsel and asks if the defense is ready. "Not ready, Your Honor," I said, adding that I was "unable at this time to provide effective counsel to this defendant." As if he hadn't heard me, the judge ordered us to appear forthwith in a particular courtroom to begin trial. I told the judge I would obey his order to appear in the designated courtroom but would not participate in a trial for which I was as yet unprepared.

I knew what might happen next; I could be held in contempt of court. The judge might claim, justifiably, that I was defying the court's authority; he was certainly capable of that, and he was equally capable of throwing me in jail if I continued to refuse to go to trial.

I was ready—both to be held in contempt and to go to jail—and a friend, Michael Millman, had recruited a prominent San Francisco attorney, James Brosnahan, to represent me should it happen. I walked down the hall to the duly assigned courtroom, resigned to the fact that I might be spending the night in the county lockup.

You did not even see cell phones in movies back then, and to the general population, they were a futuristic novelty. So I was begging a favor when I asked the court clerk if I could use the courtroom phone. "Go ahead," she said; I dialed the number of the Supreme Court clerk hoping to find out if there had been any action on the emergency petition. There had been: The legendary Chief Justice Rose Bird had granted our emergency delay. The good news was that it gave us time—and that I would stay out of jail and could sleep in my own bed that night. The bad news was that we had once again thwarted the plans of the court's presiding judge. This further postponement of the proceedings would not sit well with him, and while it is never desirable to antagonize the judge in a case you are trying, the alternative—going to trial ill prepared—was simply unacceptable. The trade-off—annoying the judge in return for gaining needed time—was worth it.

Over the next two years, we made the trade-off again and again. While doing everything I could to prepare Maurice's case, I was simultaneously occupied in beating back the judge's attempts to force us to trial before our defense was ready. I filed motion after motion, challenging the discovery process, the constitutionality of the death penalty law, the jury selection process. It worked. We managed to get multiple postponements of the proceedings—time enough to prepare a proper defense, which I would obviously have to try before a judge who was perpetually miffed at me.

But gaining that time *took* time—virtually all my time. During those years, the Keenan case was my main source of income, and I very nearly went broke working on it. The perpetually miffed judge, convinced I was holding things up unnecessarily, was certainly not above trying to squeeze me financially as a way to rush me to trial. My name was removed from the list of lawyers to whom to appoint cases, and when I applied to the court for interim payment, the judge simply said no. Once again, however, I was ready to go to jail rather than yield to the financial pressure and go to trial when I did not think we were ready. When I finally told the judge that I would have to close my practice unless payment was forthcoming, he relented and agreed to an interim payment—but he cut it by one-third.

What does it take to be "ready" to try a death penalty case? The answer to that question constituted the gist of my argument for the funding of a second lawyer before the state Supreme Court. Given that the right to "effective legal counsel"—plus ancillary services—is guaranteed to every defendant and given further that the law recognizes that the standard of protection for the preparation and presentation of a defense is higher in a death penalty case than in any other, I set forth what I had to do to defend Maurice Keenan. I catalogued the witnesses I needed to interview, the scientific and psychiatric evidence I had to explore, and the scope of the preparation required in light of the evidence the prosecution had said it would submit. To ensure the "effective assistance of counsel," I argued, the defense needed additional resources—specifically, the funds to hire a co-counsel to share the workload.

In February 1982, the Supreme Court handed down the decision that bears Maurice Keenan's name and guarantees every indigent defendant in a California death penalty case a second lawyer. The court wholly embraced our argument.[3] Moreover, in basing its ruling on its interpretation of the state constitution, it obviated the possibility of an appeal to a Federal court, since the state Supreme Court is clearly the highest authority where the state constitution is concerned. The ruling cited "a capital defendant's need for a 'complete and full defense'" and said that within the context of "the constitutionally mandated distinction between death and other penalties," that need required applying "a higher standard than bare adequacy to a defendant's request for additional counsel." In general, the court said, where there is a "genuine need" and where the circumstances warrant, "a second attorney is required."

That right is now there for all time and for all indigent defendants, and it is an understatement of the first degree for me to say I am proud

---

3. Jim Brosnahan participated in the oral argument.

of the Court's ruling. At the time, however, what it mostly meant was that I now at least had a second lawyer serving as co-counsel with me. Eight months later, the defense was as ready as the prosecution to go to trial. The trial lasted eight days. It did not take the jury long to return a verdict of guilty on all counts. It was a conviction we knew we had no chance of stopping or overturning; indeed, my strategy had been to not defend against what was all too indefensible, as the facts of the case made clear. I believed that to have argued that Maurice was in some way not guilty of the crime would have undermined the credibility I needed for the penalty phase of the trial, scheduled for a few weeks later. That was where our hope resided.

The argument I would make to the jury asking them to condemn Maurice to life in prison rather than to death was in a way a very simple one. It came out of all that I had learned in delving into the man's life, the very responsibility I had so dreaded undertaking. I would not claim that what he had been through justified Maurice's crime; nothing justifies murder. Rather, I would try to persuade the jurors that the life he had lived explained his actions; if his choice to pull the trigger wasn't inevitable, it was also not completely of Maurice's own making, not wholly within his control.

I needed expert help to make this case, and to find out where to get such help, I once again turned to my friend Michael Millman. A gentle, gracious, scholarly man, Mike had started out studying physics at Harvard, but civil rights activism turned him toward law school and a distinguished career as a defense lawyer, where he focused to his dying day on fighting the death penalty in both individual cases and state law. It was Mike who had arranged for Jim Brosnahan to be my standby lawyer way back in November 1980 when the judge threatened to throw me in jail if I didn't start trying the Keenan case the next day, well before I was ready, and it was Mike who now put me onto Craig Haney, a social psychologist with particular expertise in the social histories of violent criminals.

A professor of psychology at the University of California at Santa Cruz, Craig had impressive academic credentials, holding both a law degree and a PhD in psychology from Stanford. He was also a genius at interviewing, drawing from interviewees exactly the facts that could paint a picture for a jury, and he would prove to be the absolute exemplar of the perfect expert witness: to the point, articulate, authoritative, and personable.

Craig and I became fast friends and remain very close to this day. Under his guidance, I put together both a plan to investigate Maurice's life history and a narrative approach that I believed would show jurors that the "choice" to fire that gun had been planted in Maurice Keenan from a very early age, that it had been nurtured by forces outside a child's control, and that it had grown steadily throughout a life that was itself a form of death sentence.

I believed that Maurice Keenan was the product of negligent parents. He received meager schooling, stuttered in his speech, was clumsy in his physical movements, was beaten up by bigger boys, and showed some evidence of mental health issues. He began a life of petty theft and mindless vandalism at about the age of 12 and, it may be said, worked his way up. He left home—or what passed for home—at the age of 14; no one came after him. He was very often addled by the drugs to which he early became addicted, at first using amphetamines, as so many do, as painkillers.

My point was that Maurice Keenan had become who he had become not through choice or innate malevolence but rather through the brutalizing forces of neglect, indifference, and mistreatment. The injustice was in how Maurice Keenan had been allowed to grow up, and it was little wonder it had spurred him to injustice toward others. He had been "doing time"—serving harsh punishment—since the day he was born. As with the shooting incident the night before Opel's murder, he shot Opel while under the influence of massive amounts of methamphetamine. Killing him now via death sentence would only make all of us murderers, I contended; taking away Maurice's freedom for the rest of his life would be a just sentence for the crime to which he had been driven.

"I never understood how I became who I am until I heard your closing argument," Maurice said to me in a holding cell as the jury began its deliberations, which soon proved to be clearly troubled, even chaotic. The jurors returned frequently to court to ask for more instructions. There were rumors of contention among the jurors, and when, after several days of deliberations, the jury foreman sent the judge a note that "we have a juror who cannot morally vote for the death penalty," I immediately moved for a mistrial on the grounds that the jury was hung. The motion was denied, the judge ruling that the court was "duty bound to investigate" whether "a juror . . . had misled us on the *voir dire*," the questioning in which potential jurors were asked their views on the death penalty. I argued that there was nothing improper with a juror being unable to vote for the death penalty in this case.

It was Friday afternoon, the end of a long day, and after this glimpse into the clearly heated disputes going on in the jury room, the judge was desperate for a verdict. From the judge's perspective this seemed a good stopping point. So he dismissed the jurors for the weekend, telling them it appeared to him "that the jury has a problem" and asserting that he was required to investigate it. "I had thought the jury would have a verdict by this afternoon," the judge said with a hint of disappointment in his voice. He sent them home to spend the weekend with their families. The foreman was pleased. "We should have a verdict come Monday," he told the judge. "Good," said the judge. "Well, I'm glad to hear you say that. I appreciate that."

Was the foreman overstepping his bounds, dismissing the objections of the putative "lone holdout"? And did the judge's "appreciation" of the promised Monday verdict of death add to peer pressure on the holdout? The judge knew that the jury was 11 to 1 for death, and he certainly seemed to me to have sent a strong message that he expected a death verdict on Monday. I again moved for a mistrial, and again the judge denied my motion.

Although jurors had been ordered not to talk about the case unless they were deliberating, before deliberations began on Monday morning, the foreman told the judge that "the problem had been resolved." How would the foreman know it had been resolved unless jury members had violated their oath by discussing the case outside their deliberations? For a third time, I moved for a mistrial, and for a third time, the judge denied my motion. Shortly thereafter, the jury returned a penalty verdict of death.

———

I immediately undertook an investigation into what I suspected was juror misconduct—some kind of undue pressure applied by the foreman or other jurors, spurred perhaps by the judge's implied wish to see a verdict on Monday, intended to strong-arm the single juror—as it happened, an elderly woman—who couldn't bring herself to vote for Maurice to be executed. The findings from that investigation fueled the automatic appeal of the death sentence. At first, in 1988, six years after the trial ended, the death penalty verdict was upheld. Twelve years later, in 2000, it was reversed on appeal on the grounds of juror misconduct, the court concluding that the elderly holdout juror had been intimidated into changing her vote.

By that time, Maurice Keenan had been in prison for 20 years. As I write this, he is there still. Alive.

— 6 —

Defending the Sixties

From his lean, angular appearance to his thoughtful, deliberate manner, Stephen Bingham seemed to me a man gifted with a sense of himself and an awareness that he did not have to prove anything to sustain that sense of self.

His background was patrician and impressive. Steve was the grandson of Hiram Bingham, who served as governor of Connecticut and its U.S. Senator and was also the discoverer of the ruins of Macchu Picchu in Peru. His uncle, the elegant Jonathan Bingham, was a reform-minded Congressman representing the Bronx, New York. His mother was a member of the Tiffany family, and his father, Alfred, an ardent New Dealer, served in the state legislature and cofounded the left-leaning political magazine, *Common Sense*, which included among its contributing writers Upton Sinclair, John Dos Passos, Mary McCarthy, and Theodore Dreiser, some of the most prominent American authors of all time.

It was in this milieu, as Steve would later testify, that he first learned a sense of justice—in his home, from his parents, in a family environment in which public service and political activism were almost genetically encoded. As an undergraduate, he cut his own activist teeth reporting on the civil rights movement for the *Yale Daily News*, helped register black voters in Mississippi in the early 1960s, and served in the Peace Corps after college. As a student at Berkeley's Boalt Hall Law School, Steve was further radicalized by the growing movement against the Vietnam War and by his experience helping organize Californian farm workers for Cesar Chavez. He became a lawyer in order to advocate for those whose rights were often trampled on or shunned. He is still that kind of lawyer.

One of the people Steve became involved with was George Jackson. A young African American originally arrested for holding up a gas station, Jackson had become radicalized by his time in Soledad Prison, where an apartheid-like system of segregation was administered by a corps of racist guards. When an interracial fight broke out in the prison yard one day, the guards responded by shooting and killing three black inmates. In apparent retribution, a white prison guard was beaten and thrown off an upper tier of the prison to his death. Jackson and two other inmates—the three became known as the Soledad Brothers—were charged with the guard's murder.[1] When the murder trial was moved to San Francisco, Jackson and his co-defendants were sent to San Quentin Prison, where Jackson continued to protest the appalling conditions, especially those within the notorious Adjustment Center, or AC, the prison within a prison in which "dangerous" criminals were isolated.

But the violence surrounding Jackson's case continued to escalate. In August 1970, Jackson's younger brother, Jonathan, staged an armed kidnapping in a courtroom of the Marin County Superior Court, located in the Marin County Civic Center. Three San Quentin prisoners were freed, briefly, and Jonathan Jackson also seized a judge, a prosecutor, and three jurors as hostages in order to secure the freedom of George and the other Soledad Brothers. Guards from San Quentin were among those responding to the emergency calls from the Civic Center, and it was they who fired on the van Jonathan was driving away. Jonathan, the judge, and two of the freed prisoners were killed, and the prosecutor, one of the juror hostages, and the third freed prisoner were wounded; the prosecu-

---

1. George Jackson's prison letters were collected in the classic *Soledad Brother*, first published in 1970 and still in print today.

tor was paralyzed for life. This was the escape attempt for which Angela Davis was later charged and tried for kidnapping and murder; Davis was acquitted in 1972 in a defense crafted, to a great extent, by Sheldon Otis.

The National Lawyers Guild became involved with the George Jackson case, and when Jackson's defense lawyer, John Thorne, asked the local Guild chapter to help explore a civil rights challenge over conditions in the AC, Stephen Bingham got involved. That was how he got to know George Jackson, and it was why he was in San Quentin on August 21, 1971.

He wasn't supposed to be there, but he got a phone call from a young man he knew, John Turner, who was editing a book Jackson was writing. Turner said that Thorne's investigator, Vanita Anderson, suspected she might have trouble being "approved" for yet another meeting with Jackson—she had been to San Quentin that week already—and thought a lawyer might ease her way. Steve found the request reasonable and the goal important, and said he would be glad to help "facilitate" the investigator's visit. So he and Anderson drove up to San Quentin in Anderson's car.

As feared, Anderson was not approved for entry into the prison; neither was Steve at first, but since he was there and was known to the authorities as a lawyer for Jackson who had met with the prisoner five or six times already that summer, he thought he might as well persevere. After a couple of hours, he prevailed. Anderson had brought a tape recorder in a briefcase. A guard examined the inside of both, even opening and examining the battery compartment of the tape recorder. Steve had not intended to take either to the visit and said so to an inquiring guard. But Anderson interrupted and suggested that he do so in case Jackson wanted to dictate some notes.

Steve was a little "annoyed," when, after her visit had been denied, Anderson told him that the purpose of her visit was not about Jackson's case, but for him to edit the manuscript of a book he was writing. But, since Steve was already there, and thought Jackson had a right to write the book, he acquiesced and took both the manuscript and briefcase containing the tape recorder to the visit. He sat and watched while Jackson made notes in the margins; then he carried the pages back out to Anderson who made notes of her own; and then he brought the edited pages back for George to review. The two men spoke little. Jackson was curious, as always, about what was going on in the outside world, but Steve was running late for a luncheon at the home of his uncle and aunt, so he cut the meeting short. His role there, which had been incidental, had thus been to serve primarily as a conduit in the editing process for a book that would never be finished.

Later that day, after Steve left, George Jackson reputedly launched an uprising at the prison. As the incident was reported at the time, Jackson waved a gun and shouted "This is it, gentlemen, the Dragon has come!"—presumably a planned signal for revolt. Then Jackson effected the release of an entire floor of prisoners from the AC, thereby igniting the battle that ensued. In that battle, three guards and two white prisoner trustees suspected of being snitches were murdered before prison authorities regained control of the prison. Jackson was killed by a guard shooting down at him from an elevated catwalk; he was shot in the back, supposedly as he was running for the wall in an attempt to escape.

Before the day was out, an unsuspecting Stephen Bingham would be fingered as having hidden the gun, described as a semiautomatic pistol, plus two clips of ammunition in the tape recorder Anderson had offered to let him use, and of having smuggled these items to Jackson inside Vanita Anderson's briefcase. A wig was also said to have been in the briefcase. Prison authorities alleged that Jackson had initiated the revolt on his way back from the meeting with Steve and said they had "conclusive evidence" of Steve's guilt.

Fearing for his life, Steve fled the country. He lived the next 13 years as a fugitive, moving from place to place around Europe until settling in Paris, always looking behind him, always waiting to be caught.

———

The story could not help but be big news. Although COINTELPRO was officially ended that very year, in 1971, the fears it had stirred up did not fade quickly. On one side were the fears on the part of liberal activists over warrantless entry, bugged phones, infiltration of their organizations by FBI agents, disruption of their activities, and worse. On the other side was the terror that J. Edgar Hoover's machinations had galvanized in way too large a swathe of the population—terror of black militants, of the Black Panther Party, of calls for revolution, even of the label "dissident"—to my mind, one of the most honorable labels an American can wear. To find in the midst of this swirling maelstrom the gentle scion of one of America's blue-blooded families, and to see him disappear into thin air, chased by the FBI and the Mounties and Interpol, among others, was a tale worthy of grand fiction.

I read about it. All of us who were involved with the National Lawyers Guild read about it and took Stephen Bingham's part. I had no doubt but that he had been framed, no doubt but that he had no chance of a fair trial and little chance of remaining alive if he were convicted and sent to a California prison, where I was sure the prison guards would target him out of a thirst for vengeance and as a warning to those on the left of the political spectrum who claimed that Jackson's "escape" had been engineered by prison authorities as an excuse to get rid of him permanently. I read about who Stephen Bingham was, the kind of background he came from, and what he accomplished, and I respected what he had done with his life. He had put his life at the service of a cause greater than himself, and he had evidenced that commitment in his every action, great and small, from registering voters in Mississippi to "facilitating" the editing of George Jackson's book. In my eyes, he was living the values on which my own career had been based, the very values I tried to live by. I found him noble, and I wished him well.

Sheldon and I talked about Steve now and again. Sheldon had known him through his work with other National Lawyers Guild attorneys on the Angela Davis defense team and astonished me at one point by telling me he thought Steve and I were a lot alike. I could not imagine any two people less alike; in our backgrounds and perspectives, in our education and opportunities, and in our personalities, we were almost polar opposites. Yet much later, when Steve and I became lawyer and client, and later still, as we grew to be friends, I think I came to understand and appreciate what Sheldon meant.

Steve made the headlines twice more over the next several years. In 1974, an interview with him appeared in the Los Angeles *Times*, written by reporter Henry Weinstein, who had been a Yale classmate of Steve's. It was more a way for Steve to let family and friends know he was alive and still committed to his sense of justice than a revelatory statement. Obviously, if you are on the run, providing the normal details of newspaper reporting—who, what, when, where—is not advisable.

Then one July day, ten years later, I was walking along Market Street in San Francisco when I saw the banner headline in the afternoon paper, the *Examiner*, exclaiming that Stephen Bingham had surrendered to the authorities in Marin County. He was back, and he was ready to stand trial, and all I could think was *boy, I would love to have that case*. I could almost feel myself sinking my teeth into it, but never in my wildest imagination did I believe such a thing could happen.

A year later, it did.

———

Steve's return to the United States had been carefully orchestrated by a group of lawyers that included the one-time Attorney General of the United States, Ramsey Clark. The team assembled for the defense was an A-list of prominent leftist lawyers active in the National Lawyers Guild: Leonard Weinglass, a man of national reputation, was lead counsel, and co-counsel was San Francisco lawyer Paul A. Harris. Both participated in the preliminary hearing at which Steve was ordered to stand trial, but shortly afterwards, health concerns forced Paul to drop out, and somebody—I don't recall who—recommended me to Steve and Len, who asked me to meet with them about taking Paul's place.

The Stephen Bingham I encountered in the first moments of our meeting in the spring of 1985 was a man best described as cautious and careful, albeit also gentle and gracious in every way. Still, it was hard not to see the wary fugitive in him, and I couldn't help but wonder what it must have been like to be frightened for 13 years of your life and to assume another identity[2] altogether. Fortunately, Steve and I managed to break through the stilted first impressions fairly quickly; my sense of astonish-

---

2. Steve had lived for 13 years as Robert Dale Boarts, using the birth date and other particulars of, presumably, a child who had died young.

ment and his circumspection both faded as we connected on that person-to-person basis I needed to feel with a client.

But the legal team I joined—I would serve as co-counsel to Len Wein-glass, the brilliant, colorful lawyer famous for representing such renowned defendants as Daniel Ellsberg, the Chicago Eight, Angela Davis, and Kathy Boudin—was a bit of a moving target. From Weinglass and Harris, it had already shifted to Weinglass and Schwartzbach, so when, for a number of personal reasons, Len decided to leave the case in June, just a couple of months after I had been retained, both Steve and I urged him to stay. Len's decision to leave was final, however, and Steve was suddenly in the position of needing a new chief counsel, the absolutely essential player who would set the strategy for the trial, lead the courtroom defense, and be the final decision-maker, along with Steve himself, on all questions concerning all aspects of the case. Steve's circle of advisors urged him to replace Weinglass with another nationally known lawyer. I was seen to be satisfactory as a co-counsel, but the advisors felt that a well-known lawyer, one whose name would raise eyebrows of recognition nationwide, could bring this case the attention it deserved and imbue it with its rightful importance.

Steve came to our home to tell me all this, honestly and straightfor-wardly. Obviously, the choice of chief counsel was to him an extremely important matter; quite simply, his life and future depended on it. I understood that. And I understood the concerns of his advisors.

Now normally, I am not a man at ease blowing his own horn. It isn't that I'm not proud of my accomplishments; I am. Nor do I disdain my abilities; I believe I have a very clear and realistic appreciation of what I am capable of. But "selling" myself has never been something I found easy or did well, so I simply do not do it. Yet on this occasion, I heard myself telling Steve Bingham that I was the right lawyer for the job. "I can do this," I told him. "This is not about image; it is about who can do the job. *I* can do it." I said all this because I was convinced it was true; I knew how to win this case, and I was ready to take it on.

Steve agreed, and in the early summer of 1985, I was named his chief counsel, and the balance of the huge Stephen Bingham file was delivered to my office on Union Street in the heart of downtown San Francisco. I had double locks put on the outside office door and on the door to my inner office, and until the trial was over a year later, that inner office was never cleaned by the building janitors. A whole new level of security was now in effect.

————

Two essential understandings guided my approach to the Stephen Bingham defense. The first was necessitated by the reality that, as in every trial, but particularly in a trial that is the subject of media attention as Steve's was, there is much more involved than what goes on in a courtroom. By that I mean that there are always people with an interest in or concern for the client who are keen to offer input, and there is therefore always an array of external pressures being applied, often subtly, sometimes not so subtly. In any defense strategy, my job as a lawyer is to deal with the people and listen to the input they offer, and to deflect or resist the pressures to the extent that they may distract me from my sole responsibility, which is the best interests of my client.

Stephen Bingham is a man committed to his political beliefs, and his was in many respects a political trial. He was determined that everything done in his name and for his benefit should be consistent with his politics. I respected that demand and was sensitive to it, as I believe is required of a lawyer on behalf of his client.

But there was in addition a large circle of advisors, friends, and well-wishers surrounding Steve. They represented a nationwide network of like-minded activists, lawyers, academics, even Hollywood celebrities—a veritable Who's Who of the best and brightest activists on the left of the political spectrum. They were dedicated to the same ideals that had always motivated Steve, and they were dedicated now to his defense. Their presence and their assistance were essential; they raised the funds that supported our trial preparation and that kept Steve and his wife, Francoise, sheltered and fed, and they kept Steve's cause alive through public relations events and presentations. But there were times during the preparation and the trial itself when some of these people asked me to take certain actions and not to take others for reasons that I considered political—that is, because a particular action might set or overturn a precedent, or because it might send a message, or because it might make a statement. I understood this; idealists are as capable as anyone else of conflating their own political agenda with the cause at hand. It is a slippery slope, not easy to avoid.

My own belief, however—and this was the understanding central to my preparation of the case—was that the best precedent we could set, the clearest message we could send, and the strongest political statement we could possibly make was to gain Steve's acquittal. That was my agenda, and I was adamant that Steve's trial not become a forum for any other interest.

My insistence on this focus occasionally sparked disagreements, and when that happened, I turned to my best ally, Stephen Bingham. A lawyer himself, and a man with no need to explain or defend his political credentials, he listened carefully when I counseled against an action that I thought could compromise our defense—and he invariably agreed. But the cacophony of outside pressures was sometimes deafening nevertheless.

The second essential understanding on which I based my approach to the trial was that Steve would have to take the stand and testify in his own defense. As is true in every criminal case, the burden of proof is the prosecution's, and the proof must be "beyond a reasonable doubt." That is a high bar, so there is certainly a risk when a defendant takes the stand to try to prove his or her innocence through testimony. In both direct testimony and under cross-examination, which can be brutal, a defendant might say something or do something or leave some impression that will strike some juror or other the wrong way and that, jurors being human, might color that juror's thinking in ways not advantageous to the defense.

But in this case, there was defense testimony only Steve could supply. The prosecution was basing its case on the contention that there was no other way for George Jackson to have obtained the gun and wig except through Steve. His flight, the prosecutor would argue, was a virtual admission of that—evidence, as flight may be interpreted to be, of the defendant's consciousness of his own guilt. Steve would have to testify if only to explain his flight and his years as a fugitive.

But there was another reason for him to testify, perhaps more subtle but equally compelling, if not more so. Simply put, I needed to show the jurors the times in which the crime had been committed. For those who lived through it, I needed to remind them, and for those too young to have known or to remember the era, I needed to paint a picture of an environment in which it was rational for this defendant to believe that his only safety lay in flight and self-exile.

That meant conjuring up a time—the 1960s and 1970s—when the country was riven across a fault line of political and social and cultural contentiousness that tore families apart, fractured friendships, and made neighbors hate neighbors. There seemed to be no such thing as disagreement without disdain and discord. Violence was easily provoked, and what is perhaps the most precious right of Americans, dissent, came under systematic attack by the very institutions charged with protecting it.

It had happened in the streets of Chicago during the 1968 Democratic National Convention, when police used tear gas, Mace, and batons—the spectacle that U.S. Senator Ribicoff had memorably described as "Gestapo tactics"—to tamp down protests against the Vietnam War. It had happened on college campuses in 1970, when protesting students at Kent State University in Ohio had been shot by National Guard troops; four were killed. It had happened in the prisons of California, organized at both Soledad and San Quentin by inmates like George Jackson in protest against conditions that were unfit for humans to live in and that subverted the civil and moral rights all prisoners have. That protest, in the form of a lawsuit petitioning for civil rights, was precisely what connected George Jackson and Steve Bingham in the first place. And at San Quentin as at Soledad, it was this dissent—this lawful protest—that pitted prison authorities and inmates against each other across a chasm of distrust and sheer hatred that produced its own war with its own casualties on both sides.

This was the environment I needed jurors to understand.

It would not be easy. It was 1986 by the time the trial opened. Fifteen years had passed, and a lot had changed. Steve had come back home precisely *because* so much had changed—enough, he believed, that he could get a fair hearing. J. Edgar Hoover was by now long dead, and the FBI's Stalinist treatment of those professing beliefs Hoover abhorred had long since been discredited, although many of his tactics took a long time dying. The Black Panther Party had faded and was finally dissolved in 1982, by which time its revolutionary rhetoric had begun to sound hollow. Attitudes had changed. The counterculture and its disciples had matured; the fiery rebels of the sixties were middle-aged and mortgaged, fighting expanding waistlines and aching backs the way they once fought the "System." I am not suggesting that the issues championed by the radicals of the 1960s and 1970s had gone away, nor had the ardor of the champions dimmed. But America was a different place now, and the jurors of 1986 were going to have to understand what the America of 1971 was like if they were to give Steve a fair shot. Only through his testimony, I reasoned, could they see what he had been up against.

I also wanted to show jurors the man. You could meet Steve Bingham in a social situation and know in five minutes that this was not a man who could smuggle a weapon to a client whose civil rights case he was about to file. But jurors were not going to meet Steve at a party; they were only going to see him in a courtroom. I had to make sure they saw the kind of person he was—the character of the man, and the background and experience that had formed the character—and the best way to do that was by having him testify.

On December 20, 1985, nearly a year after the close of his preliminary hearing, a Marin County Superior Court judge granted motions we had filed and dismissed three of the five counts of murder against Steve. The charges against him were now conspiracy and the two counts of murder. In early January of 1986, jury selection got underway[3], and on Monday, April 7, 1986, the prosecution began its case against Stephen Bingham.

––––

The case proceeded against a backdrop of intense press focus that propelled me, for the first time in my career, into the national media spotlight. The Bingham trial was the political version of the O.J. Simpson trial years later—the counterculture variant of a celebrity criminal proceeding. I appeared on the *Today* show—twice—as well as on other television interview shows. It was heady stuff, the sort of thing that should make any lawyer watchful lest he or she be distracted from the goal. In

––––

3. We were fortunate to have the invaluable assistance of the superb jury consultant, Lois Heaney.

this case, there was little chance of that; I was totally focused on my client and on winning his acquittal.

I had help. My associate, Bruce Cohen, brilliantly handled the legal research and writing. Simply put, he was my right hand. In addition, an extremely bright young man named Matt Menzer, a student at Steve's alma mater, Boalt Hall, had given up two years of law school to work exclusively on this case. His very significant task was primarily organizational and focused on maintaining the massive case file, pulling together exhibits, and tracking all the details involved in making sure we were prepared for every stage of the trial. Moreover, my co-counsel Susan Rutberg handled selected portions of the preparation and trial.

We were in court four days a week, Wednesday being our off day. "Off" simply means that the trial was in abeyance and that I could exhale for a day; Wednesdays were in fact major work days. Remember that I did not become a part of Steve's team until after the preliminary hearing. Harris, Weinglass, and other lawyers had been involved with the case even before Steve's return and surrender. I did not have that background, was not conversant with all the facts going back to the beginning—and I needed to be. What's more, I have my own way of doing things—most lawyers do—and it invariably differs from that of the lawyers who preceded me. For me, this all meant long days and nights of preparation. And on Wednesdays—or often when there was a break in the trial—the entire team of us, including Steve, would head for my Union Street office and get to work on the case.

Weekends were just another variant of Wednesdays and offered little respite. I tried to take some time to relax, play with my son, go out to dinner with my wife if only for a few hours on a Friday or Saturday evening. But the trial was constantly on my mind. It always is. Your client's life or safety or future is a responsibility you simply cannot put down easily and pick up again like a set of keys. It is inescapable.

———

The case the prosecution set out to prove beyond a reasonable doubt centered on the allegation that during his visit to San Quentin on August 21, fifteen years before, Steve had smuggled a gun and a wig to George

Jackson in Vanita Anderson's briefcase. To make the case, the very able prosecutor, Terry Boren, who has since had a lengthy career on the bench, offered a step-by-step account of the uprising, accompanied by careful graphics showing the layout of the prison, and he stitched this together with a detailed recounting of the gruesome details of the murders that took place during the uprising. Theoretically, jurors were to conclude that the only way any of this could have taken place was if Stephen Bingham had provided George Jackson with a loaded gun and wig, stashing them inside the tape recorder or Vanita's briefcase. There was simply no other way.

What the defense had to do was demonstrate that the evidence did not in fact show that Steve had done any such thing. Absent such evidence, reasonable doubt existed. I intended to go beyond that, however. As I saw it, since both the tape recorder and briefcase had been searched by a guard, if the gun couldn't fit in the tape recorder—and it couldn't—then Stephen Bingham *could not* be guilty. In fact, as I would argue, the notion that Steve could have or would have committed such an act was implausible at best. The known facts made this almost easy to argue; the only thing that could be said to point to Steve was the supposition left when every other conceivable explanation had been eliminated—in other words, sheer conjecture. This was the reason I had felt so strongly that I could win this case, and it is why I had so uncharacteristically urged myself on Steve when he was looking for a new chief counsel. I won't say I believed the case was a slam-dunk; as a matter of strategy and of sanity, I never allow myself to think that about a case. But I knew the evidence to support the prosecution's conjecture did not exist, and in a fair trial based on evidence, we would prevail.

Again, it was the context—the tenor of the times—that made the accusations particularly implausible, and that is why I tried to re-create in the jurors' minds the atmosphere of violence that existed in prisons in 1971, the revolutionary rhetoric it incited, the mutual fears and hatreds between guards and inmates across lines of race and belief.

San Quentin's Adjustment Center had been a particularly scandalous example of that context. A minefield of metal detectors and bag searches preceded any visitor's entry into the prison, while inmates being brought out of the AC to meet with visitors underwent full-body searches both on their way to a meeting and on their way back to their cells. Given this, was it conceivable that anyone would have attempted to slip a weapon past guards already on high alert to challenge any visitor to the infamous George Jackson, a thorn in the side of prison guards throughout California because of what had happened at Soledad Prison? And given the rigorous search procedures—the full-body searches of inmates meant they were stripped naked and subjected to body-cavity examinations *and* to searches of their hair—was it likely that Jackson could have even contemplated, much less gotten away with, secreting a gun and ammunition in the putative wig or anywhere on his body?

That the uprising in San Quentin that day had been horrific was undeniable. The murdered guards and suspected informers had suffered hideously; their throats were slit and their bodies stacked while they bled to death. The survivors of this horror were understandably traumatized and no doubt scarred for life. Their direct testimony had been so harrowing that Steve's own father, Alfred Bingham himself, had worried that his son, whom he believed to be utterly innocent, would nevertheless be convicted. After the testimony about those deaths was presented, Alf Bingham took me to dinner to urge me to make a deal with the DA—a shorter sentence in return for ending the trial now. I assured Alf that we would win; I knew the evidence, and I knew it proved Steve's innocence.

Indeed, in questioning the guards and other prison officials who had been on duty that day, I elicited the numerous discrepancies between their first recollections as told to investigators just after the incident and their later, "refreshed" recollections delivered in court. I suggested that recollections do shift, especially in the face of the kind of horror that engulfed San Quentin prison that day, as the mind re-lives what it took in. But sometimes recollections shift as your colleagues and coworkers remember together; it becomes easier to recall an incident as others have recalled it—more comforting, easier to live with. I would further hint that the real truth of the uprising at San Quentin and of George Jackson's alleged escape attempt was something even more damning—namely, government incompetence at best, government complicity at worst.

These were the suggestions I put into the minds of the jurors even as I focused their attention on whether or not you can fit an Astra revolver into the three inches of a cassette recorder the guard who examined the recorder was unable to see. That guard had opened and examined the battery compartment of the recorder filled with four C-type batteries. He had examined the speaker. He had seen the terminal point and the diodes within the body of the recorder. All that he was unable to examine were three inches of "hidden" space. Since the Astra nine-millimeter pistol involved in the uprising at San Quentin was more than eight inches long, it clearly could not have been lodged in the tape recorder Steve Bingham brought with him into the interview room and never even took out of Vanita Anderson's briefcase. This was the testimony I had in mind when I assured Alf Bingham we would win.

Yes, the horror of that August day might easily have shaken even the most steely of prison officers. Confronted by such horror, the temptation to affix blame and to find an easy, quick target for such blame can be almost overwhelming. But temptation is not evidence, and the evidence that existed, especially in the context in which that day's deaths took place, simply did not support what the prosecution was putting forward. In fact, given the times and the man charged with the crime, it was very nearly ludicrous. That is the impression I hoped and expected Steve's testimony to implant in the jurors' minds.

———

I had taken a somewhat unusual approach to preparing Steve for testimony. Months before the trial, he and I wandered over to Golden Gate Park where we found a bench far from the joggers and cyclists and dog walkers who frequent the place. I had no legal pad, no tape recorder, no note-taking apparatus of any sort. "Tell me about your life," I said to Steve. "Tell me who you are, where you came from, what makes you tick. And when you're finished, I'll answer any question you may have about my life."

My aim was to break down any barrier that might exist between us— any lingering doubt, whether conscious or not. I knew that we liked one another. I knew that Steve trusted my legal abilities and instincts. But I was also mindful that this was a man who had been on his guard every minute of every day for 13 years of his life, and I wanted the Steve Bingham who would take the stand to have complete faith in me as a person, not just trust in me as a lawyer.

We talked for hours. Steve was unfettered in his answers to probing and often uncomfortable questions. I think we both learned what we needed to know about each other, and I came away confident that this handsome, gentle, articulate man would do very well on the stand and would more than hold his own under cross-examination.

There was only one question I did not ask Steve that day in Golden Gate Park—the one about why he came back from his self-imposed exile. I didn't ask it because I knew why. Steve's mother, Sylvia, had died in May 1981. He did not know of her death till six weeks later, and he was helpless to do anything about it except mourn inwardly. I knew that to touch this wound with a question would release a surge of emotion, and I wanted to save that for the courtroom so that the jury would see the real Stephen Bingham, the man, not the headline.

His testimony began on Monday, June 2. The lines of people hoping for a seat extended virtually the length of the hallway outside the courtroom, and the courtroom was packed. Security was at an all-time high. And when the judge instructed, "Your next witness, Mr. Schwartzbach," and I said, "Our next witness, your honor, is Stephen Bingham," a shiver of suspense whooshed through the courtroom.

I cannot recall any experience quite like what I experienced as a lawyer that day. It was as if there was an electric current passing back and forth between Steve and me. We were as one, counsel and client, as I asked and he told how he had become the man he was, how he formed his beliefs and how he acted on them, what had happened during his visit to George Jackson, why he had fled, and how he had lived as a fugitive for more than a decade. And when I asked if anything had happened within his family that had affected his decision to return to stand trial—the question I had not asked him in Golden Gate Park—Steve paused for a moment, his grief catching up with him, until I nodded to say it was okay, as if I were giving him license or dispensation to let the grief out. He did let it out—very simply. "Well, I realized that I had missed all those years with her," he began, his gentle voice breaking just a bit, "that she wouldn't be here today, and that I wanted to come back while my father was able to still be here." Alf had been in the courtroom for every session, and in that moment, as he and his son locked eyes, everyone who was there could see and feel the kind of home environment in which Steve had grown up. The newspaper stories about him rarely failed to note his family's wealth and prominence and to refer to Stephen Bingham as "privileged." In court that day, it became clear that the real privilege of having been born Stephen Bingham was to have been raised by loving, caring parents who had instilled in him his sense of justice and his desire to help heal the world. It was an emotional moment for all who witnessed it.

Steve's cross-examination began immediately afterwards and lasted through the following day, Tuesday. As I had expected, he did well. He had the gift of being nonconfrontational, a quality not always found in radical lawyers, and he was unruffled by tough questions and by Terry Boren's repeated attempts to get him to "name names" of those who had helped him flee and assisted his return. Terry was unfailingly respectful toward Steve, and Steve was unfailingly calm and careful in response. It all sat well with the jury. Or so I believed.

––––––––

Closing arguments in the case were postponed until the following week while the judge and the attorneys worked through various matters— most significantly, the content of the judge's legal instructions to the jury. Terry began his closing argument on Monday, June 16 and concluded by the lunch break the next day. Because the prosecution has the burden of proof in a criminal case, Terry would get another chance at another closing argument once I completed the argument for the defense. Starting Tuesday afternoon, in other words, I would have my last chance to address the jury person to person.

In the minds of many, the closing argument is the stuff of drama. It's where a lawyer can really shine, can strut his or her eloquence, can demonstrate passion for justice and for the client. That is all true. But the drama can also prove to be irrelevant.

Let me suggest a simplistic representation of a criminal trial as a forum in which lawyers essentially give a jury pieces of a puzzle. As with any puzzle, the pieces come in different shapes and sizes and fit together with one another in different ways. What the lawyer tries to do in closing argument is to put the pieces together to complete the puzzle, thereby showing the jury a single, integrated picture that means to jurors what the lawyer suggests it means. That makes the closing argument enormously important, but if the lawyer hasn't created all the necessary pieces and held them up clearly for the jury to see, the puzzle won't be complete no matter how dramatic, how eloquent, how passionate the closing argument may be. Eloquence without preparation is unlikely to win the case; preparation without eloquence has a better chance at victory but without a well-reasoned, well-presented final argument may not be able to close the sale. However, the opportunity to do what a closing argument can do—put it all together and get the jury to see what you see—is to many lawyers, myself among them, one of the exciting challenges of the profession and one of its weightiest responsibilities.

As with every aspect of my profession, I have a particular methodology with regard to preparing closing arguments. It is a methodology I developed and refined over the years, and it is the approach I bring to every case. Yet on every case, it is an all-consuming process and can be an exhausting one.

I have said that I am an all-out kind of lawyer. Whatever the case, however big or small, I become completely invested in my client—heart and soul, body and mind. In the Bingham trial, I was acutely aware of the vast numbers of other people who were equally invested. I don't mean just Steve and Francoise and Alf, those closest to him, but also the network of people who had spent so much time and effort working on this case with me—people like Matt Menzer, who had literally put his own future on hold for two years in order to give himself over to what he considered a profoundly meaningful cause. I was aware too of the thousands of people around the country who had contributed money and galvanized support to make it possible to bring this case to trial—to gather the evidence, pay the phone bills, keep the copier machine going, and not least of all provide me and the other lawyers and investigators and key staff a living wage. These people were both politically and emotionally committed to this case and its outcome, and while it didn't change the way I went about working on the case, I nevertheless felt that I was representing them all.

I had the feeling that when I stood up to make my closing argument on Steve's behalf, I would be serving as their voice too.

Some lawyers write out their closing arguments in full, then read them aloud to the jury. I do not. I need to connect with a jury person to person, making eye contact with each of them, as much as I need to connect one-on-one with a client. I could not do that if I were reading a script.

Instead, my standard operating procedure is to make notes—often copious notes—in my own shorthand, then to organize my thoughts by subject matter and order the subjects in outline form on a legal pad. When I deliver the argument, I can then check off each point once I feel I've addressed it.

I typically begin my presentation by talking to the jurors about the law the judge will instruct them in and by reminding them of their oath and what it means. I suggest to jurors that in being asked to presume innocence, they are being given a difficult task. The presumption of innocence is not an easy thing to achieve; to do so, it is necessary to overcome a rather natural assumption that the defendant would not be here if he or she had not done something wrong. Yet their oath requires jurors to follow the law and do just that—abandon natural instinct and presume the defendant innocent, voting to convict *only* if guilt is proven beyond a reasonable doubt. Even if they think the defendant might be guilty or is probably guilty, the law requires them to acquit, and tough as that may be, that is what their oath demands of them.

I do not run away from evidence in making my closing argument; indeed, I talk about it at length and analyze it point by point. I remind jurors that, although the prosecution will have another chance to speak to them, I will not, and I ask them to assess whether what the prosecutor will tell them is the only reasonable interpretation of the evidence. Consider, I urge jurors, what I might say in response to the arguments the prosecutor will offer, and remember that if there are two equally reasonable interpretations of the evidence, one tilting toward guilt and one toward innocence, it is their duty to decide in favor of innocence.

This was pretty much the line of the argument I was planning in Steve's case, although when I began the argument that Tuesday afternoon, I in no way had the whole thing together even in my mind, much less neatly outlined on the legal pad. But I knew I would only get so far before we were adjourned for the day, and luck was with me: The day's court session stopped just about where my outline did.

————

I dedicated Wednesday to finishing the closing argument. According to the schedule I concocted, I would work on it all day, finish up by 10 P.M. at the latest, get a good night's sleep, and be rested and fresh to deliver the heart of the argument with confidence and passion on Thursday in court.

But by 10 P.M. Wednesday night, I was nowhere near finished. It's hard to remember this now, but in 1986, computers were not yet the universal essentials they are today. I followed my traditional method of strewing the floor of my study at home with handwritten notes, both mine and Bruce Cohen's, until the study looked like the aftermath of a ticker-tape parade. At around 4 A.M., I called Matt Menzer to ask if his medical student roommate knew of a pill I could take that would keep my mind alert and my body from cramping. The answer was no, so I lay down on the futon just to rest. I was afraid to fall asleep for fear of not waking up in time. I can't imagine what Matt must have thought: Here I was, hours before what was to be an impassioned plea to the jury on the case that he, Matt, had postponed his career for, and I still had not finished the outline and had not slept at all.

Adrenaline carried me through the morning session, during which I continued my analysis of the testimony given, but when the lunch break came, I still didn't have a complete outline. I skipped lunch and cocooned myself in the law library at the courthouse to finish up.

The prosecutor's stratagem of trying to equate Steve's stated commitment to "the struggle" with a commitment to violence kept nagging at me. Yes, letters from self-styled revolutionaries urging armed uprisings used the term "the struggle." So had Steve. But use of the definite article did not mean there was only one struggle, and Steve's use of the term did not demonstrate that he was an advocate of violence. Indeed, the whole idea that "struggle" meant "violence" or condoned its use was a fallacy of logic, of language, and of substance, and this cunning attempt by Terry to muddy meaning rankled me. I was sure that Martin Luther King, an obvious and prominent proponent of nonviolence, had used the word "struggle" in the same way Steve had, and I asked our team to see if they could find such a quote while I pressed on with my outline for the closing argument. Someone came through, finding exactly what I was after in a passage in the famous I Have a Dream speech; I hastily scribbled it in my notes.

In the afternoon session, as I came to the close of my review of the kind of man Steve Bingham was, as I suggested again that prison authorities may have had reason to manipulate evidence and had done so, as I again walked the jury through the day of the incident and its awful events, as I reminded them of the terror Steve must have felt, of the self-exile he had endured, and of the courage, consistent with his actions all his life, to come home and face this trial, I pulled out that quote and recited it:

"But there is something that I must say to my people who stand on the warm threshold which leads into the palace of justice. In the process of gaining our rightful place we must not be guilty of wrongful deeds. Let us not seek to satisfy our thirst for freedom by drinking from the cup of bitterness and hatred."

"We must forever conduct our struggle on the high plane of dignity and discipline. We must not allow our creative protest to degenerate into physical violence. Again and again we must rise to the majestic heights of meeting physical force with soul force. The marvelous new militancy which has engulfed the Negro community must not lead us to distrust of all white people, for many of our white brothers, as evidenced by their presence here today, have come to realize that their destiny is tied up with our destiny."

Stephen Bingham, I said to the jury, was precisely the kind of man Dr. King meant when he spoke of white brothers who would share their destiny with those struggling to gain their rightful place in the palace of justice. That was the struggle to which Steve was committed. "You see," I told the jury, "it is okay, it's okay to struggle against injustice. It's okay to struggle against bigotry. It's okay to struggle against indecent living conditions. It's okay to care. It's okay to get involved, it really is." I felt the emotion rising in me as I said the words, for I too aspired to share my destiny in that way; I felt committed to the same struggle. It is why I so respected Steve Bingham; it is why, I told the jury, I myself had become a lawyer.

The transcript of the trial even now reveals what happened next. I choked up. For a brief moment, I simply couldn't go on. "Excuse me—" I said. Then I did go on. I went on to say that I had never been more proud to be a lawyer than I was at this moment—"to represent this fine and decent man, who has had 15 years of life ripped away, because he did struggle to care, to get involved. He struggled to fight against injustice and bigotry and poverty."

It was the struggle all those people I felt I was speaking for also waged. It was the struggle I myself had waged—or hoped I had—in Detroit, in Bayview-Hunter's Point, in every case I took on. This man's life represented the struggle, epitomized it—from the Freedom Summer in Mississippi to the Peace Corps, from the Farm Workers to the Muni transit workers, from campaigning for Robert Kennedy to bringing a lawsuit for George Jackson. He had lived his values, and they were on trial along with him.

"You can't give him back his 15 years," I told the jury. "You can give him back his good name. You can end his nightmare."

That was it.

———

The jury was out for a week. The press and courthouse prognosticators speculated endlessly on what the jurors might be doing in that closed room. Every note the jury sent out to the judge ignited a frenzy of tea-leaf reading. One day, the lunch order was for 11 tuna fish sandwiches and one roast beef; one wag suggested it meant a hung jury.

Later, we would learn that the jury had simply deliberated, as juries are supposed to, in a particularly deliberate way. Instead of taking an initial vote, as many juries do, they had spent the week sifting through the evidence, piece by piece. They did not vote until they had been through it all, and then they needed only a single vote. It was unanimous.

It came on a Friday afternoon. The corridors were lined with reporters, photographers, television cameras so thick the participants in the trial had to squeeze our way through. The courtroom was packed. Scores of Steve's friends and supporters filled the seats available to the public. In the front row, just behind the counsel table at which Steve and I were seated, were Alf Bingham and his wife, Steve's wife, Francoise, and my wife, Susan.

The ritual proceeded according to form.

"Have you reached a verdict?" the judge asked.

"We have, your honor," said the forewoman.

The judge asked her to hand the verdict forms to the bailiff. The bailiff handed the forms to the court clerk. The court clerk handed them to the judge. The judge looked at the forms, then read the verdicts aloud.

Not guilty on all counts.

The place exploded. Steve and I embraced in a kind of desperate hug as his well-wishers applauded wildly. Tears flowed from Alf's eyes, from Francoise's, maybe even from mine. I know that to me, it had seemed in a way that an entire era was on trial in this case. The sixties—lauded by some and lampooned by others, damned as naïve and defended as necessary, a cloying cliché to many and a sacred striving to others—had been on the stand along with Steve. For me, the sixties had represented a breakthrough era of freedom when real justice seemed possible, and Steve's life had embodied that era. In my eyes, his acquittal was a vindication of the values he and I both hold dear.

There was no hallway press conference; the verdict had come too late for the evening papers. It was all television and radio, cameras and microphones. Steve and his family and well-wishers managed to exit through the scrum of shouted questions and burning camera lights. Susan and I drove off to pick up Micah, now five years old, from his swimming class. We all celebrated at a party that night.

A month later, the Department of Justice of the United States of America announced through the local U.S. Attorney's office that it was considering prosecuting Stephen Bingham for falsification of a U.S. passport. It was a case the government would have won; Steve had admitted to doing just that—and doing it intentionally—in testimony that was on the record. He could have been sentenced to a term in federal prison or a hefty fine or both.

The threat was singularly small-minded, a throwback to the Hoover era when federal agents might have rubbed their hands in gleeful satisfaction to see someone they regarded as a hardened criminal behind bars. It smacked of overkill and *schadenfreude*, not to mention of pettiness.

That summer, a number of the jurors in Steve's case were galvanized into action. They wrote letters to the U.S. Attorney condemning the rumored charge of passport fraud. The jury foreman wrote that she was "saddened and ashamed" at what she saw as government "vengeance." Another said that "a prosecution of this nature" would only bring "ridicule and discredit upon the government" and asked: "What is the value of this undertaking?" Yet another wrote that further prosecution would be "disrespectful" of all the effort the jurors had expended during the trial. "Surely there are better ways to spend taxpayer dollars," the letter said.

Someone must have been listening. The charge, if ever really contemplated, died before ever being filed.

For me, the Bingham case was the one that established me locally as a lawyer of the first rank. I had had some key wins before, had won some significant Supreme Court decisions, and certainly had the respect of my peers. But this case, with its national spotlight and its significance in both legal and political circles, brought my career to a new level.

And for the next six months, the phone did not ring.

I went broke pretty fast, aided by the somewhat self-defeating financial arrangement I had made with Steve. I had no money to pay either a secretary or an associate, so both moved on to paying jobs. It began to seem to me that I was looking down a long, empty corridor stacked with bills I couldn't pay and cases I wouldn't be asked to handle.

But when the phone finally did ring, it opened the door to one of the more intriguing cases of my career—a case not yet "solved" as of this writing.

— 7 —

Someone Got Away
with Murder

It took the jury in Richard Bandler's murder trial just a little over five hours to find him not guilty, one of the fastest acquittals of my career and, in the eyes of most people, one of the most surprising I ever achieved.

It was surprising because of the weight and comprehensiveness of the "evidence" the prosecution assembled; although, as the quotation marks around the word "evidence" indicate, what looked weighty and comprehensive at first blush turned out to be less so.

What made the case so intriguing was its cast of characters. They consisted of a trio—victim, accused, and major witness—who might have stepped out of pulp fiction or a Hollywood B-movie, and an expert forensic pathologist who was simply out of his league when it came to blood spatters and gunpowder burns, essential subjects among those on which he had been called to testify.

The known facts of the case were simple. Three people well known to one another gathered in one of their homes on the morning of November 3, 1986, a Monday; the home was located in a neighborhood of Santa Cruz on the coast of California's Monterey Bay. Two people came out of the home; the third was killed.

The three were two men and a woman. Granted, that is the sort of equation that can sometimes send the mind racing to the assumption of a love triangle. Desire, betrayal, murder: an old human story, as old as the mind racing to assumptions.

In fact, the woman, Corine Christensen, and one of the men, James Marino, had indeed been sexually intimate over the course of many years. But Corine Christensen was also a prostitute, one specializing in bondage, and she had been sexually intimate with numerous customers over time. The other man, and the third person in the house that day, was Richard, well known not just locally but nationally and internationally as an author, lecturer, and consultant, the co-creator of a system called Neuro-linguistic Programming, or NLP, a technique combining linguistic processes and a kind of self-hypnosis to "re-pattern" the brain, as Richard put it, in order to improve your life, achieve business success, and/or gain personal fulfillment.

Richard Bandler was one of the leading lights of the New Age of the 1970s, when a range of spiritual or quasi-spiritual movements, often influenced by Eastern thought and focused on self-healing and alternative therapies, was in the ascendant. It was the era of hot-tub encounter groups, human-potential weekends, and primal screaming, among other exertions. California was a hotbed of it all, ground zero for all sorts of unconventional lifestyles, and a symbol, both pursued and mocked, of the growth and fulfillment they promised.

A student of psychology, Richard had joined with a well-credentialed linguist, Paul Grinder, to create NLP, but it was his notions of reprogramming yourself—as you would a computer—and of modeling the behavior you wanted to exhibit that really struck a chord. In his heyday, Richard attracted fans and adherents among corporate CEOs, major political figures, military and intelligence officials, and the requisite Hollywood celebrities as well as people eager to feel happier, do better on the job, or get a leg up on life in one way or another.

James Marino was one of those adherents—Marino would say in his testimony that he had "a natural gift" for NLP—and the two men became close. Although Richard was the guru of NLP, the older Marino became a kind of father figure—and almost certainly a supplier of drugs to Richard, a prodigious user of controlled substances. Corine Christensen, even more susceptible than Richard to the Marino "charisma," was also involved in Marino's drug trade, most likely serving as a courier and later as a bookkeeper. Marino was the centerpiece of the convoluted relationships among the three; significantly, both Christensen and Richard would care for him when he was hurt—and would do so with a kind of desperate fervor.

Christensen was murdered by a single bullet to the head fired from a .357 Magnum revolver. Marino and Richard left her house and drove in Richard's car to the wharf at Capitola, a beachfront community still farther down the coast on Monterey Bay. There, according to Marino, Richard told him to throw the chrome-plated murder weapon into the sea. Marino complied.

The two men parted ways. Richard went to the home he shared with one of his two girlfriends, Paula McFarland. Before the day was out, Marino would seek legal counsel and would report to the Santa Cruz police that Richard had murdered Corine Christensen. The following day, after a forensic team searched McFarland's home, Richard was arrested and charged with Christensen's murder.

––––––

It was around the time of the holidays, 1986, and I was driving north on Highway 101 when my brand-new car phone rang. A woman introduced herself as Suzanne Cutter and said she was calling "on behalf of Dr. Richard Bandler." He had been arrested, she told me, and was being held in custody in Santa Cruz. I was not far from San Francisco at the time of the call, but I had just experienced a six-month drought of work, hadn't a single case to work on, and had bought this car phone—my first ever—precisely so that I would be able to respond quickly should a case be referred. I did not hesitate. I turned the car around and drove hell-bent in the opposite direction to Santa Cruz, a distance of some 70-plus miles. I had never heard of Richard, and the referral had come in a roundabout way from a lawyer I had met at a recent conference of defense lawyers—a tip-off, had I only known, to Richard's extensive network of adherents. But when I entered the jailhouse in Santa Cruz that day, I was expecting to meet a medical doctor in some kind of trouble.

The Richard Bandler who rode high in the 1970s and again after his acquittal—in fact, right to the present moment—was legendary as a speaker who could hold an audience spellbound with the clarity of his thinking and the sheer power of his personality. That was not the Richard I met in the Santa Cruz jail at the end of 1986. Instead, the man I encountered, who admitted to being no kind of doctor at all, was scared out of his wits—and for good reason. The police had the murder weapon, which was registered to him, his shirt with Corine Christensen's blood on it, a finding of marijuana, cocaine, and alcohol in his blood at the time of his arrest, and for good measure, a voice-activated tape recorder, found at the home he shared with Paula, on which Richard had been recorded threatening in the wee hours of that Monday to put a bullet in Corine's brain—the very thing that took place just a few hours later. On the face of it, the evidence against Richard Bandler was simply overwhelming.

I took the case, and my first move was to get Richard's bail reduced from the half a million dollars set by the court. I filed a motion supplemented by letters from a number of Richard's many supporters and onetime consulting clients—notable among them the military and intelligence personnel he had worked with on various opaque issues—who testified to his personal probity. The judge was persuaded and reduced the bail to $100,000; Richard was now free to help in the preparation of his defense.

The heart of the prosecution's case, along with the physical evidence against Richard, was the testimony of Marino and of the forensic pathologist, Richard Mason; the several other witnesses called were only window-dressing. Marino's account of the murder had poured forth during the preliminary hearing; in exchange for immunity from prosecution on drug dealing charges, he had provided six days of testimony—incoherent, disjointed, and paranoid but insistent in its condemnation of Richard Bandler as Corine's murderer. In that testimony, repeated in all its particulars at trial, he would tell the jury that he had spent Sunday night, the night before the murder, at Richard's home. He was there because he was still suffering from injuries sustained in a beating at a Halloween party the weekend before, and he sought and received Richard's caring attention to his pain, both physical and emotional. Although it was Corine who had driven James to the emergency room after the beating and had taken care of him for several days thereafter, he had it in his mind that she had somehow been the cause of the beating, and that's what he told Richard when he arrived at his home Sunday night. Richard went after Corine in person and over the phone in the course of that night—"I want to know," he said, "who beat up my friend, my only friend." Richard's urgent insistence that Corine talk to him about the beating reached its zenith in the threat, caught on tape, to put a bullet through her head.

As Marino would tell it, Richard then insisted they drive the short distance to Corine's house, where Richard began to threaten both Marino and Christensen with a gun. Marino would say that Richard used a steak knife to saw off the top of a plastic bottle of Mr. Clean soap so he could use it as a gun silencer, but the soap spilled into the gun, rendering it useless and prompting Richard to pull out his chrome-plated .357 Magnum instead. Marino fled to the second floor and the garage in search of an escape route; in the garage, he managed to knock over a scale Corine used to measure cocaine. Richard heard the commotion, found Marino on the floor of the garage, and gently helped him to the living room sofa to lie down. Marino closed his eyes and heard a gun go off. He opened his eyes to see Corine falling backward onto the floor.

The pathologist's testimony would basically confirm Marino's story. Richard Mason cited tests showing that the gun muzzle had been so positioned beside Corine's left nostril that the pressure it produced when fired would produce precisely the blowback found on Richard's shirt. Mason identified this blowback as consisting of Corine's blood and her brain tissue. No such evidence was found on Marino.

The defense strategy against these two witnesses was simply to undermine their testimony—totally. I would show Marino to be paranoid and unreliable at best and a pathological liar at worst; I would also argue that it was he who had murdered Corine Christensen. As for pathologist Mason, the aim was to show that the tests he carried out were incomplete, that he offered opinions outside of his area of expertise, and that his conclusions were therefore incorrect and without substance.

———

The preparations for this defense were well underway when my own life took a turn. I was invited to join the law firm of Garry, McTernan,

Stender, & Walsh, and in June 1987, I did so, thereby changing the name of the firm to Garry, McTernan, Stender, Walsh & Schwartzbach. Charles Garry had been Huey Newton's lawyer and had represented the Black Panther Party and other leftist political organizations as well as serving as lawyer for The People's Temple, the quasi-religious cult founded and eventually destroyed by Jim Jones. Marvin Stender was another stalwart among left-wing defense lawyers, so the firm was a natural home for me in many ways.

True, I had never really thought of myself as a law-firm kind of lawyer, but at this point in my life and career, it seemed like a good idea. I saw the firm as providing a kind of financial security, and financial security had become awfully important. The dearth of work that followed the Stephen Bingham trial had been sobering—even frightening—and I knew I never wanted to go through it again. I had a child in school; the expenses associated with that were only going to increase as he grew up. In addition, there were the natural expenses associated with supporting a family. Being part of a firm of like-minded professionals who were all good at their jobs seemed a sensible next move, and I signed on. I was to be the criminal defense presence in the firm, and of course, I was expected to be a rainmaker for that practice.

Naturally, I brought the Bandler case with me to the firm, and I instantly had available to me the resources of our office in downtown San Francisco. But in a very real sense, being in a firm made no difference to the way I went about the preparation; it did not serve as a distraction nor did it change anything in the way I carried out my own legal practice. For me, immersing myself totally in a case is the way I focus; where I'm doing it or what the surroundings look like or the time of day or season of the year is irrelevant and immaterial to my process. So it was with the Bandler case.

For the Santa Cruz community, with its reputation for benign kookiness, the case represented a decidedly high-profile event. Yes, the area had a relatively high crime rate—it still does—a surprise to most people, even those who live there, because the place is so widely noted for its exceptional beauty and easy lifestyle. Actually, the beauty and lifestyle may be one reason *why* crime is as common as it is; Santa Cruz simply lures people of all sorts, transients as well as those putting down roots. That was certainly the case in the 1970s and 1980s, when the city became a mecca for activists of every stripe as well as a place known for easy access to drugs.

But the murder of Corine Christensen struck people as something particularly ugly and therefore somehow out of character for a place so high on peace; it seemed incompatible with the spirit of the Santa Cruz community. Moreover, the defendant in this case of murder was virtually a local boy, an alumnus of the university in Santa Cruz and one of the denizens of its hip, laid-back, free-thinking culture. So it was hardly surprising that the murder, Richard's arrest and prosection, and the pretrial period were all covered copiously in the local Santa Cruz *Sentinel* and other publications, on television, and on radio. Nor was it unexpected that the pace and intensity of the coverage increased the closer we came to the opening of the trial. *West* magazine was the Sunday supplement of the *San Jose Mercury News*, and on Sunday, November 8, the day before jury selection was to begin, it published a story by journalist Kathy Holub entitled "Mind Over Murder."

"Deadly Triangle," promised the cover copy about the story inside. "The psychologist, the coke dealer, and the party girl knew how to handle people's urges. But they lost control of their own." Sensationalist the come-on may have been, but Holub had done considerable research into the lives of the principal players and had listened at length to people who had interacted with them over the years, and her article tried fairly and in some depth to plumb the relationships among the three. I sat in on the interview she did with Richard, which was to be limited to discussion of his past and his profession—not touching the murder or the legal case— but her interview with James Marino was under no such constraint. He spoke to her readily and in extensive detail and in so doing painted a disturbed and paranoid portrait of himself. Of particular note, at least as far as I was concerned, was what Marino said about me: "This little curly-haired fucking Jewboy," Marino said—"I would love to put a gun to that son of a bitch's head. It's a wonder somebody don't *dust* him down the road. I'm serious. . . . Somebody's gonna take him out someday."

The courtroom the next day was packed with prospective jurors, while all around the town, interest in the forthcoming trial had hit a new high. My wife, Susan, was concerned for my safety; Marino had been in the drug trade for years, and rumors had long swirled of his connections with organized crime. Even a disturbed paranoiac, Susan reasoned, might have colleagues ready to carry out the kind of threat Marino had leveled at me. In chambers with the judge and the prosecuting district attorney, Gary Fry, I related her concern over Marino's threat and asked if it might be possible, even given the limited resources available, to provide some kind of security at least around the courthouse.

Fry was dubious. "Gerry, I wouldn't worry about it if I were you," he said.

"Gary," I replied, "if he were threatening to kill *you*, I wouldn't worry about it either."

The judge took my point and arranged for a modest increase in security.

Jury selection for the Bandler case was a lengthy process. As is not unusual in high-profile cases, the juror *voir dire* was individually sequestered; that is, prospective jurors were questioned one at a time before the judge, court clerk, stenographer, bailiff, defendant, and opposing lawyers only—no other jurors present. The procedure was for the judge to question a prospective juror first; I would come next as the defense lawyer, and the district attorney would go last.

As seemed to be true with everything about the Bandler case, the cast of characters among our prospective jurors was almost as peculiar as the featured players in the trial to come. I remember the judge questioning one young man about his circumstances—he was newly engaged to be married—and the young man explaining, in the most nonchalant manner, that in order to earn enough money for a down payment on a house, his fiancée was working as a prostitute in a Nevada brothel. There was a pause, and then the judge looked at me and said, "You may inquire, Mr. Schwartzbach."

I was as lost for words as the judge. "How long," I phumphered, "has your fiancée . . . uh . . . been working in Nevada?" Fortunately, for reasons other than his fiancée's line of work, this prospective juror was excused.

So was the restless fellow whose eyes darted every which way during questioning and who told me that he was looking around for cameras and hidden microphones because he knew the courtroom was bugged. "Why would the courtroom be bugged?" I asked. "It's me," he answered; "I'm being tracked by the government." After he left, excused for cause, the judge peered at me over his reading glasses. "Mr. Schwartzbach, welcome to Santa Cruz," he said.

But the aura of eccentricity that dogged the pretrial preparation went beyond the borders of Santa Cruz. One day, on my drive down the highway, my car phone rang with a call from a Los Angeles lawyer specializing in personal injury. "Have you read Richard's books?" he asked me. I told him I had not.

"You have to read them," he said. "They changed my life." He then proceeded to assure me that reading the books would provide me with a revelation that would transform every corner of my world—including my approach to Richard's defense—and would make me a better lawyer.

It was a sentiment I had heard expressed before—and with similar insistence—and I admit I was a bit weary of the religious fervor that enfolded the sentiment. I asked the L.A. guy if he played golf, and he said he did. "Well then," I suggested, "imagine that you can consistently hit a drive 300 yards down the middle of the fairway but someone points out to you that your grip is off. Would you change it?"

He conceded he would not.

"I've had a fair amount of success doing things my way," I went on, "and I don't think it would be helpful to Richard to change things now."

When I told the story to Richard, he agreed that his murder trial was no time to start experimenting. "Just do your thing," he told me.

The trial finally got underway just about 13 months after the murder of Corine Christensen.[1] The prosecution's opening statement promised a credible and comprehensive accounting of what transpired from witness Marino, the scientific evidence to back that account, and the recorded threat. I made my opening statement on December 1, 1987, and prom-

---

1. A then-young lawyer, Peter Leeming, volunteered to assist me as second chair—and did so ably.

ised that the evidence would in fact impeach the testimony of James Marino and that the science did not support his account.

Marino was to have been the district attorney's first witness, its star witness, the witness representing the heart of the prosecution's case. But James Marino was nowhere to be found. He had simply disappeared. So instead, the district attorney proceeded with the rest of his witnesses and eventually called the prosecution's next most important witness, forensic pathologist Richard Mason. Mason would go on to serve as the Santa Cruz County coroner for years, retiring in 2014 amid much sentiment, but in 1987, he was inexperienced in critical aspects of forensic science—namely, blood spatter analysis and gunpowder evidence—in which he claimed expertise. His background was as a battlefield pathologist in Vietnam, where he had indeed performed hundreds of theater-of-war autopsies, but this gave him no *bona fides* in the forensic examination of blood spatter and gunpowder burns, the two disciplines that would be all-important in the Bandler case. Expertise in how blood splatters or how it drips or trails on surfaces and in how to read gunpowder burns and instances of gunfire "blowback" was essential to understanding what happened in Corine Christensen's dining room. Mason had a healthy ego, but his analyses were simply flawed, his investigations deficient, his conclusions erroneous. He was simply out of his depth.

I had engaged Ed Miller, by now my go-to criminalist whenever possible, and forensic pathologist Paul W. Hermann to examine the science of the case against Richard, and they had prepared me at length and in depth for my cross-examination of Mason, which began on December 3. From the get-go, my questioning made Mason's inadequacies all too clear. In cataloguing his expertise, for example, he conceded that a specific book, *Bloodstain Pattern Interpretation* by Herbert L. Macdonell, was the bible of the discipline and the key text on which he relied. Yet my questioning showed that Mason had entirely flubbed a premise of blood splatter investigation that the book insisted was basic. Moreover, his exploration of the bloodstains that appeared on Corine was inexplicably partial; he had examined only the stains on her shirt, not those on her jeans.

Mason was similarly vulnerable on the subject of gunpowder burns; he simply could not explain how or why such burns existed on the right side of Corine's nose since, as he claimed, the muzzle of the gun had been held on the left side of her nose, closer than the tip of the nose. He conceded that he had been unable to repeat the stippling pattern of those gunpowder burns in his test-firing of the murder weapon.

Vague in his answers, Mason repeatedly walked back from the certainty of the conclusions he had offered in direct testimony, leaving it unclear and full of holes. Those holes would later be filled by Miller and Hermann, whose meticulously supported testimony would show that the prosecution's version of who had shot and murdered Corine Christensen was completely defective.

But before we could get there, we had to go through Marino.

———

The DA had now produced all of his witnesses except the main one, James Marino, who had disappeared. Fry requested a one-week delay so that law enforcement authorities could find and produce his star witness, and over my objection, the judge granted the request. A major hunt for the runaway witness ensued, while the media tracked every twist and turn in the chase, and the level of interest in the case and its star witness rose higher and higher. Marino was finally found and brought back to testify, repeating in court the story he had told in the preliminary hearing, to Kathy Holub, and to anyone else who would listen: His old and dear friend Richard had murdered Corine Christensen, James's longtime girlfriend and associate in his drug-dealing business, while he, Marino, napped on her sofa.

It was December 15, a Tuesday, when Gary Fry wrapped up his direct examination of Marino. "Nothing further, your honor," he said, and the judge nodded to me to begin the cross-examination.

The press had not been shy about predicting that this moment would be a dramatic confrontation between the star witness and the "curly-haired fucking Jewboy" lawyer he had made no secret of wanting to kill. The crowd that morning hoping to get into the courtroom was backed up in a line that snaked through the courthouse corridors to the outside door. It is fair to assume that those who got in couldn't wait to hear how I would begin my cross-examination.

Now I am known to be a soft-spoken man; I simply don't have one of those voices that projects well or carries far. For that reason, it is my habit to position myself in a courtroom in such a way that the jury is between me and the witness I am questioning. My thinking is that if the witness can hear me, then the jury can hear me, and those are the parties who need to hear me. But with James Marino, I didn't just want to be heard. I wanted to send a message—to both witness and jurors—that I was not intimidated, that I was not scared, and that my client had a committed fighter going to work for him.

You could have heard a pin drop as I rose from the counsel table. I moved as close to Marino as the architecture of the courtroom made possible. I was as in-his-face as I could be. "Mr. Marino," I said in as ringing a tone as I could muster, "are you going to kill me?"

"Objection!" the prosecutor shouted, although he was barely audible over the eruption in the courtroom. The judge gaveled for quiet—repeatedly. I had not asked Marino if he were going to kill me *too*, which would have been objectionable as presuming him guilty, while against the DA's objection that my question was argumentative, I countered that it went to the issue of bias. The judge was still banging his gavel when he said "objection overruled," and I went on from there.

We established that Marino hated me and said he wanted me dead, and we established further that he had conceived the hatred for me solely as a result of my questioning him at the preliminary hearing. I then had Marino catalogue the various reasons for his distrust of Corine Christensen, the disdain he felt for her, and his belief that she was plotting against him. My aim in this line of questioning was to weigh the two sets of circumstances: If he was ready to see me "dusted" because I had asked him some questions, what fate did he envisage for Corine, who he believed was scheming to destroy him?

I next set about getting Marino to admit to inconsistencies between what he had testified to in court under the DA's direct questioning and what he had said previously. Admit to them he did—time after time. I played recordings of his interviews with detectives early in the history of the case, then contrasted it with transcripts of his trial testimony. I pointed out the direct contradictions between his testimony in the preliminary hearing and his testimony in court—and he conceded the contradictions. He also admitted to lying—on five separate occasions, to both sheriff's deputies and in the preliminary hearing—when he said Richard had stuck his gun into a bottle of Mr. Clean liquid detergent. "I was mistaken," Marino confessed.

Mistakes, lies, half-truths, contradictions, discrepancies, and confusion did not add up to a reliable witness, and that is what James Marino looked like after the cross-examination. He also looked, rather pathetically, like a man with a warped mentality. Nothing expressed this better than our exchange concerning his "natural gift" for NLP.

Initiating the exchange was a bit of a risk; standard legal practice says don't ask a question to which you don't know the answer. If you don't know the answer, you won't know if the witness has lied, and if you don't know the witness has lied, you cannot impeach that witness's testimony. But with Marino, the cross-examination had gone so well that I decided to take a flier and ask about some boasts he had made to Richard.

"As of the time of Miss Christensen's death," I began, "you believed, did you not, sir, that you could actually command street lights to go off and on, didn't you?"

"Yeah," said Marino.

"And you believed, did you not, sir," I went on, "as of the date of Miss Christensen's death, that you were a leader and that people around you looked up to you and that's why they try and knock you down?"

"True," said Marino.

"And you thought that everybody could see the glow in your eyes, didn't you?"

"They did."

"And as of the time of Miss Christensen's death, you felt you had gotten into a new charisma, isn't that true?

"Yes."

The man seemed a petri dish of psychological disturbances, not someone whose testimony should convict a defendant of anything at all, much less homicide.

———

What with the holidays, the Bandler case rolled over into the new year, but when it was the defense's turn to present our case, we called an array of witnesses who reinforced that impression of Marino—testimony about the anger he directed at Corine, his paranoid fear of her, and his sense that she had abandoned him combined with accounts of his drinking and cocaine use. It got to the point that in his closing argument, the DA was forced to acknowledge that not everything his key witness said was true; instead, the prosecution would ask the jurors to excuse the man's paranoia and mental instability and to believe the parts of his testimony the DA argued were supported by Dr. Mason's testimony. It was a risky premise for a guilty verdict.

Our forensic evidence was powerful. Ed Miller's test-firing of the murder weapon was able to recreate the stippling on the right side of Corine's nose only when the weapon was held four inches away from her face and at an angle—not very nearly touching her skin as Richard Mason had concluded. Paul Hermann, who had done thousands of autopsies for the Alameda County Coroner's Office, testified that the trajectory of the bullet inside Corine's head was not what Mason had concluded. He further showed that what Mason had identified as Corine's "brain tissue" on Richard's clothing was actually from her mouth and nasal passages; it represented her few final breaths, and its presence on Richard's shirt was consistent with his statement that he had gone to her aid after she was shot by Marino. Again, the prosecution's evidence was virtually obliterated.

Richard's own testimony was articulate and delivered in a low-key manner. He attributed to Marino many of the actions Marino had attributed to him. It was Marino who insisted on going to Corine's house to confront her, he said; it was Marino who sawed off the Mr. Clean bottle; it was Marino who prowled through the house, knocking over items, even pulling the stuffing out of Corine's stuffed animals—the possible explanation for what police would call a ransacking of Christensen's house. The detergent got on his shirt, Richard said, when he yanked the gun away from Marino, and he was sitting at the table drinking Tequila and watching Corine snort cocaine when Marino walked up and fired at her. Instinctively, Richard testified, he leaped up and caught her as she fell, staining his shirt front with her blood. He explained the actions that followed—the driving around, the failure to call 911, the long hours at home drinking and snorting cocaine—as an attempt to forget the awful event and an unwillingness to rat on his friend James.

The jury got the case mid-morning of Thursday, January 28, 1988. They broke for lunch from 1 P.M. to 2 P.M., and at 4 P.M., the jurors sent a message to the court that they had reached a verdict. I was worried. Yes, the trial had gone well, and I did not think the jury could have reached a guilty verdict so quickly, but that didn't stop me from experiencing my usual pre-verdict anxiety—big-time.

But the truth was much simpler: It had taken the jurors very little time to agree that the prosecution's case in no way provided any sort of proof, much less proof beyond a reasonable doubt, that Richard Bandler had committed murder.

———

So what had happened here? I suggested early on in this chapter that just hearing that a crime had involved two men and a woman stirs the mind to thoughts of a love triangle—the very cliché suggested on the *West* magazine cover to entice readers to Kathy Holub's article.

Clichés are easy. They're overused expressions of underused thinking; in fact, they deny original thought, supplanting it with impressions so solidly fixed in the brain they have become standard responses. I think the same process that enables us to fall back on clichés is what happened to the detectives and investigators looking to solve the murder of Corine Christensen. They knew that James Marino was not a believable source, but DA Fry claimed at the time of the verdict that they checked out "every detail of his story." Really? Sheldon Otis taught me that checking something out means questioning every assumption, following every lead, and not relying on conjecture when you come to a dead end. I don't think that happened here.

Law enforcement and prosecutorial authorities are well equipped to carry out thorough investigations; they have enormous resources on hand to explore widely and deeply. They are also, of course, under pressure to solve crimes. And sometimes—actually, far too often—it is easier and certainly more expedient to take the path of least resistance and settle for the ostensibly credible solution, if not the true one. I would add that such a solution is particularly easy to find when an expert is motivated to support the case of those who pay for his or her services, rather than conducting an objective analysis and letting the cards fall where they may.

In the case of Corine Christensen, investigators did not arrive at the scene of the crime until she had been dead for perhaps eight hours. They believed the house had been ransacked; investigators could not be sure what, if anything, had been taken or destroyed. The evidence at the scene, in other words, was less than optimum for fleshing out what had happened there. But then the police divers found the gun at the bottom of Capitola Harbor just where James Marino said it was, and tests would show it had fired the bullet found in Corine's brain. There was blood on Richard's shirt and a recording on Richard's answering machine, and if you put it all together, it looked like a credible enough solution to go to trial.

I have seen it time and again. It's not nefarious. It's not about misconduct—there will be plenty of that in later chapters. I think it has something to do with the groupthink that takes over when people work closely together day after day, especially in high-pressure situations, and it has something to do with the complacency that can result when you think you're close to succeeding. But whatever the cause, it looks to me an awful lot like laziness and not bothering to go deep enough below the surface. And when a defendant's life and the public's safety are at stake, that is simply inexcusable.

Fortunately, in this case, it was all so sloppily done that it took 12 jurors only a few hours to acquit the accused. Richard has gone back to a highly successful career as a lecturer and author of such books as *How to Get the Life You Want*. I do not know the whereabouts of James Marino nor what has become of him. The case remains unsolved; Corine Christensen's murderer is still at large.

———

When the Bandler case ended, I was still a fairly new partner in a law firm. I found that I was taking on more and more civil law cases while criminal law, which I had joined the firm to solicit and practice, was falling by the wayside. I had never been very adept at scoring money-making criminal cases, and although doing so was my assignment for the firm, I felt unsuited to the task. So in the absence of the criminal cases I loved to try, I litigated the civil cases that did not particularly engage me.

I wasn't totally happy as a partner either. Accustomed to going my own headstrong way in my approach to a case, I was not comfortable with the give-and-take that is the theoretical strength of a partnership; what I could accept in theory, I had difficulty with in practice.

In 1989, after just two years as a law firm partner, I went out on my own yet again. I could not have known it at the time, but some of my biggest cases were before me.

— 8 —

Who Are the Criminals? The Cases of Murray Lodge and Buddy Nickerson

Part 1: The Crime

On the night of September 14–15, 1984, three men set out to steal cash and drugs from the home of drug dealer John Evans in San José, California. The three were Dennis Hamilton, Bill Jahn, and Murray John Lodge, the ringleader. A fourth man, Bret Wofford, known as "Wolf," had been involved in the planning from the start and would provide an essential tool of the robbery—handcuffs—but did not go along on the job.

The four men all hailed from the wrong side of the tracks in sprawling San José, from the part of the city to which you do *not* know the way. All were in some way or another connected to the world of drugs and its attendant violence, and all had been in and out of police custody or at least police scrutiny for much of their respective lives. Yet they were four

117

very different individuals with four different roles to play in the projected crime.

Wofford was a serious drug addict and a violent man; the handcuffs he supplied were intended to be used to constrain Evans and his housemate, his half-brother Mickie King, who lived in an apartment converted from the unused garage, while the three robbers gathered the goods they wanted. Dennis Hamilton was the oldest of the group at 44—the others were in their mid-20s—and the meekest; at the time, he was letting Murray Lodge live with him, temporarily at any rate, at his ex-wife's home. Not known as a particularly violent man, Hamilton needed money and looked to the proposed robbery to provide it. Bill Jahn was responsible for obtaining and driving the vehicle, a borrowed van, which would get the men to a drop-off point near Evans's house and then serve as the getaway vehicle. Like ringleader Lodge, Jahn was a sometime enforcer in the rough, drugged-out circle in which the two men ran; in fact, he and Murray frequently had acted in concert to rob and beat up local drug dealers, a dangerous occupation. Bill Jahn was also the reason Wofford wasn't present; Jahn hated him so much that he refused to do the job if Wofford was there.

While all the men either knew John Evans or knew of him, Murray Lodge had actually worked for him; the two were well acquainted. Although Evan's "day job" was as a car mechanic and car painter—he was good at both—his real profession was the drug-dealing, and in that endeavor, Murray, a scrappy ex-con who had been fighting back against anyone and everyone since he was a kid, served as useful muscle.

But Evans was also, at least in Murray's eyes, a bad guy. He was hot-tempered, violent, abusive, wild. Evans's toughness, a style of bravura expected in his profession, struck Murray Lodge as bullying, not as the kind of hardwearing steeliness that Murray himself had honed to a fine edge. Twice, Evans had held a gun to Murray's head. Both occasions were show-off moves—empty bravado—but they rankled. Just as bad—maybe worse, at least in Murray's eyes—was that Evans was disrespectful of people he considered weaker than himself—especially of women, whom he invariably treated in demeaning ways. One mark of this attitude was the explicitly pornographic "art" that decorated the bedroom in his house, but Evans also had no qualms about beating women, and in

Murray Lodge's code of honor, beating up on people smaller or weaker than yourself—and certainly beating a woman—counted as very bad indeed.

Case in point: Evans's girlfriend Barbara Payne had been beaten by Evans while in an advanced state of pregnancy with their child; pointedly, the beating had included punching her in the stomach. It's why she wasn't in Evans's house the night of the planned robbery; only recently released from the hospital, she and her infant son were staying with her sister until Payne was well enough to move back in with John Evans, which she had every intention of doing.

Another case in point was an incident that would prove particularly important to the events that would follow. An acquaintance of Evans, one Harry Nickerson, known as Nicky, had once had the idea of robbing Evans. Nicky liked to brag about what he claimed were his exploits robbing drug dealers and raping their girlfriends. Evans was one drug dealer who particularly galled him, and Nicky must have wanted to add him to his personal bragging-rights list, so he brought a shotgun along. He knocked on the door, and when Barbara answered, he gripped her around the neck and held her in front of him as a shield, walking her down the hall to John's office and yelling for Evans to come out. Evans did, holding a gun. When Barbara managed to wriggle free, Nicky's shotgun discharged into the ceiling, and Evans shot Nicky in the chest. As the bleeding man tried to crawl to the front door, Evans kicked him repeatedly. "Faster!" he commanded with each kick. Nicky was convicted on several charges related to the incident, but his most consequential punishment was the severing of his spine by John's bullet, which left him permanently paralyzed from the waist down.

Evans's disrespect, minus the use of physical assault, extended to Murray Lodge, whom he treated, in Murray's view, like "hired help," talking down to Murray and belittling him in front of others. Murray Lodge had had a lifetime of being talked down to and belittled, starting when he was a very young kid and had been encircled by a group of bullying boys, beaten to a pulp, and shoved into a garbage can. While Evans was paying him, Murray knew he had to keep his cool in the face of the disrespect, but he did not like it, and ripping off Evans, who was widely known to stash money and drugs in his house, would be gratifying payback.

———

The house was on Ronda Drive, a typical California thoroughfare of modest, low-slung houses. The street was lined with deciduous trees and the palms that "say" California to most people, even though they are imported transplants that don't really belong in the state's soil and climate. Evans's house was not far from the freeway and was just behind a condominium complex of two-story structures with a parking lot and a pool.

A longish walkway extended along the side of the house, and at around midnight on September 14, Murray Lodge, Bill Jahn, and Dennis Hamilton, wearing ski masks that covered their faces, moved up that walkway. They carried guns and the handcuffs, supplied by Wofford, which would make him culpable as an accessory, despite his absence, if ever the cops "solved" the robbery. Actually, Wofford had persuaded a woman friend to buy the handcuffs, but at his behest and with his money.

It is reasonable to assume that the three men were feeling whatever intensity people feel when they are about to do something they know might be dangerous in any number of ways. Jahn and Hamilton were there to take as much as they could of John Evans's current supply of money, drugs, and precious gems; they had no other intention and sought no other outcome. The prospect of robbery was probably sufficiently disquieting. What they did not know, because he had never told them, was that Murray Lodge intended to murder John Evans, a far more disturbing proposition than the other men had ever bargained for.

Loud music was coming from the house as Jahn kicked in the door to Mickie King's garage-apartment, hit him over the head with a gun, and handcuffed him. At the same time, Murray kicked in the door of the main house and found, not John Evans, but Michael Osorio, a longtime friend of the Evans family and the man who had taught John Evans how to manufacture methamphetamine. Evans was not there. He had gone out for a Slurpee. To Murray Lodge, already stoked on methamphetamines he'd been ingesting all day, Evans's absence and Osorio's presence added more fuel to his fire.

The commotion of Murray's entrance woke Osorio from a nap, so Murray cold-cocked him as he woke, knocked him down, and cuffed him. Bill Jahn hauled Mickie King into the living room, so now there were two victims constrained and helpless lying side by side on the floor. Murray's senses, on high alert, now quickened to the sound of Evans's car pulling into the driveway, music blaring. He ordered Hamilton to turn down the music in the house.

Cutting his car engine, Evans noted at once that the music was at a lower decibel level than when he had left. Suspicious, he pocketed his gun, got out of the car, and went to his front door. The plan by those inside the house was that when Evans arrived home, Jahn would grab him so that he and Murray together could take him down. But Evans's gun was at the ready as he came through the door, and as Jahn attempted to grab him, Evans fired, wounding Jahn. "Murray!" Jahn shouted.

Murray fired twice at John Evans. Evans was down and most likely close to death when Murray applied the *coup de grâce* and shot him a third time.

As premeditated as the shooting may have been, it is also the case that for Murray, self-defensively trained since childhood to react fast and with fury, addled by heavy doses of meth, and always mindful of how Evans had twice put a gun to his head, shooting the man was instinctive and automatic.

But now there were two witnesses who may have heard Jahn call out Murray's name. With deliberation, Murray turned and shot both Mickie King and Michael Osorio in the head. Mickie died instantly, but the bullet Murray shot into Osorio's head circled around his brain and lodged there. He was unconscious and seemingly dead, but he was alive.

Murray grabbed what they had come for—money and drugs—and ran. He knew the area and leapt over the back fence to make his escape. Jahn, bleeding from his wound, ran out the front of the house; Hamilton ran with him. They sped west on Ronda Drive and south around the corner onto Union Avenue, then split, running in different directions. All three were heading for the designated meeting place on the street near the parking lot of the condo complex. Hamilton and Jahn got there first, then picked up Murray as the van headed up the street. Jahn told the two men that he had dropped his gun when he was shot back at the house on Ronda, and since it was registered to Hamilton's ex-wife, Dennis needed to retrieve it. "Fuck that," said Murray. He jumped out of the van and took off on foot.

Hamilton and Jahn, the latter bleeding badly, went back for the gun. Dennis ran into the house, looked around quickly, did not immediately see the gun, ran back to the van, and drove it away.

Murray Lodge wandered mindlessly. From where he ended up, it seems clear he was paralleling the freeway but keeping his distance from it, and that he was heading generally westward toward the foothills of the Coastal Range. In the early hours of September 15—the middle of the night to all who slept—he broke into the home of a woman named Irene Cook, 77 years old at the time, who, quite naturally, screamed in terror. What she did not know, could not know as he grabbed her to shut her up and accidentally knocked her down, was that this was not a guy who picks on the vulnerable, and to him, a lone woman of advanced years was highly vulnerable. He managed to calm her down and apologize, and in due course she fed him pie and milk. "You'll be reading about me in the newspaper," Murray told her before leaving some hours later.

———

Lying in a pool of his own blood, Michael Osorio managed to tell the first responding policemen that he had no idea who his assailants were. Later, at the hospital, just after being wheeled out of the operating room where he had had brain surgery, he repeated to a detective that he could not identify the men, but he described them as three white males of average build, all wearing ski masks. He also related that he had been asleep in front of the television when the men entered and that he was knocked unconscious almost immediately, so his view of his assailants was brief and terrifying. Later, he would also recall hearing Mickie King say words to the effect of, "Hey, buddy, come over here and loosen these fucking cuffs."

The anesthesia given to him and the surgery he underwent, along with the beating and the brain injury, all constituted what the doctors labeled "brain traumas."

The detectives assigned to the case, at the time both sergeants in the Santa Clara County Sheriff's Department, were Brian Beck and Jerry Hall. For physical evidence, they had the handcuffs and the gun found at the scene and a trail of blood splatters that tracked west on Ronda Drive and south on Union, then darted suddenly into a kind of service driveway of the condo complex, along the wall of a garage and past a dumpster into the complex's parking lot. DNA testing and computer matching of blood samples were at a stage of relative infancy in 1984; still, the evidence sample from the trail of blood would in time be compared to blood samples from all the men arrested for the crime, none of whom matched it. Nevertheless, this defined course of blood splatters, stretching from the house on Ronda Drive right through the parking lot of the condo complex, made it clear that someone had been wounded by a gun during the crime and had fled the scene.

As for the gun found in the house, Beck and Hall traced it to Hamilton's ex-wife, Norma Goytia, who told them, as Hamilton had instructed her to do, that her gun had been stolen. In due course, however, she gave up on the lie and told Beck and Hall that Hamilton and Murray had been staying with her, that Hamilton had taken the gun without telling her, and that on the day of the murders, Murray had said he was "going to Wolf's."

That was the linchpin of the case the detectives made: through Norma's gun to Hamilton and through Hamilton to Lodge and eventually to Bret "Wolf" Wofford. The purchase of the handcuffs was traced to the woman friend of Wofford, who promptly admitted buying them for him. Hamilton, Wofford, and Murray Lodge were all fingered for the crime and were on the detectives' radar screen to be hunted down. Still missing was the wounded perpetrator, the guy who left the trail of blood from a gunshot wound he had suffered while committing the crime in the house on Ronda Drive. But since blood was the only thing tying Bill Jahn to the crime, he remained unidentified, unsuspected, and as far away as he could get.

Detectives Beck and Hall, however, had figured out a way, if not to explain this somewhat confusing situation, at least to make use of it. They put together two facts related, after a fashion, to the events of September 14–15 and came up with a conclusion they found attractive enough to embrace. One fact was Osorio's recollection, culled only a day after his brain surgery from a mind still groggy with anesthesia, that someone had called out "Hey, buddy" during the attack. The other fact was the history between John Evans and Nicky Nickerson.

Nicky Nickerson had an older brother, Glen William Nickerson Jr., called "Buddy," a character not unknown to the police of Santa Clara County. Buddy Nickerson had once served time for car theft, routinely had his driver's license suspended but drove anyway, was an inconsistent provider of child support for a son and daughter by two different women, an often disorderly drunk, and a guy who never failed to give the cops lip. They didn't like him. So when, following Nicky's ill-fated confrontation with John Evans, it was learned that Buddy Nickerson was going around saying he would get even and avenge his brother, that planted in the minds of Beck and Hall a thoroughly appealing proposition: Buddy was involved . . . Get Buddy for this and he'd be off the streets once and for all . . . Make Buddy a "fourth man" who had been at Ronda Drive the night of the murders.

And that is precisely what they did. They simply added a perpetrator and placed him at the scene of the crime.

That there was no evidence for this proposition whatsoever was but a small detail to Detectives Beck and Hall. In fact, Brian Beck had been on the lookout for Buddy to seek revenge ever since Nicky was shot; he had literally forecast retaliation, at least in his mind, and it was the first thought he had when he and Hall arrived at the house on Ronda Drive a few minutes after 2 A.M. the night of the murders. Acting on a hunch, Beck dispatched two deputies to look for Buddy at his mother's home just a few miles away in Los Gatos.

Buddy was no more at his mother's than he had been at Ronda Drive committing the crime the detectives wanted to pin on him. In fact, Buddy had an alibi for that night. He had been at a party, although witnesses said he had spent most of his time there snoozing in the front of a pickup truck parked in the driveway. Granted, alibi witnesses can be suspect, as any criminal defense lawyer will tell you. Prosecutors like to attack their credibility, and unless the witnesses are very well prepped ahead of time, this may undermine their testimony—especially if they are part of a certain crowd of people. These particular alibi witnesses, all guests or hosts at a rowdy party at which various forms of controlled substances were undoubtedly available, were likely to have credibility problems. So Beck and Hall figured they could overcome the alibi issue.

A thornier issue was placing Buddy at the actual scene of the crime, and what made the issue especially thorny was that Buddy Nickerson was hard to miss. He was 5 feet 11 inches tall and weighed 425 pounds. The man was massive—distinctively massive. Added to his size were certain characteristics of his appearance and of what might be called his style. He wore a long, unkempt beard; tattoos proclaiming a range of bigotries—pro-Nazi and anti-Black for openers—covered his arms and neck; and personal hygiene was clearly not one of his primary concerns. Even in the blink of an eye that was all that was afforded to Osorio at the time of the assault, Buddy Nickerson would have been noticed.

But he wasn't. Jerry Hall was the detective summoned to the hospital in the wee hours of September 15; his raw notes from that visit record Osorio's original description of his assailants. He could not identify any of them, Osorio told Hall, but there were three white males of average build wearing ski masks. Buddy obviously did not fit that description.

Nor did he fit the descriptions given by two other eyewitnesses Beck and Hall had found. One was 18-year-old Brian Tripp, who had just returned from a party and was standing next to his car in the condo complex parking lot the night of the murders when he saw a man running through the complex, clutching something like a towel or jacket to his mid-section. When the man caught sight of Tripp, he stopped and called out "Where the fuck am I?" Tripp told him that if he didn't belong here he should keep going, and the man did exactly that. Tripp described the man to responding officers as around six feet tall and weighing about 190 to 200 pounds.

The other eyewitness was a resident of the complex who claimed to have been bothered enough by the noise from a car in the parking lot the night *before* the murders that she looked to see what was up. The implication was that somebody was casing the area preparatory to committing the crime. This eyewitness, Sharon Silberhorn, believed she could identify the passenger in the car. Beck and Hall showed her a photographic lineup containing Buddy Nickerson's picture; she made no identification.

Now it is undeniably true that eyewitness testimony can be fickle, unreliable, and downright inaccurate. The brain is not a recording device that plays back a precise picture or the exact same picture each time a memory is recalled. Memory itself can be tampered with; indeed, false memories can be planted in people's brains. Yet the public at large and jurors in particular place a great deal of trust in the word of an eyewitness—even more trust, at least back then, than in the science of blood-matching. Sergeants Beck and Hall no doubt knew all this. Whether they did or they did not, they wanted Buddy Nickerson to have been at Ronda Drive on September 14–15, so they systematically created the myth of a fourth man at the scene and manipulated the evidence to make it say it was Buddy.

Their method was simple. They had a pliable witness in the brain-injured, traumatized, suggestible Michael Osorio; it did not take much to influence him to say there were four perpetrators, not three, and that Buddy Nickerson was one of them. In fact, by the morning of the day following the attack—that is, on September 16, 1984—Beck prepared a police report saying that Michael Osorio had claimed there were four people that had broken into the residence and that he recognized one of the suspects as Buddy Nickerson. To go from three average-sized white masked men I cannot identify in Hall's raw notes recorded the night of the murder to Buddy Nickerson and three other people in the police report a little more than 24 hours later is certainly record time, but of course, Osorio had police "guidance" for the change in recollection.

After that, the other pieces fell into place easily. In time, all the witnesses would be sufficiently influenced to believe, and would testify with certainty, that Buddy Nickerson was the man they had seen either in the house on Ronda Drive the night of the murders, in Osorio's case, or in a car in the parking lot the night before the murders, according to Sharon Silberhorn, or leaving the scene of the crime in the wee hours of September 15, 1984, *qua* Brian Tripp.

Barely three weeks after the crime, on October 3, 1984, Buddy Nickerson was arrested for the murders of John Evans and Mickie King and for the attempted murder of Michael Osorio. The arrest took place at the home of Kristin Orabona and Dion Banks, the friends who had hosted the party that Buddy had slept through the night of the murders on Ronda Drive. When Kristin told Beck and Hall that Buddy had been at her home the entire night of September 14–15, the detectives accused her of being an aider and abettor, slapped handcuffs on her, put her in a police car, told her that she was going to jail, and said they would put her child in a shelter if she and her husband couldn't find someone to watch her. When Dion corroborated his wife's story, Beck and Hall told him they knew he was lying and added that he wasn't a good liar. He too was handcuffed and hauled off to the police station. The two were eventually released and were not charged with any crime.

Before the year 1984 was out, arrest warrants were issued for Hamilton, Wofford, and Murray Lodge—the "other" three alleged perpetrators of the crimes at the house on Ronda Drive.

As for the blood that didn't match Buddy or Dennis Hamilton or Bret Wofford or Murray Lodge, it was like the classic, Sherlockian, "curious incident" of the dog that didn't bark in the night. It shouted out something important—namely, that somebody had fled the scene of the crime and gotten away with it.

———

Meanwhile, ringleader Lodge seemed to have slipped through a hole in the police dragnet. Relinquishing Irene Cook's hospitality, with apologies, Murray stole her car, then hooked up with a young guy who took his father's truck so the two men could get out of town fast. They headed east and were well into the desert when they realized they were running out of money. So in Winnemucca, Nevada, they robbed a gas station—Murray used a toy gun for the holdup—and were promptly apprehended for the crime. Murray was convicted of armed robbery and sentenced to ten years, and in January 1985, Beck and Hall drove to a Nevada state prison to pick him up and bring him back to face multiple murder charges and a potential death sentence.

Except for whoever left the trail of blood, the detectives now had their last man, or so they determined: Hamilton, Wofford, Buddy Nickerson, and, handcuffed in the rear seat of the police vehicle, Murray Lodge, about to join the other three in police custody. All were to be charged with murder, since all were involved in the robbery that resulted in the two deaths.[2] What concerned the two cops was that once they got

———

2. Participation in certain crimes that result in death subjects the participant to the murder charge even if he or she did not personally kill anybody; this is the legal theory of felony murder.

Murray back to Santa Clara County, even though he'd be under lock and key, he would have a lawyer, and the lawyer would no doubt advise him not to talk to the police. This meant that Beck and Hall had only the time of the car ride to get from Murray anything they could get that might be self-incriminating—or that might nail anyone else, for that matter.

It was January 21, a Monday, typically a fairly heavy traffic day; the detectives could reasonably expect the drive from the state prison in Nevada to the county jail in Santa Clara to take as much as four or five hours. Their hope was that Murray would volunteer information, simply in the course of conversation, and so long as the detectives asked no questions—made no attempt to *elicit* information—any information they happened to receive could be used as evidence.

But Beck and Hall had already shown they were not the kind of men to leave anything to chance or to rely on mere hope; waiting around for Murray Lodge to *volunteer* self-incriminating statements was never in the cards. The fix was in before the key was ever turned in the ignition.

Later, in sworn testimony, Beck and Hall would state that at some point in the four-plus hours of chat about the weather, women, prison food, and the scenery, Murray had "spontaneously" acknowledged having broken into Irene Cook's house the night that John Evans and Mickie King were killed. By "spontaneous" the detectives meant unsolicited by them and in no way as part of any deal or arrangement. That was a lie. In fact, just about everything Beck and Hall claimed to have learned from Murray on that car ride was obtained in return for an offer of leniency.

But it would be a long, long time before that truth would be revealed.

The preliminary hearings for the three men—Lodge, Hamilton, and Wofford—took place in 1985 and focused on the physical evidence—gun and handcuffs—and on the eyewitness testimony of Osorio, Tripp, and Silberhorn.

Bret Wofford was in due course cut loose from the proceedings. Since the case against him was the weakest among the four and since he hadn't been at the murder scene, he took a deal offered by the prosecution, pled to being an accessory to murder, and was sentenced to time served. On March 26, 1986, therefore, three defendants only went to trial on charges of multiple murders, with the district attorney of Santa Clara County seeking the death penalty for all three.

Part 2: The Path Toward Justice:
The First Four Years

From the outset, the trial was a mess. Multiple defendants, multiple lawyers, multiple petitions by the multiple defense attorneys to elicit from
stalling prosecutors all the discovery material required by state and federal law: It all added up to interruption upon interruption that stretched
the proceedings into endless months of intermittent activity.

Murray's lead lawyer was Charles Constantinides, a longtime criminal
defense lawyer with a history of progressive activism. Constantinides had
soured on defense work, however, and at the time he began defending
Murray, he was actually in the process of trying to get hired as a prosecutor in a neighboring county. Perhaps for that reason, he spent little time
with Murray, instead delegating to his co-counsel—the Keenan counsel
required because this was a capital case—the responsibility to meet with
Murray in jail and instructing her to try to calm down his frequently
belligerent behavior.

Belligerence of course came easily to Murray, and he focused some of it
on Buddy Nickerson. As it happened, the two men had been acquainted
for some time. They had grown up as contemporaries just two years apart
in age, lived in the same neighborhood, had frequently run with the same
unruly crowd, and had long despised one another on a wholly visceral
level.

But if Murray needed a specific reason to hate Buddy Nickerson now
that they were co-defendants in a capital murder trial, Buddy supplied it
when he gave a lengthy interview to law enforcement authorities under
the guise of submitting to a polygraph test. It was a rare moment of
naïveté on Buddy's part—a childish notion that a lie-detector test would
prove he was telling the truth and would lead inevitably to his release. It
did not, of course; Detectives Beck and Hall had him in their sights, and
they possessed all the power necessary to keep him there. The interview
went well beyond the limited scope of polygraph testing; it addressed
numerous issues no lie-detector could ever deal with and went on for
a very long time. Simply put, it was a sneak attack: a full-blown police
interrogation camouflaged as a polygraph test, and its only purpose, or

so it seemed, was that it was transcribed for the edification of Murray's co-defendants and their lawyers.

But when word of it got out, what it told those defendants was that Buddy was a snitch. What constitutes a snitch? In the inmate code, as inviolable among prisoners as the U.S. Constitution is among members of the Supreme Court, a snitch is someone who incriminates his or her co-defendants. It is such a no-no that anyone who talks to cops is, almost by definition, a snitch. Since you must never snitch, you must never talk to cops. Certainly, you must never sit down for a lengthy police interview with a polygraph machine recording your pulse and your breathing. To do so is to commit not just treachery but treason, for to people like Murray Lodge, law enforcement is another nation—an enemy nation.

It would not have mattered to Murray or to any of the other defendants that Buddy could not possibly have squealed to law enforcement about the crime because he knew absolutely nothing about the crime. Buddy sat for the interview in the hope—forlorn, as it turned out—of convincing the prosecutors that he was innocent. Innocent of the crime, yes, but in the eyes of his co-defendants, he had talked to law enforcement and was therefore guilty as sin of being a snitch.

It is why, during a court hearing involving all the defendants, Murray told a guard he needed a lavatory break, requested that the guard partially unshackle him so he could relieve himself, and when he returned to the courtroom, came in swinging the loosened steel chains at Buddy's head. Deputy Sheriffs finally stopped Murray by using their batons to knock him unconscious.

When he wasn't swinging at people, Murray spent much of his time insisting, to anyone in the Santa Clara County jail who would listen, that while he was guilty of murder, his co-defendants were not. He made the point well enough that on November 24, 1986, Murray's trial was ordered severed from that of Buddy Nickerson and Dennis Hamilton. The severance of the trials triggered a prosecution decision to withdraw its request for the death penalty against everyone but Murray, so when Buddy and Dennis went to trial in December 1986, it was only under the threat of a lifetime in prison.

In fact, Buddy had been offered a deal—a sentence of 12 years in prison if he would admit to the crime; with time served and time off for good behavior, he would have been out in less than a third of that.[3] He turned the deal down. "I wasn't going to plead guilty to something I didn't do," he said simply. This gave some indication, if anyone was paying attention, of a certain spine of principle in this man: He would neither deny his innocence nor bargain it away; he was simply not for sale.

But in April 1987, both Buddy Nickerson and Dennis Hamilton were convicted on charges of multiple murders, attempted murder, and use of a gun. Hamilton was sentenced to consecutive terms of 27 years to life plus 11 years for having used a gun. Buddy was sentenced to LWOP—life in prison without possibility of parole—plus two consecutive prison terms for the attempted murder and gun use counts. In other words, neither man would ever again walk free.

Meanwhile, Charles Constantinides continued to chafe in discomfort with his role as Murray Lodge's—or anybody's—defender, while the Keenan co-counsel he had dispatched to liaise with Murray may have done her job all too well—so well that this particular lawyer–client relationship eventually sparked talk that it had strayed into intimacy. She denied any impropriety and charged her accusers with sexism, then slipped quietly away to a new location where she could restart her legal career. But the incident offered a reason for the court to grant Charles' request to withdraw as Murray Lodge's lawyer; it did so on March 30, 1987.

Murray's new lawyer was Christopher Taaffe, who had been a high school football star in Santa Clara County and was well known and well liked in and out of the legal community. But Chris had never before defended a capital murder case and was simply in over his head. Defending anyone on a charge of murder is—believe me—a daunting enough prospect for any lawyer, and a capital case is light-years more difficult; as I first learned defending Maurice Keenan himself, the responsibility for another human's life is, to say the very least, unnerving.

For help, Chris had a new Keenan co-counsel, a young lawyer named Ed Sousa, who had been admitted to the Bar only the year before in

---

3. Such an offer is extremely rare in a murder case; to my mind, this indicates that the prosecutors were not confident about the case against Buddy and were afraid the weak case against him might undermine the cases against Hamilton and Lodge.

1986. The two went to work to try to understand what was going on in this increasingly serpentine case and to determine a strategy for the defense.

I got a call from Ed Sousa one day. It was 1988 or 1989, and Ed, troubled by some issue triggered by the Lodge case—I no longer remember what the issue was—had sought advice from another lawyer who had suggested that I might be able to offer some counsel. I did so, but all I really learned from the phone call was that Ed was a very decent man and a committed defense lawyer; I hoped I had provided advice he found useful.

———

Murray's case, meanwhile, was faltering—not terribly surprising given the events that had triggered the change in lawyers not to mention the change itself, with all that it meant for transfer of the defense files and the time required for the new lawyers to become acquainted with their client and get up to speed on the facts, the applicable law, and the pertinent procedures. And events had not stood still while the two freshly appointed lawyers worked to climb the learning curve.

In October, 1989, Murray's original lawyer, Charles Constantinides, joined the staff of the Santa Clara County district attorney's office, the very entity that was trying Murray for a capital crime. At the very least, this gave the appearance of a conflict of interest on the part of the prosecuting attorney's office, no matter how far from the particular case Charles's assignments were. Chris Taaffe was also conscious of the rupture of faith it represented to the defendant—to Murray Lodge himself—that the lawyer originally entrusted with saving Murray's life was now part of the office seeking his execution. Chris and Ed went to work on a motion demanding that the Santa Clara County DA's office recuse itself entirely and that the state attorney general take on the case against Murray Lodge. The two spent substantial time and effort on this legal motion, but they lost in the trial court and lost again on appeal.

At the same time, Chris had become embroiled in a fight over money with the organization that had appointed him to serve as Lodge's lead counsel. Taaffe's dispute with the organization, known as the Conflicts

Administration Program, grew especially knotty when the Program panel accused Chris of overbilling, and at the end of April 1990, he withdrew from the Lodge case. A new lead counsel, the third in less than six years, now had to be appointed.

In California, the state provides separate state funding for the expenses, apart from lawyers' fees, of capital cases, and a money judge is assigned to oversee applications for the funding in each particular case. The money judge assigned to the Murray Lodge case now decided to hold a hearing on whether or not there was a possible conflict between Murray and the Conflicts Administration Program, which was refusing to pay the bills Murray's lawyers had submitted.

———

I knew absolutely nothing about any of this, nor was there any reason on earth why I should. The distance between San José and San Francisco is only about 50 miles, but there is a world of difference between the two places. So it is unlikely in the extreme that the 1984 murders of John Evans and Mickie King were even covered in the San Francisco press, and they almost certainly would not have been covered in my local Marin County paper; if the story was covered in either media outlet, I didn't read it; if I read it, it didn't register on my consciousness.

Nor were the two legal communities in touch with one another. Any gossip among the lawyers, judges, and court clerks of Santa Clara County about the *My Cousin Vinny*-like shenanigans of the trials of these four defendants would not have made its way up Highway 101 to the court-house corridors of San Francisco.

In fact, the years in which all these events transpired were the years in which I was focused like a laser on substantive cases of my own— especially the defense of Stephen Bingham and later of Richard Bandler. For some of those years, I had of course worked as a sole practitioner, then had joined Garry, McTernan, Stender, Walsh & Schwartzbach. They were busy years: I was commuting north from my San Francisco office to the Marin County Courthouse for Steve, south along the coast to Santa Cruz for Richard, and of course in and out of San Francisco to deal with a range of other commitments. With the exception of a murder trial I tried in the late 70s—a trial that in any event was truncated in many ways—and one in the late 80s, San José and Santa Clara County just weren't in the picture.

So I was a complete babe in the woods on the day in May 1990 when I got a phone call from the clerk to Superior Court Judge Daniel Creed of Santa Clara County. Would I come to San José, the clerk asked, to represent Murray Lodge at a hearing called by Creed in his role as money judge to determine whether a conflict of interest existed that had compromised Lodge's defense? Lodge, Creed: I had never heard of them. Only the name of the defendant's lawyer rang a bell—Ed Sousa—as my brain clicked on the phone call of a year or so ago.

In fact, Ed was precisely the reason Creed called me. As he would later tell me, being Murray Lodge's sole attorney—even temporarily— was a prospect that scared him out of his wits. So when he and Murray appeared before Judge Creed and Creed asked Murray, "Who do you want your lawyer to be?" Ed whispered to Murray, "M. Gerald Schwartz-bach," and Murray, clueless, parroted the name back to the judge, who dispatched his clerk to ask me to represent Murray in the hearing. It wouldn't take long, the clerk assured me.

I went to San José. I met Ed Sousa and Murray Lodge and, knowing absolutely nothing about the case and even less about the man—except that he needed a lawyer for this particular hearing—represented him before the judge. As far as I knew, that was it. Judge Creed declared that a conflict existed and then summoned me into his chambers.

Creed was tall and big-framed, with the military bearing and brusque manner of the prosecutor he had once been, and he was known as a pro-prosecution judge. He was also regarded as a man with an inherent sense of fairness, and as far as he was concerned, Murray Lodge was not getting the fair deal guaranteed to him by the Constitution of the United States and the criminal justice system of the state of California. By declaring the existence of a conflict, Creed was able to appoint a lawyer outside the normal fee system, and that is what he was now prepared to do. He told me he that he didn't care if Lodge "fried," but he believed that he had been jerked around by the system and it had to stop. "I want somebody to come in here as lead counsel and do this right," Creed said. I felt the full force of the prosecutorial stare. "Let's negotiate your terms," he added.

I told Creed I had to think about it. The only death penalty case I had been involved in, the Keenan case, had taken a toll on me and my family, and I was not eager to revisit such stresses. Above all, I said, I could not make a decision without my wife's consent. I drove back home, and Susan and I discussed the situation in depth. "How long do you think it will go on?" she wanted to know. I shrugged. "Maybe a year," I opined.

Thus began an involvement that would last for 13 years, embrace two defendants—Murray Lodge and Buddy Nickerson—extend across two major trials and a seemingly endless petition process, make me a resident of Santa Clara County for four days out of every week for some 150-plus weeks, and consume me body and soul in the effort to help two men have their chance at life.

———

As was true in the case of Maurice Keenan and as is true in most death penalty cases in California, the Murray Lodge case had a guilt phase and a penalty phase. In the former, the prosecutors were setting out to prove murder beyond a reasonable doubt and to convince a jury that special circumstances prevailed—in this case, multiple murders and that the killer had lain in wait for the victim. If they could prove both guilt and the specified circumstances, the jurors would then have to decide in the penalty phase between a sentence of life imprisonment without possibility of parole or the death penalty,[4] and the death penalty decision would of course have to be unanimous.

It was May 16, 1990, when I was officially appointed to represent Murray Lodge. The case was in its fifth year. The case-file consisted of some 30-plus banker's boxes of documents, and Ed Sousa and I would add to that as we got down to work. Ed had now been on the case full-time for three years, the bulk of his legal career to date, and as we went over every detail again and again, we became even more convinced that Beck and Hall were dirty; we already knew that Buddy Nickerson was innocent. It was also clear to us that in its relentless pursuit of the death penalty for

---

4. A verdict of guilt without specified circumstances would result in a sentence of life in prison *with* the possibility of parole.

Lodge, on which so much time and money had already been expended, the prosecution was not about to give an inch.

On paper, Ed Sousa and I could not have been more different. Thirteen years my junior, Ed is tall, dark, and handsome with a sonorous baritone voice. I am short and compact and talk softly enough that people in general and judges in particular periodically ask me to "please speak up." Ed is level-headed and approachable; I alternate between joking around and becoming relentlessly intense. Our styles are different—we are now and were then two individuals going about things in our individual ways—but rather than dividing us, these differences complemented one another and made us a good team.

Ed was also very clearly a man deeply committed to his clients, and it was hard for me not to see in him my own younger self at a similar moment in my career. Warming to him as I did, and knowing how much we would need to rely on one another in the work ahead, I think I felt a responsibility—almost an obligation—to mentor him in the way older lawyers—most notably, Sheldon Otis—had mentored me. I wanted to pass down to him the rich lessons I had learned from Sheldon—the challenging of assumptions; the profound study of statute, precedent, and procedure; the rigorous pursuit of facts; and above all, the absolutely uncompromising thoroughness of preparation that so defined the Otis practice of law and that had become my methodology and my passion as well. The mentorship began with the Murray Lodge case, and I believe it helped Ed realize his potential to be, as he is today, a great lawyer. It's something I'm proud of.

Ed is also just a wonderful man, and it was a pleasure from the start to work with him and to get to know him as we built the friendship that still binds us today.

These relationships, forged in the heat of a shared professional goal and nurtured by long hours of thinking and debating together, are an especially valuable part of the practice of law, especially of criminal defense law. To this day, I value as priceless my own mentee relationship with Sheldon Otis; the ongoing connection I had with Ed Miller and later Chuck Morton and their team of forensic experts; and working with the people on the Hunter's Point crew, with colleagues like John Mitchell and Neil Morse when we all went to work for Sheldon's firm, with Bruce

Cohen, who was my associate for six years, with Mark Rosenbush,[5] who had been my law clerk at the Community Defender office, became a close friend and a terrific lawyer in his own right. So it was with Ed Sousa. Along with the successes I've achieved for clients in court, these associations remain highlights of my career. It is enormously rewarding to work with someone who is on the same wavelength of both thought and conviction and to have confidence in that colleague's commitment and good will. During the years of defending Murray Lodge and later of fighting Buddy Nickerson's imprisonment, Ed and I—spending more time with each other than with our families—achieved a level of collegiality and a mutual understanding that both furthered our clients' causes and were personally gratifying.

I had stipulated that a local residence-cum-office would be an essential element of any deal negotiated with Judge Creed, and the apartment[6] I rented in the city of Santa Clara was the site of many a long, long session of poring over documents with Ed and wrangling the issues together. Like college students cramming for exams, we worked late into the night—and when he went home, I typically worked on even later. But it was also the case that in between hours and hours cooped up with papers, law books, and each other, we often let off steam together too.

A routine soon developed. On Sunday, I would drive down from my home in Mill Valley, and Ed and I would go out to dinner to more or less plot out the week. Monday, Tuesday, Wednesday we would be in court all day, then go for a gym workout followed by working dinners. Thursday was the same, except that I would drive home to Mill Valley after court in time to coach Micah's Catholic Youth Organization (CYO) basketball team. As is fairly usual in long trials, court was not in session on Fridays.

The workouts and dinner breaks were important, even if they weren't everybody's idea of sheer relaxation. Our time at the gym was occa-

---

5. Mark was the first lawyer I knew who created databases for criminal defense files. I persuaded Judge Creed to let me hire Mark to do that for the enormous Lodge defense file. His work was critical in allowing Ed and me to organize and quickly reference the voluminous facts and evidence in the case.

6. It was a totally utilitarian living space that remained virtually unfurnished for the entire period of the lease. A bed, couch, table, chair, and desk constituted the complement of furniture, and as Susan remarked when she and Micah came to visit—just once—there was absolutely nothing on the walls.

sionally as fiercely competitive—this time with one another—as were our courtroom outings against the prosecution. We sometimes found ourselves contesting which of us could lift a heavier weight or do more repetitions, and the occasional ping pong game sometimes felt like a life-and-death contest. Even so, these workouts were intermissions from the case, and just getting away from our notes and outlines and all the boxes of evidence helped. Then we'd head out for dinner.

We particularly favored a seafood restaurant that had a multi-story parking lot. We'd arrive there, grab Ed's football from his car, and run patterns among the parked cars. That would get rid of any kinks our workouts hadn't. Then we'd go inside, order a couple of Scotches, and try to unwind mentally. Yet we invariably came back to the case, and probably because we were in a different setting and had refreshed our brains along with our bodies, the discussions we had in a restaurant over those Scotches yielded insights that became central to our strategizing.

I invariably carried a laptop with me, and I always asked for a table near a power outlet so I could keep it charged. But after a day in court, a couple of drinks, and the sheer adrenaline of a trial, I too was charged, too electrified to take notes that could in any way make sense the next day. But since these were the moments when my thinking took flight, some of it sharp and incisive, some of it probably gibberish, it was left to Ed to record it all. He relied on an older but perhaps equally reliable technology—namely, a legal pad—so that when either of us had a thought about the case in the middle of the salad course or dessert or with a mouth stuffed with food, he could take notes. Ed took very good notes—clear, precise, to the point. To this day, those notes testify to how extremely productive those dinners were. And they confirm that fresh surroundings, different faces to look at, varying the rhythm of the day—it all helps break the stress and clear the cobwebs for a new way of looking at things.

One of the first things I learned from Ed as we got to work was that both of Murray's previous lead lawyers had wanted to finger Buddy Nickerson as the murderer and distance Murray from him. Their "reasoning" for this conclusion was in line with what the prosecution had decided to believe—that Buddy Nickerson was a bad guy, that his brother's debacle with Evans gave Buddy a motive, and that it was time to get Buddy off the streets and keep him off. I rejected that stategy.

The prosecutors' evidence for making Buddy the killer was his having been identified by Michael Osorio, who had transformed his recollection that someone that night had cried out "Hey, buddy!" into a positive accusation on the witness stand, a transformation neatly scripted for Osorio by Beck and Hall. We knew, however, that Osorio had gotten the identification totally wrong; Ed had informed me at our very first meeting that Murray told every lawyer he'd ever had that Buddy, whom he hated, had nothing to do with the crime on Ronda Drive, and the lawyers for Murray's co-defendants affirmed that their clients had said the same thing. Since Osorio had gotten that identification wrong, how could his identification of Murray be trusted beyond a reasonable doubt? That became the crux of our strategy: to cast doubt on the identification of Murray by showing the weakness of the identification of Buddy. In a sense, I had realized that if we were going to have a chance of saving Murray, we would have to prove Buddy's innocence.

We found Brian Tripp, the young man who had testified at Buddy's trial that he was "100 percent sure" that Buddy Nickerson was the man he saw in the parking lot the night of the murders. Brian was now a deputy sheriff in Colusa County, a sprawling piece of land at the head of the Central Valley, northwest of Sacramento and well north of San José. My investigator, Cathy Kornblith, and I went up there to meet with him, finding him as congenial and gracious a young man as you could wish. I had brought with me a photo of Buddy Nickerson taken around the time of the murders. He is bare-chested, his 425-pound bulk overwhelming the sofa on which he is seated. His chest and belly are a cascade of layers of flesh, and the infant daughter he is holding in his arms looks the size of a thimble against the enormity of her father. "No," said Brian Tripp, "the man I saw that night could not have been Buddy."

"How did it happen," I asked, "that your identification of Buddy doubled the size of the man you saw?"

Brian described a subtle process of influence and innuendo. "I'm not saying the detectives told me to lie," he began, but they repeatedly asked him if the description he was giving—white man, about 5 feet 11 inches–6 feet, around 190–200 pounds—could have been of someone "bigger." In time, Brian gained the impression that "they were disappointed in me," and as he tried again to recall what he had seen as they suggested it, he began to doubt his own recollection and, over time, to believe their description. He believed it sufficiently, he now realized, to have made a totally false identification.

We were convinced that Beck and Hall had done the same with Michael Osorio, an easy mark because of his brain traumas, surgery, and lingering anesthesia, and we believed they had done the same with Sharon Silberhorn, the woman in the condo complex whose eagerness to be part of something exciting may have made her particularly suggestible.

That was not all. Ed told me that when earlier investigators met with witnesses, the witnesses told them they had been interviewed by the two detectives, but no record of any such interview had ever been turned over to the defense, as is of course required. It was not until just before the first trial in 1986 that Beck and Hall relinquished a shoebox of tapes and papers they said they had not thought relevant; in fact, the materials were damned relevant. Ed and I were convinced that the detectives had continued the practice and were withholding or had suppressed or had possibly destroyed vital evidence. As I said, these cops were dirty.

———

Cathy and I also flew down to meet with Buddy Nickerson in prison in Tehachapi, near Bakersfield, California. It was a memorable visit.

This was not a scheduled visiting day at the prison, so we were ushered into a large room and seated ourselves at a round table. Guards brought in Buddy Nickerson, who had no idea who we were and why we were there. The first thing Cathy and I noticed was the huge swastika on his left forearm; when he rested his chin on his fist, it stood out like a racist neon sign. Like me, Cathy is Jewish, and for us, there is no context in which the swastika looks anything but menacing. Nor was it meant to be anything but menacing by the huge, bigoted man before us, an avowed racist, who spent the next 45 minutes haranguing me with his indifference to anything we might say.

In a way, I could not blame him. The man was in prison for a crime he did not commit. He knew that Murray Lodge, who hated him and whom he loathed, was involved in that crime. I was Murray Lodge's lawyer and Cathy the investigator for Murray's defense. And both of us belonged to a religious tradition and a people that, along with anyone who was not white, Buddy had early been taught to hate and fear. In the vividly uncompromising language of the convict culture, Buddy Nickerson spent quite a while telling me he couldn't care less about Murray Lodge or our problems defending him. He was not swayed by my protestations that Murray's case and his were inextricably linked and that by helping Murray, he might actually be able to prove his own innocence.

My irritation was also on the rise, and my patience was in free fall. I had had enough of being polite, so I suggested a deal instead. "If you want," I began, "I'll leave now. And it's true that if you cooperate with me on this, there is no guarantee that anything I can do will get you out of prison. But I can promise you one thing."

"What's that?" Buddy asked. He was angry.

"If I leave now," I said, "so does your last chance of ever leaving this place in anything other than a box."

There was no immediate reply. In the silence, though, I could almost hear Buddy Nickerson's mind calculating the odds, the liabilities, the possible payoff. Yes, I was Jewish, which he considered despicable, and I was the lawyer for Murray Lodge, whom he detested, but right now without me, he was guaranteed to die in prison.

When he finally answered, it was with an agreement to cooperate. In fact, by the end of the visit, Buddy had committed to help in any way we wanted—including testifying. In truth, he seemed eager to testify; his lawyer had not put him on the stand at his own trial, and he wanted to go on record as denying complicity in the events of 1984 in his own voice and in his own way. It was the first inkling I had of that principled spine inside the crudely bigoted Mr. Nickerson. It was not the last.

I added one more stipulation to our deal before I left. "If I do get you out," I said, "you've got to do something about that swastika."

Part 3: Keeping Murray Lodge Alive

For lawyers trying a death penalty case, the standard rule of thumb is that it requires the same things as an ordinary trial, only much, much more. More pretrial preparation time, more motions, more experts, more witnesses, way more juror *voir dire* and therefore way longer jury selection time. But Murray Lodge's case took the cake.

Opening statements in the Murray Lodge case got underway in late August 1992, after months of trial preparation and jury selection. At the time, Murray had been in the Santa Clara County jail for more than seven years. He would remain there another three years until his fate was decided. Nobody's case lasts for ten years, but Murray's did. It was not exactly "speedy" justice by anybody's calculus.

Ed and I knew we were up against an awfully tough set of circumstances in the guilt phase of Murray Lodge's trial. Our strategy—to cast doubt on Osorio's identification of Murray as the shooter by undermining his identification of Buddy—was not easy to execute, given that Buddy had been convicted and imprisoned for the crime. We brought in witnesses who had been at the party with Buddy on the night of the murder, and they told of seeing him asleep in his truck in the driveway, his unshod feet sticking out the window of the cab. But they were not great witnesses, and neither was Buddy, despite numerous additional visits on my part to prepare him for testifying. Those visits, however, deepened the relationship between us considerably. I could not act on his behalf while I was representing Murray Lodge, but once Buddy finished testifying, I made it clear that if both he and Murray waived the legal conflict of interest between them, I would try to get his conviction overturned, and I would do it for free.

We had found one piece of important but exasperatingly incomplete evidence that would support our strategy. Kristin Orabona and Dion Banks, the hosts of the party Buddy had attended the night of the murders, had received a phone call from a friend while the party was in full swing; the friend had been arrested and called to ask for help in getting bailed out. Many of the party guests could corroborate that immediately after receiving the call, the couple had set off for the jail to help their friend, and that is when they saw Buddy asleep in his truck—the exact time at which the murders had taken place. The good news was that Kristin and Dion had a telephone bill showing the time of the jailhouse call to their home phone. The bill clearly provided confirmation of the call and of the time, so it was a critical piece of evidence.

That is why Kristin and Dion had given the telephone bill to Buddy's first lawyer, who confirmed to us that he had been in possession of the bill but claimed he then gave it to the next lawyer to represent Buddy. The next lawyer, a public defender, said he had seen the telephone bill in an envelope in the public defender's file on the case but didn't know if it was still there. So Ed and I went to see Tom Dettmer, the public defender who represented Buddy at trial, to ask him about it. Dettmer couldn't help us—he had never seen the telephone bill[7]—but in the course of our discussion, he asked: "Did you ever hear the recording with Murray?"

"What recording?" I asked.

"The one on the ride back from Nevada," said Tom.

That was interesting. Beck and Hall had insisted under oath that there was no tape recording of the four-plus hours it had taken to drive Murray Lodge back to San José from prison in Nevada. Instead, it was their sworn testimony that during the drive, Murray had simply offered the single confession about breaking into Irene Cook's house, and he had done so "spontaneously"—freely and voluntarily, not in "exchange" for any consideration of the charges against him. Beck had so stated in the police report he wrote about the ride. This was significant. Since Murray was in custody and the detectives had not "Mirandized" him, nothing he said in response to their questions should have been legally admissible in court.

———

Ed went back to his office and retrieved the shoebox so reluctantly given up by Beck and Hall in 1986. Dettmer looked through the pile of cassettes. His guess was that the tapes in the shoebox had been dumped there to be recycled, and he remembered that the recording he had in mind had been on the reverse side of an interview with another witness; it was that interview he was looking for. He found the cassette, popped it into the player. We listened as Tom pressed PLAY, and we heard Jerry Hall suggest to Murray Lodge that if Murray "provided information,"

———

7. The telephone bill was never found.

they would talk to the DA about dropping the death penalty. In the rest of the approximately 20-plus-minute tape, all that was left of the four hours presumably recorded, the detectives continued the conversation, one that, even if no specific questions were asked, was nevertheless "reasonably calculated to elicit from Mr. Lodge incriminating statements."

The words are in quotes because they were the exact words Judge Robert Foley used to characterize the taped interview when he summoned the jury in the Murray Lodge case back into court. It was February 8, 1993, more than six months after the trial had begun, and it was the end of it: Foley had spent a week reviewing the tape and taking testimony regarding it, and he now declared a mistrial. He had found, he said, that the detectives had both suppressed evidence and lied under oath. "It is my belief," Foley said to the members of the jury, "that the officers"—Brian Beck and Jerry Hall—"willfully perjured themselves in your presence."

Isn't perjury a crime? It is—a serious crime. Yet no prosecution of the detectives' perjury was ever initiated, even after the DA's office asked the state attorney general to investigate, so no criminal charges were ever filed against Beck and Hall. They suffered no consequences of having lied under oath—and in a death-penalty capital case at that.

Not too long after Judge Foley declared a mistrial, we decided to offer a deal. Murray would plead guilty and accept a sentence of LWOP if in return the district attorney would agree to raise no objection to the court considering a habeas corpus petition for Buddy Nickerson. A habeas corpus petition, officially a request for a prisoner's release from unlawful imprisonment, figures prominently in Buddy's story, as the pages that follow will make clear; suffice to say at this point that we intended it to kick off a total reconsideration of Buddy Nickerson's conviction and incarceration.

Obviously, such a precondition could jeopardize the deal, and I was not looking forward to presenting it to Murray, whose permission we would need if we were to go forward with it. It was indeed a difficult conversation, as I explained to him that we were thinking of adding a precondition—on behalf of someone he loathed—that might compromise his own chances of avoiding the death penalty. We made it clear to him that we were quite willing to make a settlement for LWOP without any precondition whatsoever—a straight give-us-LWOP-and-end-this-trial-now proposition that would not require him to do anything at all on behalf Buddy Nickerson. His reaction showed me yet again how very complex and complicated human beings can be; a confessed murderer, Murray Lodge was nevertheless a stand-up guy. Yes, he hated Buddy Nickerson, but he believed that what had happened to Buddy Nickerson was unfair. Some sense of right and wrong was at the very core of the man; he would tell me that he felt bad that the guys he had persuaded to join him at Ronda Drive, went into it not knowing his intention to commit murder. That was a wrong that he could not assuage, and it rankled him. As for his own fate, whatever it was to be, he believed he deserved it, but he was ready to go to the wall for those who did not deserve to share it—most especially, Buddy Nickerson. He authorized us to go ahead and make the offer *with* the precondition.

I told John Luft, the prosecuting attorney in Murray's trial, that I wanted a meeting with George Kennedy, the chief district attorney for Santa Clara County. We met in Kennedy's conference room—Kennedy plus two of his chief deputies, Luft, Ed, and I—and we pitched our deal. The DA and his men affected a stony demeanor and said they'd get back to us.

When they did, the answer was no. No reason was given, but my feeling is simply that they wanted the death penalty, and they thought they could get it. They wanted the win.

Eight months after the mistrial, jury selection began for Murray's retrial.

––––––

Meanwhile, life went on. Micah was about to become 13 years old. He was the son of parents with different religious backgrounds—his father a Jew, his mother, though raised Catholic but no longer practiced that religion, had been fine with my expressed wish that our son be raised as a Jew. And in fact, Micah had been attending Hebrew school for several years. But it was now time to prepare for a bar mitzvah, with all that that entails—delving into ritual, learning the prayers, memorizing the *haftorah* he would chant in Hebrew—not to mention all the details of the celebration itself: when, where, how, for how many guests, and so forth.

And who oversaw all the activity for this important milestone in the life of our son and our family, a ritual of ancient and revered tradition? Not the onetime Hebrew school boy raised in the Orthodox tradition and now wrapped up in the details of a legal case that had gone on for nearly a quarter of Micah's lifetime. No, the task fell to and was brilliantly executed by Micah's English-born, Catholic-christened mother, and on March 19, 1994, Micah's actual thirteenth birthday, we both beamed with pride as our son took his place as an adult, at least within the Jewish community, with the responsibilities that go along with that watershed event.

It was a wonderful celebration. Micah shone, and Susan and I basked in the glow, surrounded by so many people we love. The event was for me a stirring moment and a reminder in so many ways—in the happiness I was able to enjoy, in my love for my family, in my commitment as a Jew—of why I do the work I do. It renewed me somehow for the job of pursuing justice, and when the celebration ended, I went back to work on the defense of Murray Lodge.

————

We lost in the guilt phase. It was December 1994, when the jury got the case, by which time we had been at trial for a little over a year. Yet the jury deliberated for only a day and a half before rendering a verdict of guilty with special circumstances, those being that Murray had committed multiple murders and had lain in wait for his victim. It meant that Murray would face either the death penalty or a sentence of life in prison without parole. Ed and I were now focused entirely on saving Murray Lodge's life.

I was angry over the brevity of the jurors' deliberations following a multi-month trial, and I let them know it once the penalty phase got underway. "You could not possibly have looked at all the evidence we presented in the day and a half you deliberated before arriving at your verdict of guilt," I told the jury. "You simply couldn't have managed it *physically* in that short amount of time." I was intentionally confrontational; I wanted these jurors to feel rebuked, but I was also putting them on notice that they must not undervalue the gravity of the undertaking on which they were embarked. They were about to decide whether or not the state of California would execute a fellow human; I was reminding them that they needed to bring to this decision all their care and all their understanding because they would have to live with the decision for the rest of their lives. I was also mindful of the math: All I needed was one juror to vote no on the death penalty, and if I could plant a sense of unease over the momentousness of this decision in the mind of a single individual, that could do it.

But before we got to that point, the name of the game in the penalty phase was to humanize Murray Lodge. This sounds simple, but it is not. These were 12 people who had just determined, rather quickly, that Murray had callously murdered two people and had tried to murder a third. They knew he had assaulted people in jail and in the courthouse on over a dozen separate occasions. He looked and acted tough; he was not entirely likeable; it was not difficult to see him as a bad man with something dark and ugly in his nature. It is much more comfortable to regard such a man as outside the norm or beyond the boundaries the rest of us live in, as somehow not belonging to us and therefore not recognizable to us. If you can think of someone as having nothing to do with you or your life, you need not flinch at the notion that he is just garbage and therefore at the idea of throwing him out. My job was to break through that.

I had learned back in the Keenan case that to do that job right, you have to begin it at the first minute of trial preparation—starting at the penalty phase is simply too late—and dig into every aspect of your client's life. For that, I needed to talk to Murray's family, but Ed, whose bond with Murray was longer and closer than mine, had told me that Murray categorically refused to have his family involved.

I wanted him to change his mind, and quite early in our trial preparation, I went to see him about it. "No," Murray told me. "I got myself in this mess. I don't want my family's lives complicated, and I don't want them interviewed for this trial."

I argued back. "If you're executed, you're gone—you're out of it," I said. "But the people who love you will have to live the rest of their lives with the knowledge of what they did or did not do to try to save your life. You do not have a right to make that decision *for* them." Murray gave in.

It meant we could explore and present detailed evidence about the appalling and, in many ways, abusive background of Murray John Lodge.

We were going to need some form of explanation because the prosecution's evidence during the penalty phase was brutal, 42 criminal acts. Murray's numerous acts of violence, especially when related by his victims, painted a picture of a cold-blooded killer. We could neither negate nor contradict such testimony, nor—obviously—could we justify it; our only hope of a response was to shed some light on how Murray Lodge became such a man—and who he was at the core.

For help in this, I again turned to Craig Haney, the psychologist specializing in death penalty issues I had first met in the Maurice Keenan case. Since that time, Craig's career and reputation had gone from strength to strength, and he had become renowned nationwide for his policy-oriented research, particularly on the psychological effects of incarceration, a subject he lectured on and testified about all over the country. He had also become a very good friend, and he was invaluable in all these roles in helping me organize my thinking, create the right strategic approach, and find the key to just what we were looking for—some insight into Murray Lodge the man.

With Craig's help and under his guidance, we investigated and presented evidence about Murray's upbringing in a dysfunctional family on the lower end of the socioeconomic ladder, where he grew up with little exposure to what might be called the gentler pleasures of life. Small in stature, he was repeatedly bullied and beaten by bigger kids. The jury heard of the pummeling he took when that circle of boys surrounded him and more or less passed him from one to the other for blow after blow until young Murray passed out—and was stuffed into the garbage can.

This kind of evidence explained, if it did not justify, how Murray grew up to be a man lightning-fast to feel resentment or anger and to apply his fists or any other weapon he could find to express his feelings. It explained, if it did not justify, why he was at home on the other side of the divide from legality, from civil discourse, from behavior the rest of us consider appropriate. The jury was being asked to kill this man; it was important they know his life story and the events and circumstances that had brought him to this point.

More than 30 witnesses testified about the other side of Murray Lodge, drawn out initially by Craig Haney's powerful interviewing skills. Some talked about the little boy who had been helpful to his neighbors when he was growing up; others told of acts of kindness or elaborated on Murray's protective instinct—his need to shield others from the kind of bullying he himself had suffered.

One of the issues jurors in a penalty phase may consider is the kind of inmate the defendant will be if, instead of being executed, he spends the rest of his life in prison. It was a subject on which Craig would testify, and he had helped us plot the narrative we drew from witnesses who testified about Murray's previous incarcerations as both a juvenile and an adult. Correctional counselors told why they believed that Murray would be a good influence on younger inmates. A former fire captain with the California Department of Forestry, which often seeks prisoner-volunteers to help fight forest fires, testified that he "absolutely trusted" Murray with his own life and that Murray was the best inmate worker he had ever supervised. Former convicts testified that Murray had given them advice that helped them straighten out their lives. A priest who routinely visited the county jail talked about how much Murray had grown as a person while in custody over the years; he said Murray had encouraged *him* in his counseling of other inmates. And a nurse who worked in the county jail testified that, unlike most inmates, Murray had always been protective of her welfare and safety.

Murray himself took the stand for four days of testimony—direct testimony in response to questions from me, plus cross-examination. This was his chance to make himself recognizable to jury members—not as criminal or defendant, but just as a man they might, in other circumstances, have come across in the workplace or in a social situation. The goal was to try to make it that much harder for some on the jury to condemn Murray Lodge to death.

In direct examination, I deliberately asked questions only about events before and after the crime; this would enable me to argue that Murray could not be cross-examined about the acts of murder. I also wanted the jurors to think of Murray's life apart from his crime. I wanted them to picture this man securely locked away from society but living a life that was reasonable and valid and in some ways useful. Mostly, by asking about his previous prison time, I was setting the groundwork for testimony that I hoped would put the humanization of Murray Lodge over the top—for at least one juror.

I had gotten an idea months earlier when Ed Sousa told me that Murray was a singer—actually, thought Ed, a very good singer. I went up to the jail to see—or rather, to hear—for myself. "Ed tells me you can sing," I began.

Murray admitted that he was pretty good.

"Sing for me," I said.

"For real?"

"For real."

Murray grew very quiet. He tilted his head down until his chin touched his chest. Then he slowly raised his head, and, tapping the rhythm on his thigh with his fingers, he began to sing. The song was Mess of Blues— the Elvis Presley classic from 1960, my era. Murray sang it all the way through three verses and repeated refrains.

I was blown away. It wasn't just that the voice was good, although it was—a clear, smooth baritone reminiscent of that of his idol, Elvis himself. Rather, it was the way Murray gathered himself, the way he bowed his head in that moment of contemplation, as if reaching deep within himself, connecting with something there, and bringing it forth as a quality I can only describe as tenderness. The rich, a capella baritone voice, the forlorn lyrics—*I'm gonna catch the next train goin' and leave my blues behind*—the lost man doomed, at best, to a kind of death-in-life stirred me deeply, and when he had finished, I asked: "Would you be willing to sing some songs on the witness stand?"

"For real?"

"For real," I assured him.

So when I elicited the information from Murray on the stand that one of the things he had done in prison was perform in musical shows put on by the inmates, and when I then asked the judge to allow the defendant to sing three brief songs—stipulating that I would record the singing but that the court reporter need not transcribe this particular testimony— you could have heard a pin drop in the courtroom. If the judge was rendered temporarily speechless by what I am sure was the first request he had ever heard for testimony in song, so was the very experienced, normally quick-to-object-to-just-about-anything, and typically rather fluent prosecutor, John Luft, who was simply mute.

"I'll allow it," said Judge Foley.

I readied the recording machine. As he had in the jail, Murray bent his head, cleared his throat, raised his head and began to sing.

I just got your letter, Baby
Too bad you can't come home
I swear I'm going' crazy
Sittin' here all alone
Since you're gone
I got a mess of blues

When the last note of the third song faded and the courtroom returned to some semblance of judicial decorum, the point had been made. The singing was unorthodox, unheard of, unprecedented—and had shown those open to seeing it that the man on the stand was as human as the rest of us.

We saved Murray's life. We achieved a hung jury on the verdicts for the penalty phase of the trial, the jurors declaring themselves unable to arrive at unanimity under any circumstances. They voted 10-2 for death on the charge of the murder of Mickie King and 7-5 for life in prison without parole in the case of John Evans. Not enough to send Murray Lodge to death row. He was formally sentenced in March 1995 to LWOP. An appeal was automatic, and the court appointed an appellate lawyer to plead that case. But for Ed and me, our work with Murray Lodge was done; his life, such as it was, had been secured, although he would spend every remaining minute of it confined and with his actions entirely under the control of others. We now turned our attention to Buddy Nickerson.

Part 4: Exonerating Buddy Nickerson

The first thing we needed, however, was Murray's approval. Since the two men had been charged in the same crime, each had to waive any claim of conflict of interest in order for Ed and me, as Murray's onetime lawyers, to go to work on Buddy's case. It took a bit of time. We had to await the appointment of the appellate lawyer for Murray, and the lawyer needed some time to be brought up to speed on the case, for even the waiver of a claim of conflict of interest requires legal representation, and the specific language of the waiver had to be worked out.

But in due course, all the Ts were crossed and all the Is dotted, and in the early spring of 1997, we filed a petition for a writ of habeas corpus on Buddy's behalf in the Santa Clara County Superior Court.

Originating in English common law, habeas corpus is one of the oldest remedies in our legal tradition. Mentioned in the Constitution, authorized by Congress in 1789, and expanded after the Civil War, it is a legal action to determine if a particular prisoner's detention is valid. The writ seeks to bring the prisoner before the court—the exact translation of the Latin habeas corpus is "let you produce the body"—to explore whether or not his or her imprisonment is legitimate. Our argument, of course, was that Buddy's imprisonment was not legitimate on the grounds that police misconduct—the perjury, suppression of evidence, and manipulation of witnesses by Beck and Hall—had denied him due process of law and a fair trial and that the lawyer appointed for him had provided "ineffective assistance of counsel," as the term goes, both in preparing the case and during the trial itself, thereby depriving him of protections guaranteed to every defendant by the Sixth Amendment to the Constitution.[8] The police misconduct and the lawyer's ineffective assistance, we would argue, had obscured the fact that Buddy was not present when the crime was committed, for which we had the potential testimony of Murray John Lodge and alibi witnesses. In short, Buddy's imprisonment was illegitimate both because the process had fallen short—the system of justice itself—and because of his actual innocence.

In preparing the habeas petition, we had help—thankfully, as neither Ed nor I had any experience at all with habeas corpus procedures. Susan Kwan, an attorney specializing in criminal appeals—and a dear friend as well[9]—made sure that we included all possible federal Constitutional arguments along with state precedents. This was insurance: It meant we

---

8. "In all criminal prosecutions, the accused shall enjoy the right to a speedy and public trial, by an impartial jury of the State and district wherein the crime shall have been committed, which district shall have been previously ascertained by law, and to be informed of the nature and cause of the accusation; to be confronted with the witnesses against him; to have compulsory process for obtaining witnesses in his favor, and to have the Assistance of Counsel for his defense."

9. Susan was also a former law clerk of mine and was married to Mark Rosenbush. Tragically, Susan died in 2014—way, way too young. A devastating loss to both me and my wife.

could file a petition in federal court if we lost in the state court system; without such arguments in the original petition, we would not be able to appeal to the federal courts. Susan's help proved prophetic and essential.

We filed the petition in the Santa Clara County Superior Court on April 23, 1997. The DA answered the petition in September, and we filed a reply in February 1998. On April 14, 1998, about a year after the original filing, the petition was denied as untimely—that is, too many years had passed since Buddy's conviction—by a judge who had been a prosecutor in the county DA's office at the time Murray and Buddy were being prosecuted. We then took the petition to the state Court of Appeals, where it was summarily denied. We filed it with the state Supreme Court, where on December 22, 1998, it was again denied. Six days later, having exhausted state remedies, we filed a petition for a writ of habeas corpus in the United States District Court for the Northern District of California. The wheels of justice do grind slowly.

Like everything having to do with Buddy's case at this time, all this work was *pro bono;* neither Ed nor I was being paid a dime for it, and a ton of work had been involved. In addition to consulting with experts, we had to do the legal research, strategize and prepare the pleadings—that is, the legal arguments on various issues—and collect and organize all the exhibits needed to support our legal argument. Then there was the writing itself, most of which was my assignment—a difficult and laborious process. All *pro bono* by both of us.

It is not easy on a family when the primary breadwinner does work for no money. It makes a difference that filters down into the tendrils of family life, causing all sorts of consequences that can matter a great deal. Yet my wife, Susan, never wavered in her support of my doing *pro bono* work, and Buddy's exoneration was a case in point.

One weekend toward the end of Murray Lodge's trial, Susan and I had gone to see the film *In the Name of the Father,* a dramatic retelling of the story of Irishman Gerry Conlon, who was sentenced to life in prison for IRA terrorist attacks in which four people died, attacks he had been nowhere near.[10] Buddy's situation wasn't so very different from Conlon's

---

10. Ironically, the bombings were of two English pubs in Guildford, the city to which Susan's parents moved when she was a teenager and where her older brother still lives.

in important ways, including the presence, evidently universal, of corrupt policemen, and a wrongful sentence.

Susan and I were both moved by the film, by the wonderful performances of Daniel Day-Lewis as Gerry and Pete Postlethwaite as his father, also imprisoned, and of course by the recognizable parallel to Buddy's situation, now front and center in Murray's trial.

I finally broke the silence. "I've got to get Buddy out."

"I know," Susan said.

"I'll have to do it for free."

There was no hesitation. "I know," she said.

Without that kind of support, I simply would not have been able—either financially or emotionally—to do what it took across all the time that it took to gain Buddy's exoneration. It is not too far-fetched to say that without Susan's steadfast commitment to justice, Buddy Nickerson might still be behind bars.

But the Schwartzbach family did need some form of income, and to make ends meet, in 1996, I again joined a civil law firm, this time the firm of a lawyer I had successfully defended in a vehicular manslaughter and DUI prosecution; his Driving Under the Influence of alcohol had resulted in a fatal accident. The man was a genius at civil discovery and negotiations, and I learned a lot about civil litigation in the three years I worked with him—while nevertheless itching every minute to get back to criminal defense law. As intended, however, the civil work paid the bills (even if the salary didn't come close to reflecting my level of experience and my success as a trial lawyer), and I had made it a condition of joining the firm that I continue my efforts on the Nickerson case. But juggling the time between preparing Buddy's habeas corpus petition and working on the paying civil litigation was not easy.

There was one major highlight, if that word can be used, during this my second foray into civil litigation. It concerned what in my mind remains the most egregious case of premeditated murder I've ever litigated—despite its having been a civil case. It was a case brought by Juan Romo and his sisters against the Ford Motor Company. The Romos were suing the auto giant for damages on the grounds of product liability and negligence in the design, manufacturing, and advertising of the 1978 Ford Bronco sports utility vehicle in which Romo's father, mother, and one brother were killed and Juan and his sisters injured. I call it a case of pre-meditated murder because, as our evidence showed, Ford knew full well that its decision to skimp on preproduction testing and to disregard certain safety design policies in order to get the Bronco to market fast could lead to injuries and death in the case of accidents like the Romo family's rollover. Ford's number-crunchers had likely analyzed the potential costs of lawsuits and settlements for death and dismemberment, counted up the savings available from, for example, using fiberglass instead of steel in a part of the vehicle roof, and weighed all this against projected market loss if the vehicle did not get off the assembly line before General Motors produced its first SUVs.

We charged Ford with malicious conduct in the mass production and marketing of a dangerous vehicle purely for the corporation's economic betterment. We contended that Ford had brought to market a motor vehicle with a known propensity to roll over, that it had ignored its own internal safety standards while leaving the Bronco with the appearance of sturdiness, and that it had made a conscious decision not to provide adequate crush protection to properly belted passengers—in effect penalizing passengers for wearing a seatbelt. All of this we defined as "despicable conduct."

We won, and I couldn't help but compare the miscreants in this case with many of the people I had defended in my years as a criminal lawyer. Many of my criminal defense clients have been poor, disenfranchised, mentally ill, addicted to one drug or another. Some have admittedly been individuals at war with convention, with structure, with the norms of behavior that keep most of us within a certain, well-cushioned paradigm. Certainly, Murray Lodge and Buddy Nickerson fall within that category. They even looked the part, assuming the anti-fashions of the disaffected—in clothing, appearance, and vocabulary. And Murray's crime was indeed heinous. Buddy, by his own admission, had committed a range of petty crimes, but not the crime for which he had been condemned to a life behind bars.

And the managers at Ford? Lavishly compensated, fashionably dressed, and working out of plush offices, they had, at a minimum, defrauded and dispossessed customers, investors, shareholders, and lessees as they, at a maximum, gave gratuitous license for the deaths of fellow humans, dismissing such deaths as a cost their company could bear. They had done all this unmediated by any sense of responsibility to the gullible, to society, to anyone or anything except the bottom line. The jury awarded the Romos more than $296 million—$6 million-plus in compensatory damages and $290 million in punitive damages—but the figure was substantially reduced on appeal, and an eventual settlement amounting to perhaps $40 million, chump change to a corporate behemoth, meant that the company effectively got away with murder. Meanwhile, Buddy Nickerson continued to languish in prison for murders he had absolutely nothing to do with.

While the Romo trial was going on—and happily for the Schwartzbach family finances—our son, Micah, decided to attend university within the California state system rather than at a more costly private college. I now felt free to leave the civil law firm; so as not to muddy the waters, I announced my intention of doing so during the jury's deliberations but before the verdict was in. Once the trial was over and the work wrapped up, I once again went out on my own and back to the work I loved.

There was a small footnote to the whole experience: Decency and logic would have dictated that I would share in that portion of the Ford settlement designated for legal fees. But the lawyer whom I had successfully defended as a client and with whom I tried the case defied both and gave me nothing. That was a blow—and something of a shock.

Fortunately, there was plenty of work to occupy my mind and heart. A presiding judge for our habeas corpus petition in district court had been named—Judge Marilyn Hall Patel—and she gave us a very good day on February 8, 1999, when she ordered the attorney general to show cause why the petition should not be granted. It signaled to us that she saw merit in Buddy's petition.

The attorney general answered, however, by moving to dismiss our petition for federal habeas corpus altogether on the grounds that it was untimely—that is, too many years had passed since Buddy's conviction, the relevant law requiring that a defendant had one year after losing a final state court appeal to file a petition for habeas corpus in federal court. We filed a response and sat back to await the judge's ruling.

You never know and can rarely predict how long the wait will be. The scuttlebutt on Judge Patel was that she was a very thorough, very

thoughtful judge who was never less than comprehensive in her deliberations and her writing; the betting was it would take a while.

In a way, that was just as well, because something astounding happened while we were waiting.

It started with a phone call out of the blue from someone who knew
someone in the Santa Clara County district attorney's office. This individual, acting entirely on his own and in no way in an official capacity,
told me that a prisoner at San Quentin had proven to be a match to the
trail of blood left by whoever fled the scene of the Evans-King murders
in 1984. The blood evidence that had not matched Murray Lodge, Dennis Hamilton, Bret Wofford, or Buddy Nickerson matched this prisoner.
He was, presumably, the man who was seen by Brian Tripp in the condo
complex parking lot. He was the third man at the scene of the crime, giving the lie at last to the "fourth man," the phantom that Beck and Hall
had concocted so they could nail Buddy. If what I heard over the phone
was true, there went the phony card propping up the whole jerry-rigged
concoction that was keeping Buddy behind bars.[11]

The man's name, I was told, was William Carl John. That is how I
heard it over the phone, and that is how I wrote it down. Ed checked
with the Department of Corrections; there was simply no one named
William John in California's prison population. We kept digging, however, and eventually came up with an inmate named Bill Jahn, who had
been transferred from San Quentin, ten minutes away from my office,
to High Desert State Prison, 300 miles east across the state, not far from
the Nevada state line.

We also learned that an investigator in the Santa Clara County district
attorney's office had noted some scars on Jahn's body, a finding that had
prompted the DA's office to serve a search warrant for a medical examination and X-rays of Jahn; the search warrant outlined the DA's argument of
"probable cause" that Jahn had committed a crime. We obtained both the
affidavit in support of the warrants and the documentation of the search
results, which were stunning. Simply put, scars on Jahn's torso and the

---

11. My informant's motivation was simply anger that the DA's office had not seen fit to share this
information with Buddy's defense team. Needless to say, Buddy's defense team shared that anger.

remains of a bullet inside his body constituted evidence absolutely consistent with his having suffered a gunshot wound at some point in his life.

Blood match plus gunshot wound: It was not surprising that the Santa Clara County district attorney's office had obtained an arrest warrant charging Jahn with the murders of John Evans and Mickie King and with the attempted murder of Michael Osorio. What should have been surprising was that the DA's office had withheld from us, the defense lawyers representing Buddy Nickerson, any information whatsoever about any of this—the blood match, the scar, the bullet fragment tests, the arrest warrant. It *should have been* surprising, but it was not; these prosecutors had made it clear all along that they cared not a whit that an innocent man was serving a life sentence. They cared about scoring a win, and having scored one in the case of Buddy Nickerson, they were not about to let it slip through their fingers in the name of justice.

In September 1999, Ed and I went to visit Jahn. We flew to Reno, rented a car, and drove 90 miles to the prison just outside the town of Susanville. We were shown into a sparkling-clean visiting room the size of a cafeteria and absolutely empty except for us. Then a door at the far end of the room opened, and Bill Jahn was led in by a guard. He looked just like Brian Tripp's description of the man in the condo complex parking lot, only instead of clutching his gut, he was raising his eyebrows, as if to say "Who the hell are you guys?"

We told him. I introduced us both, said we were representing Buddy Nickerson, knew Buddy had not been present the night of the murder and knew further that he, Jahn, had been. I also told him we knew he was a blood match for the trail of blood leading away from the scene of the crime and that both an X-ray and scars on his body showed that he had once been shot. Then I told him something he did not know but had certainly expected—namely, that there was a warrant out for his arrest on charges of murder and attempted murder.

He was silent for a moment. Then he said, "What do you want from me?"

I gave him a simple answer: Confirm that Buddy Nickerson had no involvement in the crime on Ronda Drive.

He couldn't understand why Buddy had been convicted. After all, Buddy was innocent; he had nothing to do with this crime. Jahn began talking about that night on Ronda Drive, telling us how nobody was ever supposed to get hurt, how he had heard about the Nickerson family but had never met Buddy, and how "seeing Murray shoot John in the head is emblazed (sic) in my mind."

Jahn went on for some 45 minutes of memories. Then he stopped suddenly. "This is all confidential, isn't it?" he asked, his voice rising in pitch as he began to realize what might be at stake.

"As I told you," I said, "we are here as Buddy Nickerson's lawyer, not yours. So no, nothing you have said is confidential."

There was a tense moment of silence. We could almost feel Jahn assessing a future that suddenly looked very scary indeed. Then he said, "In that case, everything I've told you is hypothetical. In fact, seeing Murray shoot John Evans in the head is emblazed in my hypothetical mind."

There was something a little bit otherworldly about it: the frightened criminal, the air in the room still ringing with his previous volubility, the sudden silence. But for Ed and me, in a long and difficult case that held no humor and few light moments, Jahn's "hypothetical memories" stand as a comic high.

He went on. All the people who were in prison for the crime deserved to be there, Jahn said—except for Buddy. He just could not understand why we had not gotten him off since he was innocent, could not understand why all this hadn't come up long ago.

He was, he said, a changed man. He had gone straight, had married, had a family that was the most important thing in his life. That he was in prison now was an unfortunate lapse, but as much as he would like to help Buddy, he had to think hard about what would be best for his family.

In the end, however, Jahn unwittingly did give us what we came for.

We had the evidence of the interview, the Santa Clara County district attorney's investigation, and the charge of murder for the 15-year-old crime for which our client was imprisoned. I detailed it all in a declaration I quickly filed as a supplement to the original petition we had put before Judge Patel, asserting that it contained "newly discovered exculpatory evidence in support of petition for habeas corpus."

That claim of newness was at the heart of the legal issue we confronted, an issue articulated in a law known as the Antiterrorism and Effective Death Penalty Act, AEDPA, passed in 1996 and signed by President

Clinton. Among other provisions, AEDPA imposes stringent time limitations on the habeas corpus process—the requirement that you have one year after losing a final state court appeal to file a habeas corpus petition in federal court. One exception to that time limit, which of course had long ago passed for us, is proof of "actual innocence"; if such proof is substantial enough, it may open a gateway through the timeliness bar.

What makes proof of actual innocence substantial enough to open the gateway and overcome the timeliness bar? As articulated in AEDPA, the requirement is stringent. To meet it, the petitioner must present "a truly extraordinary showing" that it is more than likely that no reasonable juror would find the petitioner guilty based on new evidence *that has not hitherto been presented at trial*. In other words, only evidence of innocence not heard or seen before can get your foot in the federal courthouse door.[12]

———

That is what my supplemental declaration set out to provide—evidence that was both new enough not to have been presented at trial before and exculpatory enough that if a reasonable juror were made aware of it, it was more than likely that he or she would find Buddy innocent.

The declaration introduced Bill Jahn, detailing key facts about him—that at six feet in height and weighing about 200 pounds, he fit to a T the description of a fleeing man that Brian Tripp had first given to the police. It told how his blood matched the sample from the crime scene blood trail. It reported that he had admitted knowing Murray but denied knowing Buddy. It detailed the scars on Jahn's body, the tests carried out as a consequence, the results of the tests linking Bill Jahn point by point to the crime of 1984.

I noted in the declaration that in his original interview with Detective Hall the morning after the shootings, Michael Osorio had said he had seen three white male adults of average build. Add it up, I suggested: Murray Lodge plus Dennis Hamilton, the two men convicted of the murders

———

12. What this says, of course, is that proof of innocence alone is not a basis for relief in federal court; you have to prove you were denied a fair trial. I will have more to say about this later.

based on overwhelming evidence, plus Bill Jahn equals three white male adults of average build, while Buddy Nickerson had weighed 425 pounds at the time the crime was committed—far from an average build. Was this not sufficient to open the procedural "innocence gateway"?

I also made it clear in the declaration that while prosecutors were fighting to keep Buddy in prison, the blood match of Jahn now confirmed that Tripp had wrongfully identified Buddy, yet the prosecutors had failed to disclose that information to the defense or to Judge Patel. The failure, I contended, was intentional; surely, this deprived Buddy Nickerson of due process.

All of this I laid out in detail in the ten-page declaration filed as a supplement. So when, on December 1, 1999, Judge Patel stunned us by granting the attorney general's motion and dismissing our petition altogether, it was, to say the least, a crushing blow—emotionally and physically and in every way possible. I think I felt it more than Buddy Nickerson did. By now, he had been in prison for more than 15 years, an amount of time already longer than what he had been offered in a deal if only he would admit to a crime he had not committed; he was perhaps so accustomed to being destroyed by the system day after agonizing day that one more nail in the coffin hardly mattered. But I was in despair, and it made me more determined than ever not to give up.

In dismissing our petition, Judge Patel said that the proof of actual innocence we offered was *not* substantial enough to open the innocence gateway. The deprivation of due process through the detectives' misconduct, the ineffective counsel before and during trial, and the alibi witnesses: none of it met the "actual innocence" standard. The judge therefore deferred to the attorney general's insistence on the timeliness requirement. In other words, falling short on the innocence standard, we fell victim to the timeliness bar.

But what was utterly shocking about her ruling was that it made no mention whatsoever of the Bill Jahn interview I had detailed in my supplemental declaration. In fact, Judge Patel never referred to the declaration at all. I instinctively knew why: *The judge never saw the supplemental declaration.*

I have no idea why or how, but the declaration simply never got to her. I do know that there can be many a slip between the clerk's office, the law clerks, and the judges. A lot of papers are processed in courthouses, and humans being human, sometimes even a ten-page declaration gets lost in the shuffle. It was a matter of negligence—nobody's fault, perhaps—but negligence, no matter how benign, can be costly. It very nearly cost Buddy Nickerson his lifetime.

And there wasn't much time to counter this disaster. I had ten days in which to prepare and file a motion for Judge Patel to reconsider what amounted to her dismissal of Buddy's case, for effectively, a writ of habeas corpus was his last chance at proving his innocence.

So our last-chance motion to Judge Patel to reconsider her ruling made the case all over again. Whatever had happened to my declaration about the Bill Jahn interview and however it happened that Judge Patel did not see it, she had to see it now. I attached to the motion a copy of the declaration with the court clerk's stamp showing the date and time it had been initially filed—before her dismissal of the petition. I again detailed the interview, again asserted Jahn's exoneration of Buddy, again reported that Jahn was now being prosecuted by the Santa Clara County district attorney for the murder of John Evans and Mickie King, reported the blood match, reported the wounds on Jahn's body and the bullet still lodged within him, reported that he matched the original description provided by eyewitness Brian Tripp. I was pounding the evidence home so that this time, there could be no missing it: Buddy Nickerson deserved a chance at proving his increasingly obvious innocence.

And on September 14, 2000, Judge Patel agreed. Reversing her earlier ruling, she granted our motion for reconsideration. She would consider Buddy's habeas corpus petition—effectively, she was reopening his case in order to reconsider his conviction.

———

It was wonderful news, but I was damned if it was enough. Now that Judge Patel knew that Buddy was innocent—and I believed she fully accepted his innocence—I wanted her to release him on bail before ruling on the merits of the petition. No judge had ever done so before, and every other lawyer and appellate expert I knew told me there was no chance any judge would do so now. But to me, the idea of a man known to be innocent to continue to be confined while the justice system creaked and groaned its way to a final ruling was simply insupportable. I filed a motion seeking Buddy's release on bail.

It took a very long time—nine months, in fact, the gestation period of a human being—but on the June 1, 2001, Judge Patel granted the motion and ordered Buddy released on bail. Ten days later—the judge allowed the attorney general that amount of time to appeal the granting of bail—I was there, along with Ed, Susan, and members of Buddy's family, when he was driven out through the front gate of San Quentin. The prison van pulled to a stop outside the gate, and Buddy got out and made a beeline for me. He grabbed me, and knowing what was coming, I kind of ducked, and he kissed the top of my head. I could almost feel the elation of freedom that surged through him like an electrical current. Buddy then went home to his family and, as he told me later, spent his first night of freedom in 17 years sleeping on the floor of the bathroom rather than in the bedroom that had been prepared for him; the bathroom more closely approximated the size of the cell that had been his home for those 17 years.

But his freedom was short-lived. On June 14, just two weeks *after* the judge's order and a mere four days after Buddy had been released on bail, the attorney general filed what he called an "emergency" petition[13] in the Ninth Circuit Court of Appeals seeking to reverse Patel's granting of bail.

It was a Thursday—a bit past 6 P.M., an hour when most lawyers have gone home for the day. A fax came chugging through the machine in my office—a communication from a three-judge motions panel[14] of the U.S. Ninth Circuit Court of Appeals ordering me to file a reply to the AG's petition by noon the next day. Had I not been the kind of lawyer who routinely works long hours, I would not even have seen the order until the following morning. That wasn't all. The panel's order did not include the emergency petition to which I was supposed to reply; instead, the

---

13. What was the emergency? The AG had allowed the ten-day filing period to pass, then manufactured an "emergency"—convicted murderer loose in the streets—to put Buddy back in prison. It was a ham-fisted legal move that made a mockery of due process.

14. The Ninth Circuit Court of Appeals covers a vast area—from Montana on the east to the Northern Marianas and Guam in the west—and today includes as many as 49 judges. Federal appellate procedure mandates that a case goes first to a three-judge panel of the Court; whatever the ruling of the panel, the loser may petition the entire court for a rehearing.

AG's proof of service document, "proving" that required documents had been sent to me, noted that the petition had been mailed to me that day. So the judges were ordering me to reply to a petition they knew I hadn't seen and wouldn't receive until the next day's mail delivery, at the earliest.

But at that point, some luck came our way. I called a friend and got an after-hours number for the Ninth Circuit Clerk's Office—it was well after quitting time there as well—and was fortunate to have my call answered by a law clerk. The law clerk, in turn, was kind enough to fax me the pleading—that is, the petition to which I was being ordered to respond. I also phoned Ed. "On my way," he said, and began the drive up from San José.

I also called Buddy to warn him about the attempt to reverse his release; it was a phone call I dreaded making. "We'll be working all weekend to try to stop it," I told him, "but you may have to go back in on Monday."

There was a pause. Then: "Will I be able to spend Father's Day with my dad?"

Father's Day was Sunday. "Yes," I said. "You will."

"Then I'm okay," Buddy said.

The coming weekend was about to turn into one of our classic grinding slogs; Ed pulled together the numerous exhibits we needed, while I wrote and wrote and wrote. Just before noon on Friday, June 15, the start of the Father's Day holiday, I faxed our reply and told the panel that we would file the original response with exhaustive exhibits that day.

Within a couple of hours I received another order from the Ninth Circuit: oral argument was scheduled for Tuesday, June 19. Exhausted by the recent exertions and the prospect of the work to come, I went home and slept.

The next morning, Saturday, there was another fax, which I only happened to see because I stopped in at my office en route with Susan to Berkeley. This one was devastating: The Ninth Circuit motions panel had withdrawn the order setting oral argument and had granted the AG's petition—namely, an order sending Buddy Nickerson back to prison on Monday. We needed a rehearing by all of the judges of the Ninth Circuit, and we got to work drafting the petition. I also called Buddy and told him to be at the federal courthouse at 9 A.M. Monday, ready to surrender.

When I told Buddy that "we" would spend the weekend working, I didn't mean just Ed and me. Yes, I wrote the brief requesting the rehearing, and Ed as always organized the voluminous pages of exhibits. But Susan too was pressed into service as was Micah, home from college for Father's Day; all three of them spent much of the weekend at Kinko's copying and binding, and on Monday morning, Susan and I drove to the Ninth Circuit clerk's office in San Francisco where I filed the request for the rehearing *en banc*—that is, before all the judges on the bench, not just the motions panel. Accompanying the request were the required 50-plus copies of the brief with thousands of pages of exhibits—enough copies so that all the judges of the Ninth District, scattered throughout the states of the West and our Pacific territories, would have their own copy to read at their convenience.

I then drove to the federal courthouse. I was just entering the building when a reporter I knew called me over. "I've never seen a petition for a rehearing denied so fast," he told me. Denied? I had just filed it—maybe eight minutes ago. And it was going to every judge on the Ninth Circuit. I told the reporter he must be wrong. There was no way 50 judges could have received the petition that fast, much less have had time to read it, analyze it, and then all vote on it.

The reporter took me into the press room and showed me the denial order. Our petition never even reached the other Ninth Circuit judges. The same three-judge panel that had revoked Buddy's bail and sent him back to prison had invoked a rarely used procedural rule to deny rehearing "on behalf of the court"—in other words, without ever even circulating our brief.

So, on June 18, 2001, Buddy surrendered and went back to prison. He had polished his shoes with polish that would not dry; he wanted the prison guards to get it all over their hands. When he got back to his cell, he heard rumblings about how he had been put on a hit list by fellow inmates because the photograph of his release made it clear he had kissed a Jew—namely, me—and the photo had run on news wires nationwide. But since all the inmates realized that he was innocent of the crime for which he had been convicted, they let him live.

"Never give in," Winston Churchill told the boys of his old public school, Harrow, in 1941, when Britain stood alone against Nazi Germany. "Never give in, never, never, never—in nothing, great or small, large or petty. Never give in except to convictions of honor and good sense. Never yield to force; never yield to the apparently overwhelming might of the enemy." Stymied time after time at turn after turn—by the very people, it seemed to me, who ought to be opening every possible door to a just conclusion—Ed and I went back to work. At the beginning of August, we filed another petition for a rehearing by the full court, not just the three-judge panel, and for a reversal of the order sending Buddy back to prison until that rehearing had taken place. We charged that the Ninth Circuit panel lacked the authority to deny our petition "on behalf of the court" without even giving us a hearing, and that it had acted injudiciously in rejecting in only a few hours a decision that Judge Patel had rendered after two years of deliberation. The result was that "a factually innocent man was returned to prison, where he has been wrongly incarcerated for almost 17 years, and a distinguished judge has been rebuked for exercising her sound discretion based upon *an extensive record, which she had considered, but which the motions panel chose to ignore.*"

We argued that Judge Patel had the authority to grant bail while Buddy's habeas corpus proceeding was pending and that the three-judge motions panel of the Ninth District Court had misapplied the standard of judicial review in refusing to look at critical portions of the record. In short, the panel had acted hastily and, in my view, recklessly—exactly the opposite of the way judges should act. "In a system whose objective is justice," I wrote in our petition, "one can only wonder what could present a more compelling circumstance justifying release on bail than a 'truly persuasive demonstration of actual innocence.'"

That still sums up for me what is perhaps my most vexatious frustration as a criminal defense lawyer: the all-too-frequent disconnect between process and justice, the willingness—sometimes the insistence—to put the discipline of the process ahead of what is the right thing to do, or even to let the former supplant the latter. The discipline of the process is of course vitally important—in my practice, I am and am known to be a stickler for such discipline—but it is not the reason the process exists. Yet it has been argued by some that even factual innocence is not sufficient for release, and at least one Supreme Court justice, Antonin Scalia, has written that "this Court has never held that the Constitution forbids the execution of a convicted defendant who has had a full and fair trial but is later able to convince a habeas court that he is 'actually' innocent."[15] No matter what the truth of the matter might be, if you received a fair trial under all the laws and protections afforded by the process, then your guilty verdict stands, right up until it is carried out by lethal injection or in a gas chamber or by the latest throwback, a firing squad. Certainly, the process is aimed precisely at ensuring that the guilty are punished and that those not guilty go free. Yet sometimes—even once is excessive in my view—the process is so much the focus that its purpose becomes obscured, and you have the spectacle of law enforcement officers, prosecutors, judges, and courts working hard to deny defendants their right to prove their innocence.

————

For Ed and me, a great deal of work lay ahead. There would soon be an evidentiary hearing in which we would lay out our case point by point in comprehensive detail and present testimony from numerous witnesses.[16] Working *pro bono* had served an important tactical purpose. Since we had been Murray Lodge's lawyers, there could be no reason and certainly no motivation for us to represent Buddy Nickerson for free unless we knew for a certainty that he was innocent. In fact, that had been my intention in not seeking court appointment as Buddy's attorney; I wanted to convey an implicit message to the judge: We were working for free because we knew from Murray that Buddy was innocent. Why else would Murray tell us, in privileged conversations, that he and his co-defendants were guilty but Buddy Nickerson was innocent?

—————

15. In a 2009 dissent of the Court's order for a federal trial court in Georgia to consider the case of death row inmate Troy Davis, Scalia went on: "Quite to the contrary, we have repeatedly left that question unresolved, while expressing considerable doubt that any claim based on alleged 'actual innocence' is constitutionally cognizable."

16. One witness we hoped would help was Bret Wofford, whom we tracked down to a federal prison in South Carolina, where he was serving concurrent 25-year state and federal sentences. I traveled there with investigator Jacqi Tully, told him I was representing Buddy on a *pro bono* basis, and asked if he would give me a declaration stating that Nickerson had at no time been part of the planning or execution of what went down in John Evans' house in 1984. Wofford's response was succinct: "If I saw Buddy Nickerson lying in a gutter on the street," he said, "I'd piss on him."

But the point had by now been made, while in the years since we had first undertaken Buddy's case, I had spent thousands of dollars I did not have, had put in countless hours, and was dead broke. In the months to come, we would need to hire an investigator and launch an entirely fresh investigation, pay for travel and a range of operating expenses, take depositions, do extensive discovery, conduct the hearing, and file numerous briefs on a range of issues that would crop up, as issues always do, as we litigated our claim that Buddy Nickerson had been denied due process, was wrongly accused and convicted, was even now suffering a miscarriage of justice, and should be released from prison. It was time for us to be paid, and after the Ninth Circuit sent Buddy back to prison, we were appointed the attorneys of record in the matter of Glen "Buddy" Nickerson; we could now be compensated at least to the extent of no longer having to self-finance future work and our expenses.

While we did all these things, Buddy languished in prison for nearly two more years. He had been moved to Lancaster state prison in the northern part of Los Angeles County and—initially, anyway—was in relatively good spirits as he awaited what he believed would be permanent freedom. But the plodding pace of the justice system eventually got to him, and I could tell from his letters that he was becoming seriously depressed and was wondering if he ever would be freed after all. Ed and I flew down to see him. I tried to assure him of what I absolutely believed—that, given that Judge Patel had granted him bail, she would eventually reverse his conviction. It seemed to lift his spirits—at least for the moment.

The evidentiary hearing was conducted over three days in January 2002—January 8, 9, and 10—with a fourth day on March 28, 2002. Its highlight was the January 10 testimony of Murray Lodge, which, for security reasons, was taken at Corcoran State Prison in the San Joaquin Valley. Present were Judge Patel, her law clerk, a court reporter, a videographer, a deputy attorney general, Ed and I, and after a while a reporter from the *San Jose Mercury News*.

Murray recounted in detail the whole truth of the murders on Ronda Drive, fully and freely admitted his own guilt and the guilt of Hamilton and Jahn, and totally exonerated Buddy Nickerson.

Why, I asked him, was he finally coming clean? After all, wasn't naming names a dangerous business for a prisoner?

"It was a hard decision," Murray began, "but I had thought about it. And I thought about it more in the last two or three years than I had ever thought about it in the beginning, that ruining another man's life and putting him in prison for something he didn't do is worse than me worrying about my life and what's going to happen to me."

He admitted that at first, he had thought it "funny" that Buddy Nickerson was being blamed for something he did not do. But he always assumed that Buddy would be found innocent when he went to trial. After all, he *was* innocent.

"It's time for him to get a fair shake," Murray went on. "And as for me, well, you know what, I ruined more than just his life. I ruined plenty of people's lives."

And why should Judge Patel—or anyone—believe him now, I asked, given that he had repeatedly lied in order to protect his co-defendants in the past?

"You can call it lying if you want," said Murray, "but what I've been calling it all these years is refusing to implicate others for my safety . . . It just would have been rougher time and harder for me . . . But . . . I have thrown that caution and that worry to the wind, because I think it's only fair that this man not die in prison. I deserve to die in prison. You know, I did what I did. I got to face the music. But he didn't do anything. He didn't know anything about it. And I know he's innocent."

Make no mistake: This sworn testimony was an act of bravery on the part of Murray Lodge. He was almost surely risking his life to say what he said in court—to have it transcribed, videotaped, and covered in the press. Why his life? I noted earlier that in the inmate community, just about the worst crime anyone can commit is snitching—especially if you are suspected of trading the information for some consideration of your sentence or amelioration of your living conditions. This is a community that lives or dies—literally, in many cases—by its own customs, rules, and principles, which constitute the prisoners' own defiant way of exercising some form of control over their lives. The snitch might as well be wearing a scarlet letter S on his jumpsuit; he is fair game for anyone to exact punishment on him however and whenever they can.

I had been through this with Murray in the past. Years before, one of those 42 criminal acts he had been charged with was an attack on a fellow prisoner with whom he had been temporarily caged during the lunch break at trial. Murray took one look at the guy and started beating him up, shackles and all. Once again, it took a couple of guards to restrain him.

I could not be restrained, however. I was furious and demanded to be let into the holding cell next to the courtroom so I could give Murray a piece of my mind.

"Ed and I are killing ourselves trying to keep you alive, and you do this?!"

"I had no choice," Murray told me. "The guy is a known snitch and a rapist, and in here, if you get a chance to beat up on a guy like that, you have to." He would have been a target himself if he had not followed the code and gone after the guy.

Now he was supplying testimony on the record in open court that detailed the who, what, and where of a crime that had put other individuals, as well as Murray himself, behind bars for life. Such testimony could easily be perceived by the prison population as snitching; it would certainly be seen as turning his back on the guys trying to get out of prison for *their* participation in the crime—an equally egregious code violation.

I thought Ed should be the guy to ask Murray if he would agree to testify. They had bonded in a way I never did with Murray, and if we were going to ask him to risk his life, the request would come better from Ed than from me. And of course, he did agree, and his testimony was both riveting and convincing.

After he testified, the three of us—Ed, Murray, and I—were allowed to meet together briefly in a private room. We lawyers took the opportunity to thank Murray for his selfless act, for taking the risk and asking nothing in return. But now Murray made a single request, asking one favor for having put his own life in jeopardy to save the life of Buddy Nickerson. "When I die," he said, "don't let them bury me inside these walls." Ed and I gave him our word.

––––––

Judge Patel's reversal of Buddy's conviction came on March 17, 2003— St. Patrick's Day, yes, but also Buddy's forty-eighth birthday. In 61 closely reasoned, explicitly detailed pages, the chief judge found that "more probably than not Nickerson is innocent of the crimes for which he was convicted," while "Beck and Hall's misconduct so infected the trial with unfairness as to make the resulting conviction a denial of due process." She declared Buddy's convictions vacated and ordered that he be released from custody "within 60 days of the date this order is filed unless the State of California reinstitutes criminal proceedings against him."

I was itching for the state to do just that. Re-trying the case against Buddy Nickerson would effectively put the state of California's criminal justice system on trial. Since there was absolutely no credible evidence that Buddy had been anywhere near the scene of the crime, much less involved in any way in any aspect of it, it would show the callous indifference of the system toward justice; it would demonstrate that the detectives were corrupt and the other law enforcement players either lazy in their collusion with the detectives or themselves equally corrupt; and it would illustrate the almost frivolous way in which cops, prosecutors, and judges had closed ranks and in doing so had toyed with the life of a human being. I very nearly salivated at the prospect of trying that case.

But the Santa Clara County DA's office chose not to re-try Buddy. Several reasons were advanced for the decision, but no quarter was given on the issue of Buddy's guilt, which the state clung to like a drowning man to a life preserver that won't inflate. Later, I was not surprised to learn that the issue of re-trying Buddy had been a contentious one within the DA's office. The final decision had rested with chief DA George Kennedy, who may well have understood that the prosecution's chance of prevailing in a new, high-profile trial was slim at best and that his office would look worse than foolish when police and prosecutorial misconduct were highlighted during the trial. Or maybe Kennedy finally decided that having incarcerated a man for 19 years for a crime he did not commit was enough.

Shortly after his release, Buddy underwent the first of several procedures to remove the various tattoos that had once signaled his hates: the swastika on his forearm, the White Power sign with the accompanying hangman's noose, and more. It was his way of making amends for what he had come to see as wrong thinking, and it was this principled man's way of clearing a debt. In a letter sent to me from prison, Buddy had written: "You made me see people for who they are and not what they are. And I'll get the tattoo removed like I said, Cause I know of No Other way to show you That I have Very High Respect for you and your family." Framed and hanging on my office wall, the letter is one of my proudest possessions, for it tells me I have helped to bring about the kind of redemption of a human being that is—or ought to be—what the law is about.

———

In every society, the worst crime an individual can commit is to take the life of another human being. It is universally the ultimate offense, the unalterable injury, deserving of the severest punishment. Murray Lodge was guilty of it, and he is being punished for it with the permanent loss of his freedom.

I believe that Detectives Brian Beck and Jerry Hall also took a life—that of Buddy Nickerson. And I believe they did so wantonly and willfully. This was no mistake made in laziness. It wasn't as if Beck and Hall had conducted the kind of fair and thorough investigation in which they had been trained, the kind that starts with a blank slate and with no assumptions and pursues hard evidence as a basis for reaching a conclusion. On the contrary, they began with a conclusion—a totally erroneous one—and then twisted or suppressed evidence, intimidated alibi witnesses, improperly influenced the sole surviving victim and the key prosecution witness, and committed perjury in order to make the "facts" fit the endgame they sought, appointing themselves judge, jury, and executioner all rolled into one. This wrongdoing is all the more villainous because it was perpetrated by officers of the law, endowed with the authority of the state and the power of life and death. With callous disregard for the jobs they had sworn to execute faithfully and impartially, they used badge and gun to do a grave injustice that wounded not just Buddy Nickerson but the very fabric of a just society.

And with their suspect in hand, the whole justice system "industry," as we might call it, closed ranks around them. The prosecution must have known that these cops were dirty and that the testimony of critical witnesses was erroneous at best, perjured at worst. If they did not know these things, then they were exhibiting a phenomenal level of incompetence and sheer stupidity—and that I do not believe. Rather, I believe they went along; they had to know Buddy Nickerson was innocent from the very beginning—after all, at the very most basic level, there is no way that "three white men of average build" includes a 425-pound man—and they still tried to convict him.

Was this the notorious "blue wall of silence" that is said to grip police departments and law enforcement agencies everywhere—a kind of mindless solidarity among members of a fraternity? Was it the culture of winning that seems to infect so many professional endeavors? If numbers of convictions are what advance your career, then getting the conviction is paramount, and it becomes easier to offer a nod and a wink—apparently even to methods, like perjury and suppression of evidence, that belie the profession itself. Or was it just self-protective complacency—going along to get along?

Whatever the reason, the criminal justice system closed ranks in the case of Buddy Nickerson like phagocyte cells attacking an invading foreign infection. That is not the job of the criminal justice system; the job is to pursue justice. There was no pursuit of justice here; there was only pursuit of cohesion that compounded the corruption begun by Beck and Hall. Judges as well as prosecuting attorneys effectively consented to the injustice done to Buddy Nickerson by turning a blind eye and later by trying to deny him the opportunity to prove his innocence—even after Beck and Hall had been shown to be guilty of misconduct including perjury and suppression of evidence.[17]

Why are these people walking around free? Beck and Hall were both ultimately promoted to captain and retired at that rank, drawing down pensions subsidized by taxpayer money and living well. Beck once ran for sheriff of Santa Clara County—unsuccessfully, I am happy to report—and even more astonishingly, I have been told that Hall was placed in charge of training at the sheriff's department. Unless the aim was to instruct would-be police officers in what not to do, that boggles the mind.

Murray Lodge committed murder and is paying for it every minute of his existence. Buddy Nickerson represented a stratum of society whose

---

17. Not all judges, to be sure: Judge Daniel Creed was appalled at the way Murray Lodge was being tossed around by the system; the ever fair-minded trial judge Robert Foley made the factual finding that Beck and Hall had committed perjury and suppressed evidence; Chief Judge Marilyn Hall Patel exhibited both courage and legal acumen in allowing us to prove Buddy's innocence.

sensibilities many of us don't like to think about, committed various crimes and misdemeanors, served his sentences. Murray risked his own life to do what was right by Buddy, whom he did not like, and Buddy refused to sell his soul for a crime he did not commit. Yet the police detectives who put them both behind bars lied and cheated to do so, and the state attorney general declined to prosecute them despite a tape recording, an eyewitness recanting his identification, and a judge nailing them as perjurers on the record. I would simply ask: Who are the real criminals in the cases of Lodge and Nickerson?

Ed and I are still in touch with Buddy Nickerson. With the threat of a lawsuit, I got Santa Clara County to pay Buddy a substantial financial settlement. He has managed the adjustment to freedom well enough, and although he is still waiting for an apology for what was done to him, he pretty well accepts that one won't be forthcoming. "They don't have the class to admit they were wrong," he says. He once came to my office wearing a tee shirt with the legend, "Fat people are harder to kidnap." Anybody who can still have a sense of humor after having endured 19 years of hell has got to have some kind of inner strength. Buddy lives with his daughter and grandchildren, a patriarch—free.

Ed and I both stay in touch with Murray as well. Ed, who has known him longer and was always personally closer, is in more frequent contact with him than I, and he has kept me up to date on Murray's ongoing musical life—his participation in a prison band and his attempts, which Ed thinks pretty good, at songwriting. A few years ago, in fact, after Robert Blake's acquittal, Murray got in touch with me to ask if I could help him get some of his songs recorded. I had to tell him I did not have those kinds of contacts. Ed has a few recordings of Murray singing some of his own compositions, and I still have the recording of Murray singing on the witness stand.

— 9 —

Celebrity Trial

Palm Desert, California, is a legendary vacation retreat—a favorite getaway for Hollywood celebrities and power brokers and a famous winter playground for Canadian snowbirds. It's so different in every way from my home in the northern part of the state. Susan and I were grateful to escape there in February 2004, at my cousin Sandy's invitation, for a rare and much needed, albeit brief, vacation. In the hot, dry desert dotted with the imported date palms that give the place its name, I had just begun to unwind from the coils of my daily law practice when I retrieved a phone message that Robert Blake would like to meet with me.

Robert is almost universally known even today, but in 2004, there wasn't anyone in the country, maybe the world, and certainly in California who did not know that the actor had been charged with having murdered his wife three years before, that he had been granted bail and freed after nearly a year in jail, that he had now been under house arrest for a year while his lawyers prepared his defense, and that most of those lawyers, one after another, had quit in exasperation—the latest, just recently. The word was that Robert Blake couldn't hold onto a lawyer, a result, according to the press and media legal pundits, of his difficult and demanding personality—just what you'd expect of a Hollywood star accustomed to being catered to. The most recent defection had been by

Tom Mesereau,[1] who had lasted right up until jury selection before asking to withdraw—no public explanation given.

In other words, Robert Blake was looking for a new lead attorney. I assumed that was why I had received the call, and the assumption tied my stomach in knots.

My first reaction was to place a call to Lois Heaney, my friend and colleague, the jury consultant with whom I first worked in Stephen Bingham's case. I thought she would be familiar with the Blake case, the lawyers, and the circumstances.

"Take the case, Gerry," said Lois. "You're perfect for it."

Although attracted by the challenge of handling the controversial case, I expressed my reservations: So far from being "perfect for it," I figured that I probably wouldn't survive a preliminary interview—i.e., I wouldn't be hired. But if by some chance the job were offered, I was concerned about being in a case that would keep me hundreds of miles away from home and family for an extended period of time. "I'm finally feeling relaxed and don't want to get stressed and waste my time," I told Lois. "Besides, my beard has gotten long, and I don't have my beard trimmer with me."

"Buy a beard-trimmer," Lois commanded. "Just meet with the guy. It's on your way home, and you can swing by L.A. and have the interview."

That sounded reasonable, and when I assured Susan that the meeting would represent only a minor detour and could not possibly last longer than 45 minutes—an hour at the outside—she agreed we should make the stop.

Van Nuys, where Robert had rented a house to double as a home and legal headquarters, was about a two-hour drive from Palm Desert off an exit marked "Victory," which, if you're given to magical thinking, might have looked like an omen. I try to be rational and eschewed the magical thinking as we drove up to a simple one-story house—very nice but nothing fancy—and parked across the street.

The man I thought of as a glamorous Hollywood star was sitting on a lawn chair near his front door, dressed in gray sweatpants and sweatshirt

---

1. A talented lawyer, Tom soon thereafter became well known for successfully defending Michael Jackson against child molestation charges.

and wearing a baseball hat. He looked frail, and as he rose from the chair to greet Susan and me, he appeared depressed—and weighed down by the depression.

But Robert's smile, as he approached us, was as winning as when I had watched him in *The Little Rascals* years before and as "Baretta" more recently, and he was as gracious and welcoming as he was understated. He led us through the house and out the back door, past a minute, leaf-strewn pool, and into a smaller house out back. This was the operational nerve center of the defense, for it housed the defense file, a very substantial collection of boxes and binders filled with documents, records, references, reports, notes, audio and video recordings—everything that had been collected having to do with the case of the *People of the State of California v. Robert Blake.* There was barely room in the house for the private investigator who used it as her "hotel" on her frequent visits.

By now, what with introductions, pleasantries, and the first look at the file, Susan and I had already been in Van Nuys for half an hour, and we still had a six-hour drive ahead of us. So, leaving Susan in the hands of the investigator in the little house, Robert and I returned to the living room in the front house and sat down to talk.

Four hours later, Susan and I began the drive home.

A four-hour preliminary interview is certainly not standard. In this particular case, however, it was as necessary as it seemed natural. For one thing, Robert's life was on the line. For another, he was nothing like the conventional-wisdom idea of him that I admit I had carried with me into our meeting—a difficult guy, a Hollywood *divo* who was simultaneously high-handed and petty. I saw nothing like that.

It's worth remembering that by the time of our meeting, Robert's wife had been murdered, he had spent 11 months in jail, and, with his future uncertain, he had agreed to allow his young daughter, whom he adored, to be adopted by his adult daughter and her husband. He had also lost his reputation, his ability to practice his profession, and his standing in his community. He had gone through much of his wealth, with little chance of replenishing it. His past life had become an open book that was fodder for endless grazing by television's entertainment shows, while his name had become the punch line of endless jokes. He was fair game for psycho-babblers, legal commentators, and pundits of every stripe. For reasons that were the subject of yet more speculative gossip, in the three years since the crime for which he was being charged was committed, the legal team going to work for him had looked like a constantly shifting tableau of dropouts and replacements. He had spent nearly a year of his life in jail and was now tethered to an electronic tracking device that could not be removed.

It was therefore perhaps not surprising that Robert felt battered—let down by the justice system and, in his eyes, taken advantage of by the legal community. Add to this the justifiable insecurity that many celebrities harbor that there is a difference between people wanting to be close to them—perhaps just to bask in their reflected glory—and genuine affection, and you have a recipe for mistrust with a capital M. Simply put, the man I met with that day in Van Nuys was vulnerable, and he didn't try to hide it.

But he also had a lot of questions. I had been recommended to him by Chuck Morton, the forensic scientist who was my go-to criminalist[2] after Ed Miller retired. Robert had gone to great lengths to investigate my record and vet my resume. I would learn that he had met with a considerable number of nationally prominent lawyers and had plans to meet with more; presumably, he put them all through the same exercise. With a possible life sentence in the offing, you take no chances.

The truth is that Robert Blake and I connected almost at once. There was an instant rapport between us, built, I think, on mutual trust. I saw a combination of street smarts and legal naiveté, and he saw my honesty, and we took it from there. Our conversation was candid, mature, to the point. I believed Robert. And I liked him.

Within an hour of leaving L.A., Susan, whose total time with Robert was about 30 minutes, said: "He wants you."

She was right. The next day, Robert called and said he wanted me to represent him. Three days later I was officially hired. Four days after that, on March 1, 2004, I made my first court appearance as Robert's lawyer.

---

2. Chuck was so highly regarded in his field that he was named to the forensic team that investigated the assassination of Robert F. Kennedy.

That first day in court was my baptism by fire into the proverbial media circus, excessive beyond anything I had ever known, and I was determined to get ahead of the phenomenon before I lost control of it entirely. Keep in mind that this was the sensational murder trial of a famous Hollywood celebrity, taking place virtually in the Hollywood community, home to more paparazzi and "entertainment reporters" than possibly anywhere else on earth. Interested as they all were in Robert Blake, they were particularly interested that morning in seeing who Blake's next lawyer-victim was going to be. For the moment, I was an unknown quantity, a Bay Area defense lawyer for 1960s' radicals, battered women, and wacko personal growth gurus. Nobody in the L.A. media knew me from Adam.

Court was due to start at 9 A.M. I instructed Robert to get there by 8:30; the press awaited him at his usual parking spot. I arrived at 8 A.M. under cover of my own anonymity, which was about to end, had a leisurely breakfast in the cafeteria, entered the packed courtroom at five to nine, walked down the aisle, and took the empty chair next to Robert at the counsel table.

The press swarmed us at the post-court press conference. I had no statement but said I would take a few questions. The last came from a reporter wanting to know how I had managed to maintain my cool against the verbal tirade delivered to me, once the judge had walked out of the courtroom, by Deputy District Attorney Shellie Samuels. "You folks don't know me," I replied, "but it would be a mistake to interpret my civility as a sign of weakness."

My aim was to let them know that I would not be bullied and that, unlike some lawyers in high-profile cases, I also had no intention of trying to exploit the press. I was there to defend my client in court, not in interviews or through shouted questions. By making this clear up front, I made it possible for both Robert and me in the coming months to pass through the phalanx of reporters and photographers without getting involved in the circus of it all.

We were off and running.

———

Robert Blake was Bonnie Lee Bakley's tenth husband, the last in a line of often vulnerable older spouses. She made a living off of seducing men and persuading them to give her money, but her goal was to either be a celebrity or be married to one. Bakley had been dating Christian Brando, son of Marlon Brando, at the same time that she had a brief sexual affair with Robert and told both men she was pregnant with their child, a daughter born in June 2000. Bonnie named the child Christian Shannon Brando, but in September, a DNA test proved that Robert was the father of the child, who was renamed Rose Lenore Sophia Blake, before Robert and Bonnie were married in November of that year.

About six months later, on May 4, 2001, the couple dined out at a restaurant, Vitello's, a place Robert had gone to so often for so many years that the restaurant had named a popular pasta dish after him and kept a special booth reserved for him. After the meal, the two walked around the corner to where their car was parked on a side street. But just as they got to the car, Robert remembered that he had left his gun, which was legally registered, in the restaurant. He had placed it beside him on the banquette of the booth and had covered it with his sweater. Now he realized that when he picked up the sweater, he had missed the gun, so he headed back to the restaurant to collect it. Bonnie had gotten in the car, and when Robert returned, he found her immobile in the passenger seat, shot in the head. Although she was still alive when the ambulance arrived, she could not be saved.

Bonnie Lee Bakley's family was convinced that the murderer was Robert Blake, and they stayed away from Bonnie's funeral, protesting that Robert's presence at the grave with Rose was nothing but a Hollywood publicity stunt. It made for sensational tabloid copy.

The Los Angeles Police Department fingered Robert as the murderer on the night of the murder but knew they didn't have evidence to prove it. Along with the district attorney's office, the LAPD spent nearly a year investigating the case. Bolstered by the statements of two former stuntmen, who would testify that Robert tried to hire them to kill his wife, cops and prosecutors compiled what looked to them like an overwhelming collection of circumstantial evidence, and on April 18, 2002, arrested Robert and his friend and bodyguard, Earle Caldwell, for the murder of Bonnie Bakley.

The arraignment four days later charged both men with conspiracy to commit murder, while Robert was also charged with one count of murder with special circumstances, a potential death penalty offense, and, based on the stuntmen's statements, with two counts of solicitation of murder. Both men pleaded not guilty to all the charges. Three days later, the district attorney's office declared it would not seek the death penalty against Robert but would ask for a sentence of life imprisonment without parole. Caldwell was released on bail of a million dollars, but Robert was denied bail and instead went to jail, un-convicted of any crime, for very nearly a year.

By the time I came on board, the case had gone through even more twists and turns. Robert had been freed on bail of $1.5 million and was banded with an electronic monitor around the ankle, limiting him to the area of the rental house in Van Nuys from the driveway next to the house to the back wall of the little house holding the file. The conspiracy charges against both Robert and Earle Caldwell had been dismissed by a judge, and Caldwell stepped out of the picture altogether. The tabloids continued to have a field day.

———

Even a first cursory look at the copious materials in the file brought home to me that our case was in terrible shape and that the task the defense confronted was massive and complex. After a few weeks of commuting by plane, I rented an apartment in Sherman Oaks, a stone's throw from Robert's place, and turned it into a home office. I was here to stay.

Then I proceeded to fire many of the existing defense team in order to build my own. I hired jury consultant Lois Heaney, lead investigator Jacqi Tully, and trial presentation expert Ted Brooks, and I retained a database specialist and forensic scientists, among others. One holdover from the previous team was a young lawyer named Bridget Daniels to whom I assigned the task of inventorying the materials in the file from top to bottom. I wanted to make sure we had everything the prosecution claimed to have provided. Bridget was to check everything we had against every communication from the district attorney's office. The inventory made it clear that there was a huge gap between what the

DA said it had produced and what was in the file. So step one was to close the gap.[3]

We also needed to get all the physical evidence examined and tested by the forensic laboratory retained for that purpose—something that, for reasons I didn't understand, had never been done by Robert's lawyers. Critical among the essential forensic tests to be conducted was to test-fire the murder weapon—found in a construction dumpster parked in front of Robert's car—so we could compare the results of gunshot residue tests on the hands of the person carrying out the test against the results of tests the police had done on Robert's hands on the night of the murder.

We had to investigate the stuntmen the police had managed to rope in and scrutinize their similar stories of having been approached by Robert to do a hit on Bonnie. Although investigation had been done, I thought there was much more to be done.

I also wanted to examine other possible suspects—Christian Brando, for one,[4] not to mention those nine previous Bonnie Bakley husbands and numerous other men Bonnie had taken for a financial ride. I wanted to know whether they harbored enough ill will to be potential suspects.

The police investigation into other possible candidates for the role of Bonnie's murderer had been superficial at best, secondary to their aim of bolstering the conclusion at which they had so quickly and satisfyingly arrived. Yes, statistically it makes sense to suspect a husband in the murder of a wife, and cinematically, it makes for a gratifying narrative arc to fix responsibility for a shooting death on a movie actor, especially one who has played the role of an unconventional cop in the TV series *Baretta* and a killer in the movie version of *In Cold Blood*. But as our investigative team kept digging, it became clearer and clearer that the police had pinned the murder on Robert on the night of the murder because they decided—or more precisely, jumped to the unsupported conclusion—that he had the motive and opportunity to kill his wife.

---

3. I hired another young lawyer, David Christensen, who worked alongside Bridget throughout the trial, providing valuable backup.

4. The judge denied my request to present detailed evidence about what I believed was Christian Brando's involvement in Bonnie's murder. At the hub of a wheel of very detailed evidence to this effect was a well-respected businessman, Brian Allan Fiebelkorn. Brian, generally known as Brian Allan, had been a longtime supporter of the LAPD but became completely disillusioned with the police and the DA's office as a result of their failure to investigate adequately Brando's culpability.

Also, they couldn't find anyone else to pin it on. In the artful scenario they constructed—this was Hollywood, after all—Robert Blake had never wanted to marry Bonnie Lee Bakley; he barely knew her, and what he knew he didn't much like. But he fervently loved the daughter born to Bonnie and him, and making Bonnie disappear was a surefire way to gain custody of his Rosie.

In truth, the bare outline of Robert's feelings toward both Bonnie and Rosie—up to the point of committing murder—was not far from the truth. It was in that final leap of logic, from loving your daughter to murdering your wife, that the fantasy lay, and it was sheer fantasy not so much because this was Hollywood, but because there was no evidence to support the accusation. None.

It takes a special kind of logic—call it "police logic"—to make this cognitive leap, but as I believe this book demonstrates, it happens far too often. Unable to determine the identity of a perpetrator through investigation of evidence, and being in the business of identifying perpetrators, police sometimes eliminate those they determine clearly not to be perpetrators and settle on whoever is left. As in Buddy Nickerson's case, the Los Angeles police convicted Robert on the night of the murder—before they had an opportunity to conduct an investigation.

But in rushing to judgment in this way, the police didn't just fail to do their job properly and thoroughly, they also suppressed evidence and manipulated witnesses. To confirm their initial conclusion that Robert had murdered Bonnie, they simply closed off all other lines of inquiry, dismissing or distorting anything that led away from that conclusion. It's what happened in the cases of Suzanne Wickersham and Buddy Nickerson; it's what happens every day in police departments and legal jurisdictions around the country—and it clearly happened in the case of Robert Blake.

Why does it happen? The motivations are as varied as the people involved, starting with perhaps the most obvious motivation—that of taking the easy way out. Suffice to say that in the case of Robert Blake, positioning him as guilty put certain people in the spotlight, might have been good for a few careers, may have gratified some bizarre popular yearning or quenched a public resentment, and fulfilled the need to provide an answer. Perhaps even more fundamentally, I believe that the LAPD and the district attorney's office as well felt a need to make up for having bungled a similar case of celebrity wife murder some years previously—the O.J. Simpson case. Justifiably or not, the police and prosecution emerged from that experience looking like fools; it rankled, and I think they felt that Robert's case was a chance for a do-over. The bottom line was that both police and prosecutors really wanted to nail this one, and it may have been this that blinded them into investigative "work" that was sloppy, mendacious, unworthy of the job of policing, and a body blow to justice. And my team and I were not about to let them get away with it.

But it required an awful lot of work. With critical parts of the file missing and an enormous amount of investigation and scientific work still to be done, I knew we could not be prepared to go to trial by the September trial date Judge Darlene Schemp had declared fixed, and not about to be changed for any reason. In July, I asked her for a postponement of the trial date, submitting along with the motion a huge declaration, filed under seal so that only the judge could read it, not the prosecution and certainly not the press, detailing what was missing from the file—that is, the discrepancies between what the DA's office believed it had turned over to the defense and what was actually on hand in that little house behind Robert's rental. In open court, I told the judge that because I was from another jurisdiction, I had consulted with a number of L.A. lawyers on the best way to convince her that a postponement of the trial was necessary. They were unanimous; I told the judge, that I should ask for twice as much time as needed because she would cut the request in half in any event. To my relief, the judge smiled. I then told her I had never lied to her and would not start now and that I needed exactly what I was asking for: two months. And I assured her that the reasons were spelled out precisely in the declaration I had submitted.

The judge's ruling gave us what we needed, and we got ourselves in gear to go to trial in November 2004.

———

It's no secret at this point in this book that getting in gear for a trial is my life's work. I know how to do it and had done it many times before the Robert Blake case. But on a personal level, in this case, I was utterly miserable. Mostly, I was lonely. In the year of my life that I lived in Los

Gerry in college baseball game

Washington & Jefferson College Yearbook

Gerry and Lester Stiggers leaving Wayne County Jail

Detroit News

Gerry, with Micah at his side, speaking at Bingham fundraiser

Susan Homes Schwartzbach

Stephen Bingham on the witness stand

Susan Homes Schwartzbach.

Gerry speaking to the press
during Bingham trial
Susan Homes Schwartzbach

Gerry waiting for
Bingham verdict
Susan Homes Schwartzbach.

Stephen Bingham and
Gerry at reading of
last verdict

AP

Stephen Bingham and
Gerry embrace at
last verdict

AP

Gerry and Susan hug after Steven Bingham verdict

Courtesy of the author

Gerry and Richard Bandler

Susan Homes Schwartzbach

CONFIDENTIAL & LEGAL From: Buddy

NOT To Be OPENed UNTiL DAY OF Judges FINAL RuLiNG

From: Glen Nickerson
D-66169 · D-3-148
CSP-LAC
44756 60th St West
Lancaster, California
935-36-7619

FOR: M. Gerald Schwartzbach
Attorney At Law

CONFIDENTiAL & LEGAL

To: Mr. "M" Gerald Schwartzbach.   March 5, 2002

Just, wanted to say Thanks. For all you've done, for me and my Family. And what a Great Job, you did in Court. I can Live with the Judge's dission. I can now get on with my Life. And get out of this Limbo Stage. I've been in for the past eighteen years. I am Very **Honored** to have met you. And have you as a Friend. And you've made me, see people. For who they are And not what they are. And I'll get the tattoo removed. Like I said. Cause, I know of NO Other way to show you. That I have Very High Respect for you. You and your Family. Did a Great Job in Court. And you all Should be Very, Very Proud of it. I know I'm proud of all of you. And Remember, What I've Always Said. This is My Distiny. And I Can Handle it. Life is still Good. What a Journey, its been. Ya Hooo! ☺ And My The Sun Always Be on Your Face. And the Wind at Your Back. And at the End of Your Journey. May the Stars See You Safely to Your Loved Ones. IT HAS Been A HONOR KNOWiNG **you!**

P.S See you in the funny papers.

                                    With Much Respect
                        Glen William Nickerson Jr.

        (OVER)

Buddy's letter to Gerry

Courtesy of the author

Buddy kissing Gerry when released after being granted bail

AP

Buddy leaving
San Quentin
after exoneration

Susan Homes Schwartzbach

Gerry when Buddy released from prison
Susan Homes Schwartzbach

Buddy having
racist tattoos
removed
Susan Homes Schwartzbach

Gerry and Robert
Blake on weekend
Susan Homes Schwartzbach

Gerry and Robert Blake at
surprise 60th birthday party
Courtesy of the author

Susan, Robert, and Gerry at 60th birthday party

Courtesy of the author

Gerry wearing
Badger jacket

Susan Homes Schwartzbach

Robert Blake kissing Gerry at post-verdict press conference

AP

Gerry and Dr. Roozrokh at verdict

San Luis Obispo Tribune/David Middlecamp

Gerry, Dr. Roozrokh, former patient Joe Quiroz, Ken, and Micah
outside courthouse immediately after acquittal

Courtesy of the author

Gerry and Susan

Courtesy of the author

Angeles, I saw my wife maybe a dozen times; I saw my son, who at any event was in law school, just a few times. I knew virtually no one in the area, had no close Angeleno friends, and while I was fond of all the members of our newly formed legal team and very occasionally saw my nephews Mitchell and Neil, there was really no L.A. pal with whom I could go out and have a meal and talk about old times. I had experienced no old times with anyone in L.A.

And I was homesick. The wide cultural gap between San Francisco and Los Angeles is so storied as to be axiomatic, and while it has become something of a self-fulfilling prophecy that owes more to legend than to reality, I felt the difference acutely. It wasn't just style; the air was different down there, and I missed the scent of the forest and the fog. Adrift in a culture of striving go-getters, movie people, and relentlessly mild weather, I worked seven days a week, mostly in my apartment, and then would go to Robert's house to oversee more work and spend time with Robert. I came home each night to my little apartment—a world away from my comfortable home in my comfortable community—eminently ready to feel sorry for myself, but knowing nobody in the courtroom would.

There wasn't time for self-pity anyway; I simply didn't have the luxury of not coping. A client's life was on the line, and his money was in my pocket. We had a deadline and a clear task—a huge task—and it required of me, as lead attorney, absolutely everything I had. So I gave it that, for long hours every day, seven days a week. In fact, if there can be said to have been an upside to my loneliness and homesickness, it was that I was freed to hone in one hundred percent on the task at hand while I put my emotions to the side.

Not that there weren't light moments as well as moments of real companionship and connection—most of them with Jacqi Tully or Ted Brooks, but also with other members of the defense team as well as with Robert himself. In the years following his acquittal, Robert became a disenchanted and embittered man, and his once-warm attitude toward me apparently grew cold, although a voicemail message and letter in 2015 reiterated his gratitude and showered best wishes on Susan, Micah, *and* me. And in those months of preparing for his trial, when we worked so closely together, the connection between us was fraternal, and I found him a congenial presence and a benevolent friend.

I remember in particular Robert's good-natured "participation"—off-stage—in my wife's birthday celebration some months after I had been named lead attorney. Since we first met, Susan and I had never been apart on her birthday, August 31, and in 2004, the year of Robert Blake, it was pretty clear that my absence meant we would have to be. We both expressed unhappiness over the idea, but what Susan didn't know was that, with Robert's encouragement and connivance, I was plotting a Bay Area surprise appearance at a restaurant where a birthday dinner had been arranged with Micah and his girlfriend, Maria.

Meanwhile, when I lamented that I had no time to shop for a gift, Robert offered to teach me a song to sing to Susan instead.

"But I can't sing," I protested.

"Sure you can," he said. "You sing in the same key as Frank."

"Frank? You don't mean Frank Sinatra."

"That's exactly who I mean," said Robert, possibly on the grounds that if you are an Italian American from New Jersey, there is only one Frank.

"Robert, all these months I've been trying to figure out our defense, and now I've got it: Insanity!" For comparing my singing to that of Sinatra seemed utter insanity to me.

Robert was unperturbed. "You'll sing *It Had to Be You.*' You know? 'It had to be you, it had to be you, I wandered around and finally found somebody who . . . Remember?"

So I practiced singing *It Had to Be You*—presumably in the same key Sinatra used. I practiced it in the car; I practiced it standing in line to board the Southwest Airlines flight from Burbank to Oakland on the night of my wife's birthday; I practiced it standing in line when the flight was delayed and I frantically called Micah with instructions to somehow delay the arrival at the restaurant; I practiced it in the rental car when I had finally arrived in Oakland and was on my way to the restaurant.

I was the first one there, and I took a quiet booth in the back. I saw Micah leading Susan and Maria; the two women were engrossed in conversation and never saw me at all until they arrived at the booth, and when Susan noticed me, she burst into tears.

Once we were all seated, I told her I had "a somewhat unusual gift for you."

Susan doesn't miss much. "Is this Robert's idea?" she asked.

"Actually, yes." And I launched into *It Had to Be You.*

Susan again burst into tears, this time joined by Maria, while Micah kept muttering, "Dad, please don't."

But at least, according to Robert Blake, it was in the same key as Frank.

———

Jury selection got underway in the second week of November. Both lawyers and the judge had already culled the juror questionnaires to weed out those individuals who were obviously unsuited. Now we began the *voir dire*, the lawyer for each side questioning prospective jurors on their backgrounds, biases, and qualifications and deciding whom we wanted to reject and, by extension, whom we wanted to select.

My strategy in the forthcoming trial was going to be to destroy every bit of the prosecution's evidence and the credibility of their witnesses, including the stuntmen's claims of being solicited to kill Bonnie. My worry was that while the prosecution's case was circumstantial and we could beat back every bit of it, the volume of it was so great that it might simply overwhelm members of the jury, blinding them with sheer heft.

Poking holes in the stuntmen's testimony, for example, would not necessarily destroy the accumulated impression the prosecution would try to foster—namely, that Robert was the kind of a man who could talk about "whacking" or "snuffing" or "popping" people, even his wife, and that he was therefore a guy who just might ask someone to do her in. I could discredit each witness's testimony until I was blue in the face, but perception piled upon perception is hard to battle, and my main weapon in proving Robert's innocence was going to be highly technical, highly scientific, admittedly boring data about gunshot residue. That meant that when it came to jury selection, I would be looking for people who were intelligent and patient, people who could stay awake through a dull recitation of scientific facts about infinitesimal particles found on skin and clothing, people who could then process the information, for it was this evidence that proved that Robert Blake did not fire the gun that killed his wife. The prosecution might persuade jurors that Robert was a bad guy, as low a thug as the tabloids painted. Jurors might be convinced that Robert disliked Bonnie Bakley and that he had thought about, even talked about getting her out of his life one way or another. They could build a case around Robert's personality, character, his likes and dislikes, the people he associated with. But the scientific evidence would show inescapably that he was not the guy who killed her. That was our trial strategy, and, expertly directed by Lois Heaney, it guided our jury selection process.

On December 1, the process ended. I went to my apartment satisfied with the jury's composition and confident that Robert would get a fair trial. So it was a real jolt to my system to see my apartment door ajar and the lock clearly broken. The reason was evident the moment I stepped across the threshold. Things were missing—the golf clubs Susan had brought me on a recent visit and, more to the point, my laptop computer, which of course contained everything about the case.

I called the local precinct and was told that it might not be until the next day that officers could get to my place to investigate. This obviously had a huge bearing on the case, so I phoned the judge's emergency number, told her what had happened, and explained my concerns about confidential information getting into the wrong hands and about my ability to try the case now that the entire computerized file was gone. Then I called Shellie Samuels and told her the same thing. "What's your address?" Shellie demanded. I told her. "The police will be there in ten minutes," she said. And they were.

In fact, the local cops were soon followed by officers of the elite downtown LAPD, and pretty soon, there seemed to be a swarm of police officers at the site, yellow police tape was stretched around the building, and crime scene evidence technicians came to my apartment.

Clearly, Shellie had made a phone call or two. Though I didn't realize it at the time, she was convinced that Robert was responsible for the break-in in order to cause a delay in his trial. There was no other explanation for the extraordinary amount of police attention given to the nonviolent burglary of an apartment. [5]

As panicked as I was at first, I told myself to think like a lawyer. I didn't trust the police and didn't want them in my apartment where they

---

5. Shellie maintained that belief even after her own office prosecuted the burglars, who had absolutely no connection whatsoever with Robert.

could see my physical defense file, which included confidential information and documents. I refused to let the police enter my apartment and instead called the judge again. She promptly appointed a lawyer to come to my apartment and monitor what the police could look at and touch. He and I used bed sheets to cover parts of the legal file I didn't want the police to see. Only then did I allow the police to enter.

The evidence technicians found fingerprints on my front door jamb. The prints took them fairly quickly to a couple of young guys who had been told by their cocaine dealer friend that they could score cash and valuables in Apartment 202. But the guys got the apartment number wrong and went to 302, where they found the empty apartment of a nice little old lady who had virtually nothing that could be fenced, so instead they broke into the apartment next door, mine, and thought they hit pay dirt. Little did they know that by doing so they would guarantee themselves time in prison. They quickly pawned my laptop and very shortly thereafter were rounded up, taken into custody, and charged. The only bright spot in the whole tawdry episode was the wonderful example of chutzpah exhibited by the pawnbroker who had taken the laptop off the two burglars' hands. He told the investigating detective that I ought to reimburse him for the hundred bucks he paid to the young guys who had obviously stolen my expensive computer. When the detective relayed the pawnbroker's message, I sent a message back: "That's not happening."

The laptop was scientifically vetted to certify that it had not been opened or its data tampered with, and at long last, on December 20, 2004, opening statements began in the case of the *People v. Robert Blake.*

The way you make a circumstantial case is to create a chain, building it link by link until the chain wraps around the jury's collective brain leaving them no other conclusion but the one you have drawn for them. The charges of solicitation of murder were based on the claims of former stuntmen Gary McLarty and Ronald Duffy Hambleton that Robert had offered each of them money to kill Bonnie for him. On the charge of murder, the prosecution forged links of means, motive, and opportunity—he owned guns, he wanted his wife gone, and he was there that night—

to leave the jury with the conclusion that he was the only one who could have murdered her.

It was Robert who had parked behind a dumpster in which the murder weapon was eventually found. It was Robert who claimed he had left his gun behind in the restaurant and went to collect it, thereby providing an opportunity for the murder to take place. A few witnesses testified that his behavior walking to and from the restaurant and before and after Bonnie was found was bizarre. Was it feasible or even reasonable to believe that Robert was *not* involved? After all, *who else could it have been*?

To counter this, we presented evidence that point by point broke each link in the chain. Why, for example, did Robert park the car behind the dumpster? Well, for one thing, the restaurant parking lot was full, as we showed in testimony from other patrons who had also hoped to park in the lot that night. In fact, finding any parking space was not easy; it was Friday night, after all, a busy time in that neighborhood. We also demonstrated that Robert usually parked on a side street when he dined at that restaurant, and we showed that other patrons had parked on the same street and on nearby streets that same night; it was sheer chance that he parked where he did, not premeditated design.

A retired LAPD detective who in the past had dined with Robert at the restaurant testified that Robert had once left his gun behind and had to return to the restaurant to collect it. In other words, even leaving his gun in the restaurant booth—*his* regular booth—was not a freak occurrence; it had happened before.

Against testimony from some bystanders that Robert had acted "bizarrely" walking back to his car, we countered with testimony from other patrons, bystanders, and an experienced Fire Department captain that there was "nothing bizarre" about the way he acted after he had retrieved his gun. In one instance, we rebutted a doctor's testimony that Robert had walked back toward his car in a strange manner; the rebuttal included establishing the fact that the doctor, rather than rendering medical aid, had hidden behind a tree even after learning that Bonnie lay mortally wounded a short distance away.

The prosecution also mocked Robert's claim that on finding Bonnie, he had run across the street and had knocked frantically on the first door he saw to find help but got no response. Well, he wouldn't have, as we proved, for the owner was away on vacation at the time, a fact

Robert could not have known when he spoke to the police. What was confirmable the night of the murder was that in the next house he ran to, there *was* a person who responded to his terror and called 911; in fact, we played the 911 tape, on which Robert's freaked-out pleas that the ambulance hurry could be plainly heard—and Bonnie was still alive at that time.

In short, the defense left nothing unanswered in the accumulation of claims through which the prosecution attempted to forge its chain of evidence.

We also completely demolished the testimony of the stuntmen, proving that both were drug addicts, seriously ill mentally—to the point of having frequent hallucinations—and liars who had perjured themselves on the stand. We did this by locating and subpoenaing previously undiscovered medical records, as well as by finding critical witnesses who had never been interviewed by the defense. It is one thing to prove witnesses took drugs; it is much more significant to prove they are mentally unstable and have repeatedly lied. That is what the newly obtained medical records and newly interviewed witnesses accomplished.

In smashing these links of "evidence," we also clearly showed the bias and corruption of the police. Then we produced the gunshot residue evidence, linchpin of proof against Robert's culpability, and showed the police's rank and inexcusable incompetence.

———

Every time a gun is fired, residue is dispersed out both ends and both sides of the barrel. The residue is composed of three chemical elements, and all three of them must be present in a particle if that particle is to be identified *specifically* as gunshot residue, or GSR; if a particle has only one or two of the elements, it is considered *consistent* with GSR but just as likely from another source.

On the night of the murder, Robert's hands had been tested for GSR by the police; they found five particles *consistent* with GSR on his hands. *No particles specific to GSR were found on Robert's hands.* On the basis of these test results, the prosecution claimed that Robert had fired the gun, tossed it in the dumpster, then wiped his hands on the grass and washed them with water to get rid of any traces.

I had had the murder weapon test-fired under forensic laboratory conditions; surprisingly, none of Robert's lawyers had done that before I was retained. Celia Hartnett, a gunshot residue expert, testified as to the results. She told the jury that the murder weapon that had killed Bonnie had left 2,440 *consistent* GSR particles on the hands of the person shooting the gun—as against the five found on Robert's hands—and 537 *specific* GSR particles versus zero specific particles found on Robert's hand. Had he washed off the evidence? As our expert testified, GSR residue doesn't wash off easily, and there had been neither the time nor the opportunity for him to do so "properly." As for particles on his clothing, even the LAPD forensic science procedures warned against such analysis because there was simply no way to specify the date or time of the contamination—especially in this case because the cop who picked up the clothes the day after the murder tossed them in the trunk of his police car and drove around with them all weekend. This was incompetence piled on top of incompetence.

The science, in other words, not only discredited the prosecution witnesses but also proved that there was absolutely no physical evidence connecting Robert to the murder. And if that weren't enough, the GSR evidence, which nobody had adequately explored, showed conclusively that Robert Blake did not fire the murder weapon.

The prosecution's assumption that Robert had to have been the murderer because it couldn't be anyone else was turned on its head: Since Robert could not have been the murderer, it could be just about anybody else. Moreover, there was absolutely no evidence that anyone Robert had communicated with was involved in the murder.

Case closed? Not quite.

———

My all-out, full-on, virtually 24/7 work on this case, which had consumed a year of my own life and over which loomed, at all times, the threat of my client spending the rest of his life in prison, had brought me to a point of utter exhaustion. It's not as if I didn't have help. There was jury consultant Lois Heaney. There was our team of investigators led by Jacqi Tully with assistance from Linda Larson and a support staff that included two young lawyers, Bridget Daniels and David Christiansen, as well as nonlawyers Gus Ramirez, Elena Perrotta, and Joanne Lichtenstein. There was Ted Brooks, a computer trial presentation expert who made the evidence come to life on large screens in the courtroom. And there was Allison Shalinsky, who had joined Robert's legal team of a couple of lawyers earlier and had stayed on. Allison is one of the best— and best-organized—case preparation lawyers I've ever come across, a genius at crystallizing research, a superb writer, and excellent at creating outlines for examination and cross-examination. But she is a woman who cannot stand to be in a courtroom, so I was particularly grateful that, for this case, she allowed herself to be persuaded to come to court, although she would not sit at counsel table. Still, for me, knowing she was there and available for consultation and that I was backed by the other terrific team members was a comfort and a help.

But I was still exhausted. The stress of such a trial is oppressive. It wasn't particularly surprising that earlier in the trial, I had passed a kidney stone that caused a tear requiring minor surgery, or that by now I was exhibiting the classic symptoms of physical and mental fatigue. Add to it the fact that I had uprooted myself, that I missed my wife and son something fierce, that I longed for the comforts of home and the world I had left behind, and that I am constitutionally a guy who can get very emotional, and you have a potentially explosive situation.

However, I know this about myself, and over a long career as a lawyer, I have developed ways to deal with it. We all still had a ways to go before this case was closed, and I was the lead attorney, so I couldn't afford to let up; there could be no diminution of effort, no scaling down of our intensity. Sleep was not a possible antidote because I had to work until the wee hours to get done all that needed to get done—my outline for closing argument, for example, ran to more than 160 typed pages. Instead, there was a particular morning routine that I applied to prepare myself for the days in trial.

It started when I got in the car each morning. The minute I turned the key, I punched the button on the car radio tuned to a classical music station. To this day, I have no idea what the station's call letters were, but in the morning, they tended to play soothing symphonic music— one day Mozart, the next day Haydn, Brahms, Mendelssohn, Schubert, Beethoven. It did what great music is supposed to do—uplifted me, took me out of my exhaustion, and calmed my overly feverish brain and being.

With this as background, I exhaled deeply, then began talking to myself: *You're ready. You're prepared. You know how to do this, so go in there and do what you know how to do and what you do well. Be a lawyer. Stay professional. Don't let your exhaustion or your emotions make the decisions; only the lawyer in you makes decisions.* And so on—until I arrived at the underground garage where I would meet Robert and the others. Restored and revived, I walked to the courthouse with our legal team.

———

I delivered the closing argument before a packed courtroom. At one point, the judge asked me to speak louder. "Those in the back of the courtroom cannot hear you," she said. "With all due respect, Your Honor," I replied, "I will try to keep my voice up, but these"—I turned to the jury—"are the folks who really matter." I looked them in the eye as I said it. I had worked hard to establish their trust throughout the trial, simply by being honest about who I was and who Robert is, and the payoff to all that was the attention they were giving me now. I wanted them to know I valued that attention and would not fritter it away in grandstanding for the media.

The media circus, which had never let up, hit a new peak as the trial wound down. I had sworn off any on-the-record contact with the press for the duration of the trial, but I was still stunned by the chaotic carnival atmosphere at its end; I really had never seen anything like it in my professional experience.

There was something else in the air as well, and that was the public's presumption of guilt that had dogged Robert from the start. He had been unaware of this until I showed him the numbers culled from the questionnaires potential jurors months before. They showed that more than 70 percent of prospective jurors—and, by extension, of the public at large—thought him guilty. It terrified him, but it made him more than willing to get on board with my planned trial strategy and to comply with anything I asked of him.

Why did so many people feel this way? Partly, I think, it was the general belief that if you're charged with a crime, you must have done something wrong—i.e., where there's smoke, there's fire. Partly, it was and is an assumption that the rich and powerful can buy their way out of trouble, with a special resentment for celebrities who "think they can get away with it."

It also goes to the heart of why I believe the police in this case failed to follow their own procedures, showed such incompetence when they did follow procedure, withheld exculpatory information, violated court orders, and generally lied and cheated when the facts didn't conform to the conclusion they had reached before conducting a thorough investigation. Again, in my view, both the LAPD and the county district attorney were hoping in this celebrity wife murder to regain the credibility they lost when they were perceived to have botched the O.J. Simpson celebrity murder case. In a word, for the prosecution and the public at large, it was payback time, and they wanted Robert Blake to go down.

———

The jury was out for nine days. The length of time did not particularly worry me. I was still counting on the slow, patient absorption of all the evidence, including that scientific evidence. I thought the prosecution had erred in showing an excerpt from a television interview Robert had done on ABC's *20/20* with Barbara Walters before I was retained. He had done the interview against his lawyer's advice—Tom Mesereau was his lawyer at the time—and while he was still in jail. The prosecution thought that the interview excerpt it showed would paint Robert as a liar. But because the prosecutor had introduced the interview, that allowed me to play an excerpt as well, a much longer one, and one that I believe humanized Robert. He looked frail, vulnerable, and anything but murderous. And he proclaimed his innocence—in his own voice and in his own words.

The moment a verdict is read is always a heart-stopping one, whatever the charge.

In this case, where my client's life was on the line, where so many of us had invested so much and sacrificed so widely, those seconds seated next to Robert while the pre-pronouncement formulas were recited were as full of dread as anything I had ever known.

Robert put his hands on my knees and swung our chairs toward each other. "Gerry," he whispered, "you did everything you possibly could." It was the only time in my entire career that a client tried to comfort *me* before a verdict was read—and this client was about to learn whether he would spend the rest of his life in prison. I was blown away.

"Not guilty," read the court clerk to the charge of murder. "Not guilty" again to the first count of solicitation. Hung eleven to one for acquittal on the second solicitation count, the jury declared itself unable to come to a verdict on that count, and, on a motion by the prosecutor, the judge dismissed that last charge. Robert was free to go.

So was I.

———

The size of the exhilaration I felt at that moment not only equaled but wiped away the dread I had felt seconds before. All the pent-up intensity of a year of work and worry burst out of me in a split second; my physical exhaustion dissolved; I felt like a lion of the law.

During the course of our trial preparation Robert began to call me "the badger." In fact, at a surprise 60th birthday party he arranged for me at his rented house, Robert gave me a World War II Air Force pilot's leather jacket, with, in huge letters, "The Badger" on the back. In truth, it wasn't lionlike strength that had won this case; it was tenacity. It was the process of harrying the evidence, clawing down for every scrap, questioning every assumption, hassling and pestering the authorities when necessary, teasing out every fact. We did the job the police should have done but didn't.

If evidence is at the heart of the criminal justice system, and it is, it is worth remembering how utterly essential the often tedious process of examining and reexamining the evidence is, weighing it, sifting it, shaking it until it gives up all its secrets. Like a piece of art, evidence reveals more the more you look at it. And as with a piece of art, others will see things in it you have missed. The key with evidence, therefore, is to keep coming back to it. Badgerlike, we dug into every bit of evidence. We kept coming back to it and digging some more. We didn't rest until we got to the bottom of the truth, and, although there are still many people who refuse to see it, it was the truth that set Robert Blake free.[6]

———

6. Robert later lost a factually related civil wrongful death trial that was more a circus than a serious legal proceeding. Although I did not participate in that trial, in my view the flawed verdict was the result of the failings of the lawyers who first represented Robert, the limited time his trial lawyers had to prepare and develop as deep a rapport with him as he and I had, the trial judge's erroneous rulings, and juror misconduct.

—10—

A Little Like Saving the Whole World

The case I consider perhaps the most important of my career started unexceptionally enough with a phone call in 2006 from a close personal friend, Ken Freeman. Susan and I had met Ken and Jeanie Freeman in 1980, when Susan and Jeannie were both pregnant. The Freeman's son Nick was born 15 days before our son Micah in March 1981. Through those shared extraordinary experiences our two families became lifelong friends.

After a stint as an attorney in the State Attorney General's Office, Ken had opened his own practice representing health care professionals in regulation cases—licensing, credentialing, and the odd disciplinary issue. I was quick to catch the note of concern in Ken's voice when he called that day to tell me about a case he had taken on and to enlist my help.

Kaiser Permanente, the huge healthcare consortium that runs health plans, medical groups, and its own hospitals, had retained Ken to represent a young organ transplant surgeon, Dr. Hootan Roozrokh, against allegations by the Medical Board of California; they were accusing Dr. Roozrokh of violating ethical protocols in the attempted harvesting of organs from a dying patient in a hospital in San Luis Obispo.

Ken's first step, normal in any such situation, was to phone the San Luis Obispo investigator assigned by the local district attorney to investigate Dr. Roozrokh to learn more about the nature of the charges. What he heard shocked him. The local DA's office was considering criminal charges—specifically, attempted manslaughter or, maybe even attempted murder. To Ken, whose judgment I trusted, either charge would be a travesty; even more, a travesty looking suspiciously like a politically motivated prosecutorial over-reach—somebody was hoping to turn the organ donation aspect of the case into ghoulish publicity and a high-visibility climb up the career ladder.

Ken wanted me on board—initially, to persuade the DA not to file any criminal charges. I tried but was met with a stone wall. The DA not only filed criminal charges but they also issued a press release about this first of its kind prosecution. Kaiser retained me to defend Hootan and Ken to assist me. We, along with Micah, who by then was a lawyer in his own right and my associate, were soon embarked on a full-time effort to defend Hootan. We would spend the next two and a half years consumed in that fight, working flat-out, subordinating just about every other aspect of life to this case and this trial. The final verdict came at the tail-end of 2008—when Hootan Roozrokh was acquitted of all the charges against him.

Why was it so important to me? After all, this was not my usual sort of case. Someone even described it as "a bit of an outlier" among the kinds of criminal cases I had taken over the course of my career. It was not, for instance, a capital case. Dr. Roozrokh was not in the end accused of having committed murder. So this was not about saving a defendant from a death penalty or a life in prison.

Nor did Hootan himself fall into that category of defendant I had long given my all and staked my reputation to "save." There was nothing downtrodden about this man, nothing helpless; he was not disadvantaged, had not been exploited, was no one's lackey. On the contrary, Hootan is a brilliant young man who at the time was already climbing with ease to the very top of his profession. Abundant resources were available to him. For him personally, a conviction would have been a disaster but, in my opinion at least, not a death. His punishment, had he been convicted of any or all of the abuses with which he was charged, would have resulted in a felony conviction and perhaps confinement in prison. Worse, the California Medical Board would no doubt have stripped him of his medical license and therefore of the livelihood for which he was so well suited, and his life would have turned downward in such profound ways that he himself might have felt it was over. But this was not a man to be wholly undone even by such a crushing defeat; he had the means— mental and material—to re-create himself, had that become necessary. So, on the one hand, Hootan's acquittal did not save a life *per se,* but, on the other hand, perhaps it saved many more than one.

In my view, Hootan's acquittal may have saved hundreds, thousands, and as time goes on, even more lives. For what hung in the balance in the trial of Hootan Roozrokh was nothing less than the future of organ donation, both in this country and around the world. Long a dream of medical science, the idea of harvesting viable organs from the just-dead in order to save those whose lives are at risk had come a long way since the first known transplant in 1954. But for all the technological and medical progress and for all the efforts—by government above all—to loosen the psychological and/or religious constraints on organ donation, it remained a slightly taboo issue that people didn't like to think or talk about; it was an issue that made many people feel a bit queasy, while the donation and transplant process was little understood, often even by those involved in it.

The trial of Hootan Roozrokh brought the issue to the fore and thrust it into the public arena, firing up the debate, igniting people's interest, and yes, letting loose the bugaboos that lurked beneath the surface. Those were fears about selling organs, buying organs, stealing organs from people who were not really dead just yet. The trial opened doors into what really happens when organs are harvested, into how suffering is defined, and into what doctors do and do not do. It also shone a light on what they may not do and must do in dealing with the immediate issues of the dying and those with a chance to live.

This was a unique case—the first of its kind, I believe, in the history of law. It is rare enough that science and criminal law intersect; the case of Dr. Roozrokh represented a near-collision of medical science, ethics, and the protection of the individual under law, and the acquittal was a victory for all three. That is why it was perhaps the proudest moment of my career.

Here is the story:

———

At any moment, there are approximately 120,000 Americans in need of an organ transplant and waiting for a donation. The names of those waiting, along with their associated medical data, are all on a list so that the individuals can be matched, on the basis of various criteria, to suitable donors, the number of which is far smaller than the list of those in need. The agency that governs how donated organs may be procured and distributed is called the United Network for Organ Sharing (UNOS), and its job is to regulate the nation's Organ Procurement Organizations (OPOs), organizations serving specific geographic areas and responsible for allocating available organs within their designated service area (DSA). When organs become available, the appropriate OPO offers them to transplant centers where the donor information is evaluated and a provisional determination made for possible recipients. A transplant team from the transplant center is then dispatched to the facility where the donor is, harvests the organs through surgery, and distributes them as needed for transplant into the bodies of recipients all over the country.

The majority of organ donors are accident victims; they have suffered a fatal brain injury and have been declared brain-dead, but as long as they remain on a respirator, their organs continue to function. The transplant team can operate with deliberation and without particular urgency as the surgeon retrieves the body parts; the organs will only stop functioning when the donor is taken off the respirator. Hootan Roozrokh, despite being the youngest transplant surgeon in the country, had been involved in a number of such surgeries.

A much thornier and far more controversial situation is donation after cardiac death, or DCD. In this case, the patient is typically in a coma but is not brain-dead, and the attending end-of-life doctors must determine that the patient has no chance of surviving if disconnected from the respirator—extubated, to use the medical term. If the determination is made, what you are then talking about is the withdrawal of life support with the intention of causing cardiac death—pulling the plug. In the case of a patient who is a candidate for organ donation, once the next of kin consents to the organ donation, time and timing become factors, for the moment the donor is extubated, his or her organs will begin to deteriorate from lack of oxygen.

So here's how events proceed: The attending end-of-life physicians determine the patient will not survive off the respirator. The next of kin consents to organ donation. Potential organ recipients—from one to perhaps as many as half a dozen—are identified. A transplant team is assembled and transported to the hospital where the donor is being treated. Upon the team's arrival, the putative donor's attending physician—or a designated practitioner acting on the physician's direction—disconnects the respirator. The transplant team waits for the donor to be declared dead—that is, all respiration and circulation totally stopped—and then proceeds to retrieve the organs surgically.

A sense of urgency—even of anxiety—invariably suffuses the members of the transplant team as they wait for the declaration of death. Time is limited once the extubation takes place; the organs have begun to deteriorate, and no one can be sure how long it will be before they are useless to save any other lives. But it is all very clinical and anonymous, directed at a distance by the OPO. Transplant teams are assembled, then sent to hospitals to which they typically have no connection to harvest organs that will be transplanted into patients they have nothing to do with. It is as if walls are thrown up as ethical divides between each stage of the process; indeed, the walls are intentional, aimed at establishing ethical divides.

One obvious wall, in either brain death or DCD, is that between the transplant medical team and the end-of-life medical team. Obviously, you don't want the doctor who is there on assignment to retrieve body parts to declare the patient dead; that is the responsibility and the duty of the attending physician. You also just don't want even a scintilla of possibility of any kind of cooperation or collusion between the two unrelated medical tasks. At the time of the Roozrokh trial, just such a wall was a rule in some hospitals and health centers, but not everywhere, and the truth is that the nation as a whole offered a patchwork of protocols and procedures for end-of-life organ donation and transplant situations. There was certainly no national protocol for DCD procurement. The trial itself would succeed in shining a light on the need to rationalize these protocols and procedures.

———

Ruben Navarro was nine years old when he was diagnosed with adrenoleukodystrophy, or ALD, a rare neurological disorder that also affects the muscular system, often leading to a tightening of muscles that causes excruciating pain in the limbs and spine. He lived most of his life thereafter in institutions; from the age of 20, he had been living in an assisted-care facility, and that is where he was when, on January 29, 2006, he suffered a massive respiratory and pulmonary arrest and a severe loss of oxygen to the brain. He was comatose when he was admitted that same day to Sierra Vista Regional Medical Center in San Luis Obispo, a small, attractive college town on the central coast of California.

Ruben was 25 years old. His prognosis was grim. Contacted by the relevant OPO in this case, the California Transplant Donor Network, CTDN, his mother on February 2 consented to the withdrawal of life support from her son and to the donation of his organs after death. Later on in this story, I would have occasion to come face to face with Ms. Navarro, but she was a single mother whose main purpose in life had been her only child, and, as a parent—as a human being—I cannot imagine what it cost her to make this decision. Since Ruben's life could have been prolonged for as long as he was maintained on the respirator, she was agreeing, in essence, to accelerate her son's death. Indeed, only if he died quickly after extubation would there be a donation.

Once Ms. Navarro's consent was given, the process was expedited, and the California Transport Donor Network swung into action, advising the attending physician that his patient was to be a candidate for organ donation, identifying an organ match with a patient at California Pacific Medical Center in San Francisco, and organizing a transplant team, to be quarterbacked by transplant team coordinator Carla Albright, who worked for CTDN.

Hootan Roozrokh was next in line on a rotating list of transplant surgeons maintained by CTDN. He was employed by Kaiser Permanente, as was a senior transplant surgeon, Dr. Arturo Martinez, who agreed to assist Hootan in the operating room at Sierra Vista.

In all, in fact, the team CTDN assembled that night was highly professional but utterly devoid of experience in donation by cardiac death, and

CTDN had done little to deal with the deficit. Hootan had completed an organ transplant fellowship less than a year before, and during the fellowship, he had observed one DCD. He had been the primary surgeon in a number of brain-death procurements but never at a DCD procurement. Likewise, Carla Albright had never coordinated a DCD transplant team. CTDN, meanwhile, gave no DCD training to either Hootan or Dr. Martinez, nor did it provide a complete DCD protocol to the team.

Once assembled, however, team members, aware that they might be harvesting organs that could possibly save multiple lives, raced to the airport and took off for San Luis Obispo. Delayed by fog and re-routed to another airport, they didn't arrive until nearly midnight, and when they entered Sierra Vista Hospital the night of February 3, 2006, prepared to get to work, they found their own DCD deficit compounded.

There had never been a DCD procurement at Sierra Vista hospital, and while CTDN had scheduled a training session on organ donation in January 2006, it was not well attended. In any event, no one on the Sierra Vista staff who would be present in the operating room February 3 and 4 had ever received any training in DCD procedures, nor had any of them been prepared in any way for the emotional trauma that can come from participating in a DCD procedure.

No one and nothing was really ready for this organ procurement. Ruben's attending physician had left for the weekend, although doctors were of course on call, and only minimal orders for administering pain medication to Ruben were available to the nursing staff. No one knew what to do next; not only was there no protocol in place, there were no written rules for guidance. Nobody was in charge of Ruben's care. It was like getting all dressed up for a party, only to arrive and find that no party has been scheduled. Granted, Sierra Vista was no big-city hospital with vast resources, but the hospital management knew this was coming, and they certainly knew the donor patient was in their care. Finally, someone phoned the on-call attending physician; by this time, it was the middle of the night. Disturbed at home and apparently unhappy about having to leave her family, the on-call doctor nevertheless agreed to come to the hospital.

Hootan took a look at Ruben in the Intensive Care Unit, the ICU, and saw a man curled into a deep coma, weighing about 70 pounds, and on life support. His immediate concern was about possible suffering once the respirator was disconnected, so he asked the staff what pain medication had been ordered for administration in the operating room (OR). None, he was told; the departed doctor had left no instructions at all for pain medication in the OR. Hootan consulted with the transplant coordinator, Carla Albright, reviewed Ruben's long history of pain and pain medication, then, considering his inevitable high tolerance to such medications, wrote an order for morphine and Ativan for the attending end-of-life physician to administer in the operating room once she arrived, as in due course she did. Two operating room nurses were also brought in to help, along with an ICU nurse. The nurses, the transplant coordinator and transplant assistant, a respiratory therapist, Arturo Martinez, and Hootan constituted the team that more or less put itself together in the absence of any guidance by the hospital itself for this its first-ever DCD transplant procedure.

The lack of guidance extended to these participants' behavior as well. Transplant surgeons are not supposed to be in the operating room until the donor is declared dead, but neither Hootan nor Arturo Martinez was aware of this. There was an absence of any instructions on who should be doing what and when they should be doing it, and the transplant coordinator in charge of such behavior, the CTDN's Carla Albright, was doing precious little coordinating. There was simply no one and nothing to stop the two doctors from doing what surgeons normally do once they have suited up and scrubbed in: They walked through the operating room door. Both men were there, seated against the wall, waiting, when the respiratory therapist extubated Ruben Navarro. Authorization to do so came in a nod of the head from the end-of-life attending physician. This was her bailiwick, and she had the authority and the responsibility to call the shots. She called this one on extubation. The next shot she called was to turn all further decision-making over to Hootan Roozrokh.

In a way it was understandable. This was the first time she had seen this patient; she had no training in DCD procedures; her hospital had established no rules to guide her. She seems to have felt herself unprepared for the task ahead of her, so she transferred the responsibility for it to someone else. In effect, she abdicated the care of Ruben Navarro in favor of the designated transplant surgeon in the room.

How do you know if a dying, comatose patient is suffering? You don't. There is no way to discover absolutely whether or to what extent a person who is not conscious and not able to communicate is feeling pain. In such situations, the Hippocratic Oath replaces its first precept—Do No Harm—with another precept, Prevent Suffering, if such is suspected, even if doing so might hasten the patient's death. And Hootan suspected suffering in the case of Ruben Navarro. When they had first laid Ruben down onto the table in the OR, the nurses felt resistance in his arms, a possible signal of pain. Vital signs, tracked by transplant coordinator Albright, gave indications of distress that the administered drugs had mitigated only briefly. Against this background, Hootan, left in charge by the attending physician, wrote orders for more drugs. His aim was to overcome the tolerance for medication that Ruben had built up over the 15 years of his illness; until and unless it was overcome, there was reason to believe that Ruben might continue to suffer while he died. Hootan's aim was to do all that could be done so that Ruben Navarro would not suffer as he died.

Half an hour after extubation, Ruben was still alive. Hootan phoned the doctor attending the intended organ recipient up at California Pacific Medical Center. The two physicians were in accord that the organs had likely deteriorated to such an extent that they should not be retrieved. The surgery was called off, and the transplant team packed up its equipment and left the hospital. Ruben Navarro was taken to the ICU. It took him nearly nine hours to die.

───────

It was one of the nurses who set in motion what became the allegations against Hootan Roozrokh. A fundamentalist Christian, whose experience in operating rooms was to save lives, she had been uncomfortable with participating in the intentional acceleration of a patient's death—like everyone else there, she had no familiarity with DCD. She was certainly uncomfortable with Hootan. In the story she told police in San Luis Obispo, "Dr. Hootan" refused to leave the OR and was responsible for administering potentially lethal doses of drugs to Ruben Navarro.

The Medical Board of California initiated administrative proceedings to assess whether Hootan's medical license should be suspended or revoked, and that is when Kaiser referred him to Ken. After Kaiser agreed to bring me on board, I wrote to Karen Gray, the prosecutor assigned to the case—sending a copy of the letter to her boss, the district attorney—and offered to go to San Luis Obispo with Ken to meet personally with them so that we could head off this nonsense at the pass.

Karen impressed me as tense and inflexible, and I thought I detected a healthy dose of ambition in her. True, she might be looking at a high-profile case that would likely attract serious national attention for its hot-button issues, but whether or not this was her reason for stonewalling, I got nowhere with her or with her boss; they rejected the offer of a meeting.

In June 2007, a civil lawyer who saw the chance of a payday in Rosa Navarro—an immigrant, a single mother, poor, bereaved—filed a civil lawsuit against Hootan, Sierra Vista hospital, CTDN, and Kaiser Permanente, among others, charging wrongful death, assault, battery, fraud, civil conspiracy, negligence, medical malpractice, and intentional infliction of emotional distress—basically, everything the lawyer could think of. The filing was accompanied by a press release, and the content of the complaint was a mishmash of bad English, un-lawyerlike writing, and fabrications. One of the most outrageous fabrications, downright amateurish in its flagrant disregard for what lawyers are supposed to care about—namely, facts—was the allegation that Hootan, meeting with Rosa one-on-one at the hospital, had coerced her into the decision to withdraw life support and donate Ruben's organs. Of course, Hootan never met or spoke to Rosa Navarro. She had actually taken a train home—she lived hundreds of miles away—the day before he and the team arrived in San Luis Obispo; the "meeting" was entirely made up—a fantasy.

Also outrageous was that Rosa's lawyer had been given more than 200 pages of discovery by the DA's office. Of course, such material is not intended for public consumption, but the lawyer managed to insert parts of it into his press release. It was obvious that he had been working closely with the district attorney's office and Karen Gray.

On August 14, 2007, Hootan was officially charged with three crimes: dependent adult abuse, administering harmful substances, and prescribing controlled substances without a legitimate medical purpose. In my opinion, it was a prosecution that no competent, ethical prosecutor would have filed, and I was determined to tear it to pieces.

––––––

Hootan Roozrokh was in his early 30s when all this was happening, and it is safe to say it was the first stumbling block on the upward trajectory of his life. Born in Iran, he was a toddler when his family emigrated to this country and eventually settled in Wisconsin. By the time he turned 16, he had been accepted simultaneously to college and medical school at the University of Wisconsin. He excelled at both. In so many ways a quintessentially Heartland-of-America kid, Hootan was a scholastic All-American athlete as well as an A student, and he was a serious sports fan, especially when it came to the Green Bay Packers and NASCAR. His successes piled up—in academics, in his professional aspirations, in life. By the age of 33, accomplished, brilliant, happily married, Hootan clearly had a sparkling future stretching before him. Apart from the sadness of losing his mother, who died waiting for a liver transplant, it must have seemed that nothing could ruffle this perfect life.

But as the press began reporting about the "San Francisco transplant surgeon criminally charged," and as the national and international head-lines and TV coverage grew more sensational, Hootan and his wife could feel even their neighbors looking at them in a new way—with a kind of fear—while he also found himself the target of that special invective some Americans reserve for people they decide are "Islamic terrorists." Stones were thrown against the windows of the Roozrokhs' apartment. The fact that Hootan was Christian, not Muslim, was irrelevant to the bigots.

Hootan was now on paid leave from Kaiser Permanente. Although some in the organization had balked at the idea of funding Hootan's defense, I reminded the Kaiser leadership that if the case were lost, the headline would declare that a "Kaiser doctor" was convicted, and that's what people would remember. Those in charge agreed, and Kaiser paid the bills for the case from start to finish.

It was clear, once we had the go-ahead, that the preparation for the trial was going to be a tremendous amount of work. Because it involved an area of expertise about which I knew virtually nothing, I was going to have to become very educated relatively fast. Ruben had been extremely sick for a long time, and the collective medical documentation on his disease and his treatment was voluminous. Obviously, Hootan was a primary source—a walking, breathing textbook of the science and medical procedures involved—so I gave him a desk in my office, and he became part of the team dedicated to preparing his case, joining Ken, Micah, and me.

What a pleasure it was—and what a source of pride—to have my son working with me. The Roozrokh case would be the third in which he occupied the second chair as my co-counsel. Micah is wonderful at legal research, excels as a writer, is highly organized, and is a great brainstorming partner. He also has a special grace with people—defendants, prosecutors, judges, witnesses, you name it—and is so well liked and respected that everybody around him just naturally tries to up their game a notch or two. I was thrilled to have his help and to have him with me.

The task before us was massive, exacting, and time-consuming as I prepared myself, with Micah's help and under the rigorous tutelage of Hootan and Ken, to examine a range of witnesses with all sorts of medical and scientific credentials and direct, hands-on experience in administering medication and caring for very sick people. I put aside all other work and rejected all other offers.[1]

Also involved in the defense were a number of the people I routinely relied on: Jacqi Tully for investigative work, Lois Heaney for jury selection, Allison Shalinsky in charge of the overflow of research and writing, and Ted Brooks to prepare the big-screen, computerized displays of various forms of evidence that were going to be so important in this case.

We would of course look for jurors who could absorb a lot of very difficult medical material, but as the Robert Blake trial had shown, Ted's displays could be relied on to grab and hold the jury's attention and, through various techniques like zooming in and out or highlighting with

---

1. Among the people asking me to represent them at that time was music producer Phil Spector, the legendary creator of "the wall of sound." He was charged with murder, and although he had a reputation as being mentally unstable, he was infinitely polite with me. I told him I was committed elsewhere and that, if I took his case, I would not be able to give my all to either one of my clients. I believe he understood that.

a marker, keep jurors interested—essential in a case like this. After all, it doesn't matter how good your evidence is or how much of it you have if the jurors snore through its presentation because they just don't get it. This is why the jury selection work of Lois Heaney, which helped us find jurors capable of understanding what they would hear, and the presentation work of Ted Brooks were so crucial.

No case exists in a vacuum, of course, and some of the ancillary issues in this one fed into our approach to the trial. One issue was the prosecution's motivation. Now prosecutors are as human as the rest of us and therefore just as susceptible to aspirations for success and glory. To this day, I believe that the prosecution of Hootan Roozrokh sprang to a great extent out of a belief on the prosecutor's part that the case would attract worldwide attention and was a sure bet for a conviction. And if getting that conviction meant stirring fears about shady doctors killing people for their organs, even if those fears were tinged with racism, so be it.

That is why in the Roozrokh case I departed from my usual practice and made myself available to the press, establishing my *bona fides* as a reliable source for the responsible press and countering some of the fantasies that began pouring out of the gutter press almost at once; two weeks after Hootan's arraignment, for example, the inimitable Nancy Grace had given Rosa Navarro's civil lawyer a TV platform to strut his stuff. It is also why I was quoted in one such encounter as saying that if Hootan's name were Joe Smith, the case might never have been brought at all.

———

A funny thing happened as we delved deeper into the heart of the case. I had always known we were dealing with huge life-and-death questions, but I began to see how far-reaching the answers to the questions could be—certainly well beyond Dr. Roozrokh's professional life. Fundamental matters of science and ethics, of individual responsibility, and social accountability had woven their way through the story of what had and had not taken place in the OR at Sierra Vista Hospital the night of February 3–4, 2006. How is suffering measured? How can you be sure when to pull the plug? How much pain medication is too much, and how much is not enough? Who is responsible for making these determinations?

Obviously, these are all profound philosophical questions that demand and are worthy of serious contemplation and debate. But in an operating room, they have to be answered on the spot. And as I was coming to understand, how the questions were answered that night at Sierra Vista and how those answers fared in the trial would have consequences for the entire process of organ donation and transplantation. For all the people now and in the future who might be depending on organ transplants for their very lives, and for those who might suffer as they died, what happened in our courtroom was a matter of life and death. For doctors and nurses and medical ethicists, what happened in our courtroom was almost equally significant, for it would provide guidelines for action and responsibility. The responsibility on us lawyers was also huge, for only the law can tell us how to answer such questions where they happen—in the very practical arena of human experience.

As I began to see where this case was going, I understood that what was at stake was something way beyond my professional career. The realization of the wider societal implications added to my burden of responsibility, but it also made me yet more determined, and it intensified my commitment even further.

The preliminary hearing was scheduled for February 27, 2008, in the main San Luis Obispo courthouse. It confirmed for us that the prosecution's trial strategy would consist of a parade of both expert witnesses and, often contradicting one another, those who had been present in the OR at Sierra Vista Hospital the night of February 3–4, 2006. The hearing went on for an unusually long time, but on March 19, the judge dismissed for lack of evidence the charges of administering harmful substances and prescribing controlled substances without a legitimate medical purpose. That we were now fighting only one charge did not make the work much easier.

We all moved down to San Luis Obispo even before jury selection got underway in October 2008. It was going to be a lengthy trial, and we were going to need living space for a number of people, so after we failed to find a house to rent, I decided to lease seven suites in a hotel, with additional suites rented as needed when Lois, Jacqi, and various witnesses were in town. It meant we had room available not only for the permanent players—me, Micah, Ken, Ted, and of course Hootan—but also a double suite that housed our enormous defense file and served as a defense team conference room. It was a good solution.

Jury selection was, as it always is, of the utmost importance. As noted, we wanted a conscientious jury—12 people who would take seriously their duty to understand both the science and the ethics at the heart of this case. The science alone was difficult and extensive; it would not be easy to listen to, understand, and process, but we somehow had to find people who could do all of that. We also looked for people whose views on criminal justice and whose experience with medical practitioners were at least not negative. Almost at the top of our list of desirable jurors were those who showed a sensitivity to human suffering and to the idea of dying with dignity.

To find such people, we had an overriding reality on our side, for there was one thing we were absolutely sure of: Everybody dies, and everybody has known somebody who has died. So finding a way to elicit thoughts and feelings about how people die was a good pathway to finding jurors we felt comfortable with.

One of the prospective jurors was a captain at a nearby prison—precisely the sort of pro-prosecution occupation virtually every defense lawyer would automatically reject, especially since this man had the linebacker appearance that went with his job. But when I questioned him during *voir dire* about any experience he might have had with someone dying, he answered by telling about the wonderful treatment his mother-in-law had received in a hospice facility. His voice remained steady as he spoke, but a solitary tear squeezed its way out of his eye and coursed down his cheek. I alone was in a position to see this. I returned to counsel table where Hootan and Micah were seated. "We're taking this guy," I said. And we did.

———

Opening statements were on Monday, November 3, 2008. Karen Gray opened dramatically, lining up a convoy of empty vials labeled morphine and Ativan to demonstrate what she called the "excessive" amount of drugs given to Ruben Navarro. "The only purpose for that medication," Gray said, "was to hasten his death so that [Hootan Roozrokh] could do what he was there to do and harvest his organs." That was the gist of the prosecution's argument—a quite deliberate and emotionally powerful horror-movie suggestion aimed at stoking latent fear or stirring it up where it hadn't existed before. To make the legal proposition stick, however, the prosecution would have to prove that the dosage given to Ruben *was* excessive, and to do that, the evidence would have to show that Ruben was not suffering. Only someone not suffering would have no need of medication to alleviate pain.

The prosecution's big guns were the expert witnesses brought in to educate the jury about these issues. The chief of transplantation at the University of California Irvine Medical Center, Dr. Clarence Foster, testified about standards to be followed in cases of DCD surgery. In cross-examination, I showed that he had lied about his training and transplant experience, and I wondered aloud if he was testifying in this case for the purpose of getting publicity. By the end of cross-examination, he was toast.

I grew very angry at the Santa Barbara neurologist who testified for the prosecution that there was "no way" Ruben could have experienced any suffering at all because he was so deep into a coma. First, I challenged this doctor's qualifications for the statement; he was not Board-certified in pain management, palliative care, or toxicology. Second, I offered a catalogue of medical records and testimony from doctors who had treated Ruben, the weight of which clearly suggested that despite being in a coma, he could indeed have experienced suffering. I wanted the jury to confront the issue of whether anyone, even the most credentialed expert, can possibly know with certainty what an individual unable to communicate may be sensing in the most extreme circumstances. No one has the capacity nor does any measuring instrument exist that can reach deep enough inside human physiology to assure us that Ruben Navarro felt nothing in his final hours. It is beyond our capacity to find out, and we are left with guesswork, religion, and a physician's oath to alleviate suffering if at all possible.

I was speaking from the heart when I confronted this neurologist, informed by the crystal-clear memory of my own mother's death in 1977. As I've written earlier, I was in mid-trial in San Jose when a phone call summoned me to what I understood was her deathbed. I flew across the country to Philadelphia, greeted my brother and sister, my aunts and grandmother, and went into my mother's hospital room. She was in a coma, hooked up to various drips and tubes, and as I stood for a moment in the doorway, I could see that the monitor beside her bed showed a flat line. But as I walked toward her, the line began to flutter up and down; in a very real if metaphoric sense, it sprang into life. A moment later, as I walked back to the door, it flat-lined again. I was taken aback by this, and I walked back and forth a few times to test it. Was her inert body responding in some way to a shift in the room's air pressure? Or was there something somewhere within her that sensed that her youngest child had walked into the room? Perhaps there was some other reason altogether. I have no idea. Neither does anyone else. But you can't tell me that there isn't some level of what we call consciousness or at least sentience so long as a person lives.

Something very similar happened with Ruben Navarro, as I would prove in the case we presented. It happened after the surgery had been cancelled and Ruben had been taken back to the ICU. When the nurse on duty there saw that his monitor had flat-lined, she went over to the bed where he lay and held his hand; she did not want him to die alone. As she took his hand, the flat line flared into life again, just as it had with my mother. No awareness? No capacity for suffering? Ruben would not die for a few more hours; could anyone really swear that he felt nothing?

The defense of course also presented our own expert witnesses in transplant surgery, neurology, palliative care, and pain management.[2] All were nationally prominent experts in their respective fields. Their testimony reaffirmed the argument that there is a possibility that a comatose, dying person suffers, even if in a way we do not comprehend, and that the amount of medication Ruben received was not at all excessive.

So my final argument to the jury came down to a very simple question: What was Hootan Roozrokh to do in that operating room that night? He had been sent to a hospital where a potential organ donor lay dying. He had every expectation that the hospital had prepared for the organ transplant procedure and that protocols would have been set in motion. He arrived to find nothing like that. Nothing was prepared. There wasn't

---

2. They were Drs. John J. Fung, Michael Aminoff, John Luce, and Ray d'Amours.

even an attending physician. There was only Ruben Navarro, dying, and, in Hootan's considered medical opinion, giving indications of sensation and suffering. And when a doctor did finally arrive, seemingly disgruntled at having been plucked out of bed and worried because she had no training in transplant procedures, she deferred entirely to Hootan.

At that point, a doctor concerned about protecting his career—perhaps an older doctor—would have walked out the door and flown back to San Francisco. For theoretically, it is true that Hootan should not have been involved in what turned out to be end-of-life care. What he saw, however, was a man dying and *nobody taking care of him*. And Hootan did not believe he could let Ruben Navarro suffocate to death. He carried out the oath every physician takes; when you can no longer cure, palliate and provide comfort.

As to the amount of medication given, we provided testimony about how markedly dosage recommendations can differ. Dr. d'Amours, an expert in pain management, testified that "tiny old ladies sometimes need an enormous dosage," depending on how long they have been taking a drug and the tolerance they may have built up. "What's important is to give the drug until it works. That's how you know what the right dose is," Dr. d'Amours told the jury.

And of course, the ultimate truth of the matter was that the drugs neither killed Ruben nor hastened his death. He died long after the drugs were administered of what the coroner determined were natural causes. You didn't need to be a doctor to realize, I argued, that the amount of medication administered was not excessive. If it had been, Ruben would have died in the OR.

Nor did Hootan Roozrokh gain anything from Ruben's death. No organs were harvested. Even if they had been, they were not for patients Hootan was caring for; as the transplant surgeon, he was only the conduit. And he had no financial interest in whether any organs were procured.

I did acknowledge in making our case that what had gone on in Sierra Vista Hospital on that night—the failure of preparation, the minimal and untrained staff, the confusion—was not the healthcare system at its best. But it underscored that what Hootan had done was to step into a breach; if in doing so he theoretically overstepped his authority, it was because no one else was giving Ruben Navarro the end-of-life care he deserved.

Even the very fact that Dr. Roozrokh had been charged with a crime, I told the jury, had been a grave mistake, the effects of which could be felt far outside the courtroom. It had not made this country a safer place to live, I said. Rather, it had made it a more frightening place to die.

The case went to the jury December 15. The jurors deliberated for two and a half days. I worried over the enormity of the technical details we had asked them to master. However, the prosecution failed to produce the testimony of transplant coordinator Carla Albright, the "quarterback" responsible for organizing the procurement, which was certainly part of their obligation if they were going to prove guilt. What was clear from the evidence was that she had not done what she was supposed to do as transplant coordinator and had not ensured that procedures were in place and that all staff knew precisely what was expected of them. The records she compiled of what went on in the OR on the night in question had disappeared, and Albright had moved to another state and did not testify. I knew the jury was wondering why, but I made sure the jurors knew it was the prosecution that had the burden of proving guilt beyond a reasonable doubt.

———

On December 18, 2008, the jury returned its verdict of not guilty. Hootan was joyous, as were we all. The other pins fell quickly: After Ken and I met with the Medical Board's attorney, the Board rescinded its administrative complaint, so Hootan's license was never suspended, and Rosa Navarro dropped her civil suit—with an apology from her lawyer, lest Hootan counter-sue for malicious prosecution.

This was, nevertheless, a case that in my view should never have been brought. Once again, a prosecutor's attempt to ride an emotionally charged issue to political power had knocked a human life off its moorings and degraded the justice process. And none of it came cheap. The personal toll on all of us involved in the Roozrokh case was huge—in the long hours spent, the stress on our bodies and minds, the impact on "normal" family life. For Micah, this was his first taste of the impact of such a commitment on a personal relationship, as he and his girlfriend—now his wife, Maria—struggled to find time and space for one another and for their life together.

I, by contrast, was an old hand at this kind of all-consuming work experience, but that did not make it any easier for Susan or me, since I was distanced, in mind even when not in body, from home life. Freud is reputed to have said, "Love and work, work and love. What else is there really?" Certainly, both make life worthwhile, but when the two are at war with one another, it can be difficult, and after decades of a career that often presented me with just such a conflict, I found I wasn't getting any better at it. My intensity—the fervor with which I approached a case—often made me difficult to be around and was exhausting as well. The Roozrokh case seemed to me so important, so profound in its potential impact, that as thrilled as I was with Hootan's acquittal, I was also emotionally wrung out, drained of resources, and I began to wonder: How many times can I continue to draw from this well?[3]

But a fine doctor had been exonerated and vindicated. Hootan could and did return to his profession, which he practices to this day. Also vindicated, I believe, was the whole process of organ transplantation, with all that means for the people hoping and waiting for transplants and for the doctors who serve them. Correlation does not mean causation, but it is a fact that the number of donors and of transplants flatlined during the period of Hootan's legal troubles, then began to rise again after his acquittal.

For of this I am sure: Had Hootan Roozrokh been convicted, it would have been even bigger news than his acquittal, which was headlined on the front page of the *New York Times* and shouted across the airwaves. A conviction would have dealt a body blow to organ transplantation, with donors withdrawing their names from the sign-up sheets and fewer individuals volunteering than ever before. The mismatch between potential donors and those needing transplants would have become a gap too wide

---

3. It was probably not unconnected that in due course Micah, who had certainly seen and felt the effects of my stress over the years, bowed out of trial work entirely. Today he is the managing editor of a legal publishing company, a keen observer, a sharp analyst of the changing legal environment, and a writer who makes it easily accessible to readers.

ever to fill, and organ harvesting and transplanting might well have gone underground.

The trial also highlighted the need for clarification of the entire harvest and transplantation process. It spurred UNOS to develop and adopt new bylaws defining the separation of responsibilities between the transplant team and the end-of-life team, a start, one can only hope, toward a universal rationalization of protocols and standards governing the wall between the two.

Nor was transplantation the only issue that benefited. New light was shed on the whole question of palliative care, an increasingly crucial issue as lifetime longevity increases in populations around the world. Caught between the rock of alleviating suffering and the hard place of prolonging life, what, after all, is a doctor to do—especially when the patient cannot speak for himself or respond meaningfully? When patients are comatose and you cannot know what they are feeling, how do you apply the dual dictates of the Hippocratic Oath to do no harm *and* to prevent suffering? Just a few years before Hootan's trial, in a civil lawsuit in Oakland, a family had won a judgment of $1.5 million against a doctor on the grounds he had not given the patient *enough* pain medication. The Roozrokh trial helped doctors find a way between not enough and too much: When you cannot know what is happening inside a person in a coma, the physician must err on the side of preventing suffering; that is the overarching principle and must be the overriding practice.

––––––

As I hope this book has demonstrated, I'm a man who only ever wanted to do good in the world, to make it a slightly better place, even if infinitesimally. Almost accidentally, the law became my instrument for that effort. In case after case, on behalf of defendant after defendant, I sought to lean on the arc of the moral universe a little bit, to help bend it—even just nudge it—toward justice. I succeeded often enough, and because I knew that each courtroom win was a life saved in some way or another, and because I believe what I quoted earlier in this book from the Talmud that "whoever saves a single life, it is as though he had saved a whole world," I considered myself a success. But the Roozrokh acquittal that "saved" one man's professional life also kept alive a new chance at life through organ donation for untold numbers of people I'll never meet or see; in fact, the chance may even have been renewed, stronger and better than ever. It is gratifying to be able to say that it was the practice of law that made that happen, and it is a point of enormous pride for me to have been involved in making it happen.

—11—

Closing Argument

After more than 45 years toiling in the criminal justice system, I suppose I qualify as an elder statesman. The experience has left me with scars as well as callouses, and I expect I have caused a few of the same in some of my colleagues and, I hope, in several of my adversaries. My greatest challenge has been to be the best lawyer I could be while simultaneously being the best husband and father I could be.

I can say of my career something that I don't think all the people I know in a number of other professions would say of theirs—namely, that I hold the same ideals and adhere to the same standards of right and wrong today as when I started. If anything, I believe even more strongly that we are all the same at our core, that the potential for goodness exists in all of us, and that if we can get to the core of goodness in those who have committed crimes, they can be redeemed. It sounds as corny as it always did, but 45 years of seeing it happen before my very eyes seems to me to be irrefutable evidence.

Objectifying human beings is what keeps us from doing this work of redemption, because of course it takes time and effort to plumb to the core of a human being who finds himself or herself a defendant in a criminal case. By the same token, many of those who need redemption the most have suffered the kinds of isolating detriments that don't make them easy to approach or deal with. Poverty, prejudice, physical abuse, sexual assault, drugs, mental illness can make people withdraw from a society indifferent to their plight, can make them angry, can twist their minds, can break their souls. For protection against further injury, they encase their emotions in a shell, a carapace that hardens over time. For the attorney defending such people, that makes the work of relating to them particularly difficult—a matter of patiently splintering the shell, bit by bit, until it falls apart. Over the course of my career, my commitment to this task never flagged, and I still place it at the heart of the job I do.

There are realities surrounding the job, however, that are probably never going to go away, and it would be naïve to suppose they might. Political animals are never going to stop using a criminal case to stoke fear and prejudice and ride them to power. Some law enforcement officers are never going to stop looking for a quick resolution. Some judges and prosecutors are never going to stop rushing cases along as if they were widgets on an assembly line, forgetting that the wheels of justice are supposed to move with all *deliberate* speed. This is why there may be no greater realist on earth than a criminal defense attorney; we are, after all, the final bulwark still standing for our clients—their last chance.

The responsibility of that can sometimes seem almost paralyzing. The antidote to such potential paralysis is the work itself—making your way through the facts until you find the truth about your client and his or her case.

For me, the image of a forest is what always comes to mind when I think about how to approach a criminal case. From outside, the forest is dense and dark; the details, especially underfoot and high up in the canopy, are obscured. The defense lawyer venturing into the forest needs to stop and look at every tree, every branch of every tree, and every leaf on every branch. But you must also be able to walk out of the forest, gain some distance from it, and see the totality of it all over again, this time noting how each of the details you have observed fits into that picture of the whole. Until and unless you can make sense of how all the details fit into the big picture—and until and unless you can articulate how they do—neither you nor a jury will understand the essence of the case; neither you nor a jury will be persuaded that the details create the picture, and that the picture is simply not complete without appreciating *all* the details in it.

But for how to look at those details, I rely on another image, one I've mentioned before—that of a work of art, specifically, an abstract painting. For me, the more I look at a work of abstract art, the more I see in it. The more times I come back to it, the more I see. The more I listen to what other people see in it, again, the more I see. Just so with the events, the statements, the timelines, all the facts and every detail of a criminal case and every criminal defendant. Look again—and again and again—and more will be revealed with each look.

It is all a part of that almost insanely thorough preparation of which Sheldon Otis was the prime exemplar. Sheldon looked under every rock, pebble, even grain of sand for the truth, and when he walked into a courtroom, he had put all the disparate, abstract pieces together and was ready for anything and everything. I always tried to do the same.

To be sure, Sheldon and I were far different personalities, but if there is one truth I have learned, it is that there is no one personality—and certainly no single style—that fits us all. If I ever tried to ape my heroes—and I probably did as a very young lawyer—I quickly got over it. It simply doesn't work in the world of criminal defense. A jury can sense when a lawyer is acting, and if that happens, it will be your client who loses. It's probably true of every profession, but lawyers need to stay in their own skins; if they don't, the consequences are inevitably adverse.

Of course, that means knowing who you are—your strengths and weaknesses—so you can comfortably excel at what you do best and find ways to fill the gaps where you don't. I always felt insecure about my intellectual capacity and my research skills. I still do. So it has always behooved me to rely on great colleagues, who often became great friends, and to reach out to those who have expertise in areas that are not part of the lawyer's training. In every way, knowing that those people were at my side, complementing and supplementing what I could provide, both gave me confidence and was personally rewarding.

By the same token, I learned early on in my career that I had a gift for relating to people, and the ability to relate to clients and witnesses is a boon for a criminal defense lawyer. I also always knew that I was emotional in my commitment and intensely competitive—qualities that in a lawyer could go either way, serve as either a strength or a weakness or sometimes both at once. When I could bring my fervor to heel and fold it into my work ethic, it could be a strength exerted on behalf of my client. But there were certainly times when the sheer heat of my emotions and my zeal threatened to become disruptive, and that was something I learned to guard against.

There are thousands of dedicated criminal defense attorneys in the United States today, as committed as I am to the fight for justice. We take pride in and draw enormous satisfaction from ensuring, when we can, that the innocent avoid conviction, from helping those who have committed a crime to turn their lives around, and, when necessary, from exposing the flaws in the criminal justice system. There are also thousands of law enforcement officers, prosecutors, and judges who are equally dedicated to the pursuit of justice and equally concerned about the system's flaws.

But one would have to be blind to deny the reality that many in the criminal justice system, on both sides of the adversarial divide, do not honor their ethical obligations. When we do deny that reality, we make it all the more possible for the innocent to be convicted,[1] and we put off for yet another day the need to address the root causes of crime, not just the terrible consequences of those causes.

That is what I have seen in a career that has been more personally rewarding than I can express. I'm a criminal defense lawyer: As always, I say what I think, not what I think people want to hear.

---

1. According to the National Registry of Exonerations, more than 1,700 wrongfully convicted people have been exonerated in the United States. Since 1973, 156 of them were freed from death row. Aside from the devastation to the lives of innocent people, what is often lost in the publicity about exonerations is the fact that, whenever an innocent person is convicted, the real perpetrator remains free to commit additional crimes and victimize more people.

Acknowledgments

D. Danielle Svetcov, my literary agent, without whose guidance, encouragement and persistence this book would not have been possible.

Susanna Margolis, an exceptional writer, who made it possible for me to convey the reality that has been my personal and professional journey.

Nina Martin, who wrote about several of the cases I litigated, and who found me a literary agent willing to take a chance on a lone-wolf criminal defense lawyer.

Lynn Weiss, a superb publicist who has been tireless in her advocacy for this book.

ABA Publishing, and in particular Jonathan Malysiak, for valuing the work criminal defense lawyers do to protect the Constitutional rights of all Americans, and for allowing me to shine a light on the dedication required and the personal toll it takes to help the arc of the moral universe bend toward justice.

The enumerable people who have provided invaluable assistance to me over these many years. No trial lawyer does it on his or her own, and I certainly didn't.

My parents, Sanford Schwartzbach, and Rachel Finkel Schwartzbach. Each in their own way gave me the moral and personal foundation upon which my value system was built. Coming from distinctly different socio-economic backgrounds, my father and mother taught me to be a person of principle and to understand that the potential for good lies at the core of every human being.

My brother Stephen and my sister Barbara who took pride in and supported the unexpected journey their kid brother has travelled. Also, my brother-in-law Ed Felder and sister-in-law Sherry Schwartzbach who have consistently encouraged me during my journey.

Micah Schwartzbach, my son and for six years my associate. Micah came to work for me so that I could teach him how to be a criminal defense lawyer. Although he has moved on to a career as a legal writer and editor, during the time we worked together Micah became my teacher. He was a crystal-clear mirror by which I improved as both a lawyer and a person. Now married to the wonderful Maria Arieta and the father of our precious grandson Jeremiah, he is a constant source of pride and uncompromising love.

My wife Susan. Susan Elizabeth Homes was born in Middleton-on-Sea, a small village on the south coast of England. Her own personal journey eventually led her to San Francisco. My book often, but not nearly enough, acknowledges Susan. She has stood by me for thirty-seven years at great personal and professional sacrifice. As we enter a new phase of our lives together, we will share it with friends and family, but most of all with each other, and with Micah, Maria and Jeremiah. Susan is an extremely talented artist who forewent her own ambitions to make my career possible. She has been an extraordinary wife, mother, and now grandmother whose own legacy will endure. She is, and will always be, the love of my life.